SWEET AND LOWDOWN

SWEET AND LOWDOWN
Woody Allen's Cinema of Regret

Lloyd Michaels

WALLFLOWER PRESS
LONDON & NEW YORK

A Wallflower Press book
Published by
Columbia University Press
Publishers Since 1893
New York • Chichester, West Sussex
cup.columbia.edu

Copyright © 2017 Columbia University Press
All rights reserved
Wallflower Press® is a registered trademark of Columbia University Press

A complete CIP record is available from the Library of Congress

ISBN 978-0-231-17854-9 (cloth : alk. paper)
ISBN 978-0-231-17855-6 (pbk. : alk. paper)
ISBN 978-0-231-85093-3 (e-book)

Columbia University Press books are printed on permanent
and durable acid-free paper.
Printed in the United States of America

Cover design by Elsa Mathern
Cover image: *Husbands and Wives* (1992) © TriStar Pictures

Contents

Acknowledgments ix
Preface xi

Chapter 1 Regret and the Problem of Shallowness 1

Chapter 2 Apprentice Works 21

Chapter 3 The Relationship Films 39

Chapter 4 The Murder Quartet 61

Chapter 5 The Reflexive Films 81

Chapter 6 Nostalgia 103

Chapter 7 To Remedy Regret 125

Postscript Speculations 137

Bibliography 149
Index 154

For Mary, Dee, Jack, Emily, Callie and Tyler

Acknowledgments

The impetus for scholarship while teaching at a liberal arts college has always been, for me, a product of what happens within the classroom. The best ideas emerge from dialogue with students, followed by engaged research, extended contemplation and further discussion. Although I have been teaching the films of Woody Allen for more than thirty years to a generation of undergraduates, I had not published anything about his work until recently, when I offered a full-year, non-credit course covering twelve movies to a group of elder learners at Allegheny College. Inspired by curiosity rather than degree requirements or the hope of a high grade, these adventurous, uninhibited new-old students challenged my ideas about Woody Allen and brought fresh life to my teaching. This book is deeply indebted to the persistence of the group's leader, Jan Hyatt, the organisational skills of her colleague, Nancy Sheridan, and the insightful contributions of the dozen or so participants in that class who have since persuaded me to present two similar classes on contemporary international and American cinema.

Soon after that first class concluded, which coincided with my retirement after forty-two years at Allegheny, I submitted an essay on 'Woody Allen's Cinema of Regret' to the *Quarterly Review of Film and Video*, which promptly published it. I am grateful to the journal's editor, David Sterritt, for accepting the article and to the publishers, Taylor & Francis, for permission to re-print a substantial portion as part of Chapter One of this book. I also want to acknowledge the support of my longtime friend and unofficial mentor, Dudley Andrew, who prodded me to continue working on the manuscript as I approached the potential indolence of retirement. The isolation imposed by academic research and writing does not come easily to me, and without the early motivation provided by these two esteemed film scholars I might not have persisted in my ambition to produce a new book. Among the many excellent authors who have written about Woody Allen, I remain especially indebted to Peter J. Bailey, whose *The Reluctant Film Art of Woody Allen* (University Press of Kentucky, 2001) remains the ideal study of the director's reflexive cinema that I had once imagined writing myself and the single best scholarly book about Allen I have read. Bailey's collaboration with Sam B. Girgus on *A Companion to Woody Allen* (Wiley-Blackwell, 2013) has also proven to be a valuable resource, particularly on Allen's work in the twenty-first century. In addition, I want to acknowledge Tom Shone's *Woody Allen: A Retrospective* (Abrams, 2015), an astutely written and beautifully illustrated addition to any film library that I consulted before beginning every sustained analysis of a specific film. My exploration of the topic of regret used Janet Landman's comprehensive study of the topic, *Regret: The Persistence of the Possible* (Oxford University Press, 1993), as both a touchstone for research and a constant resource through the writing and revision process.

Two colleagues from the Philosophy and Religious Studies Department at Allegheny substantially influenced the development and refinement of this project: Eric Boynton team-taught two interdisciplinary courses in film and philosophy with me and encouraged me in the early stages of this project; Steven Farrally-Jackson read the manuscript and contributed valuable suggestions for its improvement. Their meticulous, informed efforts on my behalf define the kind of collegiality that first attracted me to academic life at a liberal arts college but that, sadly, seems to have receded with the passage of time and competing professional demands. I also want to thank Yoram Allon, Commissioning Editor at Wallflower Press, and the anonymous readers at Wallflower Press for their constructive advice and editorial efficiency. This is my fifth book, each with a different academic publisher, and, by far, my happiest experience from proposal submission to publication.

I have loved being a teacher, editor and scholar for what is now exactly half a century. In addition to the joy of communicating my appreciation of literature and cinema to so many gifted students, I feel blessed to have shared the good company of such smart and dedicated people as I have known on the faculty of Allegheny College. Among these lifelong friends, I count Jim Bulman, Richard Cook, Shannan Mattiace, David Miller and Carl Olson as the most insightful, productive, generous and steadfast, without whom I could not have sustained an enduring intellectual life. Finally, there is my family to thank, a small coterie of six – Mary, Dee, Jack, Emily, Callie and Tyler – to whom this work is lovingly dedicated.

Preface

In what was, at the time I began this study, Woody Allen's most recent feature film, *Irrational Man* (2015), the protagonist, a burned-out philosopher named Abe, laments his inability to complete his current academic project: 'Just what the world needs, another book on Heidegger and fascism.' I confronted a similar dilemma as I stared at the blank manuscript. What is left to be said about such a prolific filmmaker after a career that has spanned more than a half century, a celebrity who has generated countless newspaper and magazine articles that first revered and then reviled him, a cinematic auteur who has been the subject of numerous scholarly books and journal articles, a putative 'recluse' who is the topic of at least three books of interviews and regularly appears for promotions and press conferences upon the release of each new movie? Who needs another book on Woody Allen, not to mention the familiar emotion of regret?

The answer, as I have convinced myself and the editors at Wallflower Press, is twofold. First, Allen continues to add stylish, thoughtful and, frequently enough, engaging new works to an oeuvre as impressive as that of any other American filmmaker. Everyone will have a slightly different list, but I am confident that Allen has written and directed at least a dozen films that will continue to be studied and enjoyed into the foreseeable future. I count *Annie Hall* (1977), *Manhattan* (1979), *Hannah and Her Sisters* (1986), *Crimes and Misdemeanors* (1989), *Husbands and Wives* (1992) and *Match Point* (2005) as masterpieces; as you will read, I also consider *Broadway Danny Rose* (1984), *The Purple Rose of Cairo* (1985), *Sweet and Lowdown* (1999) and *Cassandra's Dream* (2007) to be vastly under-appreciated accomplishments. Allen's critical reputation abroad, despite his misfires and cinematic datedness, remains much stronger than in his own country. In short, like Heidegger, he remains a worthy subject for serious discussion.

My contribution to that discussion lies in the reverberations of the concept of regret, which, unlike the topic of fascism in relation to Heidegger, has been all but ignored in the literature about Woody Allen's cinema. The expression 'I made a mistake' and its variants resound like a mantra throughout his films, although the theme of regret has never figured prominently in any extended study of his work. Moreover, despite being a universal emotion, regret itself has received relatively short shrift among philosophers and psychologists when compared to related feelings such as guilt, shame and depression. So I stake some claim to originality in centring my analysis on this recurrent concern and hope to clarify both the parameters of regret and to suggest its value as an alternative to the attribution of scepticism or misanthropy that pervades most current criticism of Allen's cinema.

Usually portrayed comically, as in Virgil Starkweather's resolution to lead a life of crime (*Take the Money and Run* (1969)) or Cecilia's infatuation with the movie star Gil Shepard (*The Purple Rose of Cairo*), the motif of error and consequent regret in drama originates with Aristotle's notion of *hamartia*, a mistaken action or lapse of judgement that leads to an unfortunate fall. For schlemiel characters like Virgil or Leonard Zelig (*Zelig* (1983)), the mechanical repetition of the compulsive mistake, following Henri Bergson's formula in *Laughter* (2008), produces slapstick; for fundamentally unrepentant criminals like Judah Rosenthal (*Crimes and Misdemeanors*) and Chris Wilton (*Match Point*), the superficiality of their regret produces melodrama that borders on nihilism; for narcissistic artist figures like Isaac Davis (*Manhattan*) and Emmet Ray (*Sweet and Lowdown*), the epiphanies of deeper regret they ultimately experience touch on tragedy and hint at redemption. In every case, however, the emphasis remains on the shallowness or transience of their self-reproach. Among the dramas, the single exception – the exception that proves the rule – is Terry, the tragic hero of *Cassandra's Dream*; among the comedies, it is Broadway Danny Rose.

This volume therefore focuses on both the frequency with which the director deploys the idea of regret as a plot point and yet the superficiality of its effect on character. What we typically see, with varying degrees of emphasis from the one-dimensional Monk (*The Purple Rose of Cairo*) to the morally troubled Judah, to the self-deceived Jasmine (*Blue Jasmine* (2013)), is Allen's depiction of *shallow regret* – the absence of deeply experienced, sustained remorse – that may well apply to the author as much as his characters. Similar to the auteur's signature theme of God's silence in Ingmar Bergman or the motif of the wrong man in Alfred Hitchcock,

Allen's repeated invocations of regret do not comprise a consistent philosophical argument but rather an ongoing meditation that invites the audience to engage with the epistemological (*what can we know?*) and moral (*what is the good?*) questions that mark human existence. Perhaps this practice is most evident in the penultimate scene in *Crimes and Misdemeanors* when Cliff and Judah discuss (somewhat drunkenly, it should be remembered, thereby devaluing the seriousness of their conclusions) the tragic implications of Judah's scenario for the perfect crime; but, as we shall see, this Socratic dialogue continues across several films – comedies like *Manhattan Murder Mystery* (1993) and *Bullets Over Broadway* (1994) as well as dramas like *Match Point*, *Cassandra's Dream* and *Irrational Man*. The permutations of regret/remorse/guilt will diverge from film to film, not surprisingly given that, as Janet Landman concludes in her book-length study of the topic, 'Regret can lay claim to no one single, fixed set of laws that universally describes its nature or its natural history' (1993: 247).

Insofar as I occasionally cite psychologists like Landman to define regret and remorse and philosophers like Jean-Paul Sartre, Emmanuel Levinas and Gabrielle Taylor to illuminate guilt and shame, I apply an interdisciplinary approach to what remains fundamentally a literary and cinematic study of Woody Allen's films. I am especially cautious about my forays into philosophy, where I have no academic training and only qualified confidence in my ability to parse primary texts. Nevertheless, I have team-taught film philosophy classes during the late stages of my career and, like Woody Allen himself, have maintained a lifelong interest in philosophical questions as well as the cinema of ideas. At the least, my knowledge of philosophy and my working vocabulary of the pertinent terms seem likely to equal the director's own.

For those attuned to the autobiographical implications of art, like the morally outraged readers in *Deconstructing Harry* (1997), the pattern I delineate might seem revealing, particularly in light of the enduring apprehensions about Allen's moral character following his scandalous break-up with Mia Farrow in 1992 and subsequent charges of child abuse that have plagued his personal reputation to the present day. Although I will on rare occasions allude to the subjective ramifications of this reiterative gesture of regret, my intent is never to judge Woody Allen the person, whom I do not know except through his films and writings. Trained (long ago) as a New Critic, I have little interest in the distinction, central to *Another Woman* (1988), *Bullets Over Broadway* and *Deconstructing Harry*, between 'the artist' and 'the man'. Although I do frequently cite interviews with regard to establishing the director's sources, intentions or technique – matters relating to the *genesis* of the film text – in matters of *interpretation* I tend to adhere to D. H. Lawrence's famous admonition in *Studies in Classic American Literature* (1923): 'Never trust the artist. Trust the tale.' In a brief post-script, however, I allow myself to speculate about the human dimensions of a man I have never met.

With shallow regret providing what Henry James called 'the figure in the carpet', this book is organised into seven chapters that can be read independently as essays on a particular aspect of the director's career. The first of these defines the key terms and applies them to a range of movies, culminating in a detailed analysis of *Sweet and Lowdown*. By using Allen's early short story 'The Shallowest Man' (from *Side Effects*, 1980) as a touchstone, I survey several examples before concentrating on *Sweet and Lowdown* to outline the book's thesis. Initially constructed as the product of a 'screw-up' that is the unwitting act of the schlemiel and later becomes a measure of the protagonist's superficiality, Allen's recurrent depiction of regret reveals not the moral self-condemnation of authentic remorse but only the necessity of living with unpleasant outcomes; in short, being a victim of fate rather than its agent. Even the crudest and most calculating of his protagonists, of whom Emmet Ray and Chris Wilton may serve as paradigms, experiences the feeling of being 'dishonoured in his own eyes', which is Taylor's definition of shame (1985: 57). But these introspective moments are nearly always transitory. With few exceptions, Woody Allen's characters remain fundamentally *shameless*.

The second chapter covers Allen's stand-up career and apprentice works, culminating in the transitional *Love and Death* (1975). I argue that his astonishing talent for joke-making imperfectly conceals an insecurity about his limitations as an artist. His early films are all parodies, dependent for their comic effects on the preexisting classics of geniuses he can only approximate or imitate for laughs. Thus he labours under the shadow of Robert Benchley and S. J. Perleman, Albert Camus and Samuel Beckett, Ingmar Bergman and Federico Fellini, whose formal virtuosity and philosophical profundity threaten to expose his sense of his own relative shallowness. In Chapter Three, I look at the so-called 'relationship' films that continue to sustain Allen's critical reputation. Personal relationships – girlfriends, wives, friends, mentors – are forever fleeting in these works. Even in earlier lightweight movies like *Play It Again, Sam* (1972; written by and starring Allen, directed by Herbert Ross) and *A Midsummer Night's Sex Comedy* (1982), the hapless hero obsessively regrets the 'missed opportunity' to declare his love to his presumed soul mate, only to do so with disappointing or impermanent consequences. The sad truth of *Annie Hall* prevails: 'Love fades.'

Chapter Four focuses on the perfect murder tetralogy – *Crimes and Misdemeanors*, *Match Point*, *Cassandra's Dream* and *Irrational Man* – and the rationalisations, intellectual ('It wasn't easy, but you can learn to push the guilt under the rug', Chris says in *Match Point*) and offhanded ('You just push a button', to borrow a phrase repeated in *Crimes and Misdemeanors* and *Cassandra's Dream*) employed by various perpetrators of homicide. Like the philanderers and adulterers in the relationship films, Allen's murderers may experience a modicum of guilt but never shame (always excepting Terry), and never the 'infinity of firmest fortitude' that characterises Ahab's tragic resistance to conventional mores in Melville's mighty book (1992: 135). Following the essay on murderers, Chapter Five turns to Allen's representation of artists, whom he apparently regards with similar suspicion. On the one hand, what passes for art, including magic, fortune-telling and communication with the dead, is 'just a trick', as Rain describes her precocious writing talent in *Husbands and Wives*; on the other, even the illusions created by the crudest performers remain as 'necessary as the air' (*Shadows and Fog* (1991)). The artist's compulsion to perform, combined with the audience's need to be enthralled – or at least to be distracted – accounts for the natural antagonism between them that Allen dramatises in several films, most notably *Stardust Memories* (1980). In countless personal testimonies in interviews and festival press conferences, the director seems to side with his cynical avatar Dobell in *Anything Else* (2003) by denying the revelatory quality of art's representation of truth: 'Work gives the illusion of meaning.' This chapter also explores two related themes that resonate throughout Allen's work: the difference between talent and genius and the distinction between the artist and his art.

Chapter Six extends the analysis beyond agent regret, with its inherent negative self-assessment, to consider nostalgia, which is a form of regret for a bygone era that implies neither responsibility nor remorse. Allen's films, of course, are suffused with this emotion, most notably in the musical soundtracks that usually accompany the credits and punctuate the narratives. In his award-winning short story 'The Kugelmass Episode', he brilliantly depicts the dilemma of being 'stuck' in an idealised fictional past, an idea that was reprised with equal success in *The Purple Rose of Cairo*. Several other films – *Annie Hall*, *Another Woman*, *Crimes and Misdemeanors*, *Alice* (1990) – incorporate extended flashbacks in which the protagonists return in memory to their old home, recalled as a site of simple pleasures and happier times. Some of Allen's characters, like Gil in *Midnight in Paris* (2011), yearn to live in an earlier 'belle époque'; others, like Alice or Bobby and Vonnie in *Café Society* (2016), wonder about their own lost and better self: 'Where did that part of me go?' Alice asks. A movie like *Radio Days* (1987) has itself become an object of cinephiliac nostalgia, as *Midnight in Paris* may prove to be for a later generation. Nevertheless, Allen seems acutely aware that nostalgia, however tempting, remains the Shallow Man's version of history and memory, a point that becomes the explicit moral of *Midnight in Paris*.

The prevailing critical discourse about Woody Allen in late career generally recapitulates the charges of misanthropy and despair that have dogged him since *Stardust Memories*, and yet no artist, certainly not one with the creative persistence over time as Woody Allen – someone who has famously remarked on how success is largely a matter of 'just showing up' – can truly remain a nihilist. Art might not serve a social good or grant the artist immortality, Allen insists, but that does not excuse the artist from putting forth his or her best effort to express a truth about human experience. The concluding chapter therefore underscores the humanist implications of the director's persistent interest in regret. To be conscious of regrets, Janet Landman argues, 'signifies that you have standards of excellence, decency, morality, or ethics you still care about' (1993: 26). 'I affirm life,' Juan-Antonio says in *Vicky Christina Barcelona* (2008), 'despite everything.' Nowhere is Allen's commitment to the imperative of acting in good faith in the face of absurdity and diminished expectations more clear than in *Broadway Danny Rose*, a fable for adults of secular sainthood confirmed by the community Danny creates among his troupe of marginal performers, the redemption he grants for Tina's guilty conscience, and the good will he evokes among the comedians re-telling his story.

In tracing this through-line of regret that marks so many examples across time, I begin with a cautionary note to myself about reducing the variety and complexity of these works to a simple paradigm, one that denies the contributions of Allen's talented collaborators, ignores the nuances of plot construction and cinematic technique, or suggests a psychoanalytical analysis of sublimated confession. Instead, I am interested in uncovering a pattern that threads through a prodigious artistic output, a motif that helps to define both Woody Allen's persistent concerns and, perhaps paradoxically, the universality (despite nagging complaints about his parochialism) of his cinema's appeal.

CHAPTER ONE

Regret and the Problem of Shallowness

'My one regret in life is that I am not someone else.'
— Woody Allen

A fter nearly five decades, Woody Allen's filmmaking career seems to have entered a fourth stage. Following what might be called his apprenticeship – the movies culminating in *Love and Death* in 1975 that exploited Allen's stand-up persona of the neurotic *schlemiel* – his second act, what some now call his 'classic' period, produced an astonishing string of nuanced comedies (along with the occasional disquieting drama) from *Annie Hall* through *Husbands and Wives* (1977–1992), films that served to separate him from his onetime comic rival Mel Brooks, establish him as an international auteur of the highest regard, and reinforce his status as an original American talent and cultural treasure. The features of this period – including *Manhattan, Zelig, Broadway Danny Rose, The Purple Rose of Cairo, Hannah and Her Sisters, Radio Days* and *Crimes and Misdemeanors* – were neither box office smashes nor above critical reproach, but they were generally recognised at the time and stand today as an exemplary body of work nearly unprecedented in American cinema. Few readers of this book, in fact, will be unaware of Woody Allen's sustained achievement during the otherwise uneven, commercially-driven movie decade of the 1980s.

Allen's status as the epitome of artistic integrity and icon of intellectual hipness met its demise with the scandal over the break-up with his star and longtime romantic companion, Mia Farrow, following the revelation of his affair with Farrow's adopted daughter, Soon-Yi Previn (who, it still needs to be said, was not Allen's legal step-daughter), and the subsequent custody battle over their children in 1992. Although he never broke stride with his professional schedule of writing, directing and releasing one film a year, Allen responded to the public opprobrium with a series of seemingly repetitive and 'minor' (to use a favorite adjective from *The Purple Rose of Cairo*) movies, starting with *Manhattan Murder Mystery* in 1993 and concluding with *Melinda and Melinda* (2004). With few exceptions – most notably, *Sweet and Lowdown*, which will be discussed later in this chapter – these products of the 'post-scandal', 'post-classical' period were scorned by ticket-buyers and, until quite recently, virtually ignored by film scholars. It seems fair to say that by 2003 Woody Allen (at least in America) was dead in the water.

But then came *Match Point* and a revival of Allen's critical reputation. Although it has been marked by duds (*Scoop* (2006), *To Rome with Love* (2012)), the filmmaker's fourth act – call it his 'late' period – has also garnered commercial success (*Midnight in Paris* became his all-time top-grossing film), renewed acclaim (Academy Award nominations for *Match Point*, *Vicky Cristina Barcelona*, *Midnight in Paris* and *Blue Jasmine*), and a general reappraisal of his lifetime achievement, as evidenced by the four-hour *American Masters* documentary aired on PBS in 2012 (d. Robert B. Weide) and the nearly-600-page scholarly anthology *A Companion to Woody Allen* (2013). Co-editor Peter J. Bailey's introduction to the *Companion* succinctly states the current respect for the filmmaker's oeuvre: 'How easy it is to type or say that Allen has made 41 films in 41 years; how difficult it is to grasp fully the consistently indefatigable creative energy that that accomplishment enshrines' (2013: 4). And now, as I compose this draft, two new coffee table books have appeared: Jason Bailey's *The Ultimate Woody Allen Film Companion* (Voyageur Press, 2014), intended largely for film buffs and bloggers, and Tom Shone's *Woody Allen: A Retrospective* (2015), more elegant and erudite.

While Peter Bailey likens the director's artistic productivity to three contemporary American writers, Joyce Carol Oates, Philip Roth and the late John Updike – given their shared urban Jewish experiences, recurrent self-referentiality and injection of alter egos into their work, and mordant wit, the comparison to Roth seems most appropriate – perhaps the arc of Woody Allen's career might be more strictly compared to that of another New York filmmaker of an earlier generation, Elia Kazan. Like Kazan, Allen enjoyed early acclaim within New York's cultural avant-garde (Kazan in the Group Theatre; Allen in Greenwich Village nightclubs), then migrated west for even greater fame and financial rewards (Kazan in Hollywood; Allen in Las Vegas); both directors worked in literature as well as theatre and film (Kazan as a best-selling novelist; Allen as playwright, screenwriter and *New Yorker* humourist and essayist). Their prolific careers were both interrupted at the height of their celebrity by a notorious public indiscretion (Kazan's infamous HUAC testimony was given in executive session, but he immediately announced his motives for naming names in *The New York Times*) that influenced the work that followed (for Kazan, *On the Waterfront* (1954); for Allen, *Deconstructing Harry*). Neither man expressed public remorse in the face of scandal. Instead, that remorse – and its corollaries, regret and guilt – seems to have been sublimated into the art of their later years.

This book explores the permutations of 'regret' throughout Woody Allen's long filmmaking life, arguing that while this emotion may be properly defined as seminal to an extraordinary variety of works covering nearly a half century, it is actually the *shallowness* of his characters' response to their own bad behaviour – *regret at the very absence of authentic remorse or guilt* – that holds the key to understanding both Allen's philosophy of existence and of cinema itself. Regret, so the argument goes, is the shallow man's emotion, and film, so Allen apparently believes, is the shallow art. For all but a few geniuses or saints, life becomes intolerable without distraction from the inevitable regrets that follow living, be they artistic or ethical. With this theme in mind as a background, a movie like *Sweet and Lowdown*, perhaps the most neglected of Allen's post-classical works, emerges as a case study, a meditation on regret and its relation to consciousness, creativity and the possibility of redemption.

Modes of Regret: Remorse, Guilt and Shame

When Woody Allen says that his one regret is not being someone else, he is, of course, making a joke, transforming a singular misgiving into an ontological dilemma. His 'regret' reinforces his comic persona, a *kvetch* who laments his fate rather than taking responsibility for it. Were he to feel actual remorse about his identity, we would expect him to change it; were he truly to feel ashamed, we would expect him to hide himself from our judgement; were he to feel guilty, we would expect his confession to be followed by some form of recompense or punishment. To regret something – one's bad behaviour, one's appearance, one's circumstances – carries with it either the inability or the unwillingness to change it. Thus, we might 'regret' being short in stature or near-sighted without feeling remorse; we might regret not living in a 'golden age' like Paris in the 1920s or Manhattan in the 1940s without feeling ashamed about it. Alternatively, we might regret having an affair with our girlfriend's teenaged daughter without feeling sufficiently guilty to give up the object of our love or repentant when others find out about our conduct. Regret may be sincere, as when we decline an invitation or offer condolences, but remorse runs deeper, acknowledging as it does a moral responsibility. Thus, remorse always involves a wish to undo the wrongful action, whereas regret sometimes involves the acceptance of necessity, the 'screw-up' that comes with simply living. Shallow regret in Woody Allen's cinema, as we shall see, serves to foster comedy; authentic remorse, which only rarely appears, allows for melodrama and approaches tragedy.

To begin with a broad definition, regret may be described simply as the painful wish that one had, or could have, acted differently or that, regardless of our actions, things had turned out more favourably. In other words, regret presupposes a *counterfactual* awareness of the discrepancy between things as they are and the more pleasant thought of what might have been: 'how much better if it had been otherwise' (De Wijze 2005: 459). Despite the disclaimers found in retirement speeches, losing teams' locker rooms and popular music, where 'no regrets' is a cliché that follows from doing it 'my way', everyone experiences regret. 'Because it is not possible to have it all, and because we know it,' Janet Landman writes, 'regret is inevitable' (1993: 40). Although philosophers and psychologists vary in defining the proper balance, they appear to agree that regret involves a synthesis of thought and feeling, a combination of cognitive self-assessment and emotional disappointment. In contrast to disappointment or sadness, however, what ethicists call *agent* regret is a response to undesired outcomes for which one feels responsible rather than simply to the state of things. Typically, the recognition of one's misguided behaviour leads the agent to experience some level of remorse or guilt, as when Isaac (Woody Allen) acknowledges the hurt he caused Tracy (Mariel Hemingway) at the climax of *Manhattan*. When the agent concludes that his mistaken action is less the product of poor decision-making but rather something essential to his selfhood like cowardliness, selfishness, repression or simply evil, he exhibits what Amelie Rorty (1980) cites as *character* regret, quintessentially expressed in Allen's paradigmatic joke about wanting to be someone else. Among Allen's characters, only Terry (Colin Farrell) in *Cassandra's Dream* feels this kind of sustained regret for *who he is*.

Agent regret, the principal topic of this study, involves a dimension of personal responsibility lacking in nostalgia (the topic of Chapter Six) or regret at the acts of others. One may yearn for the good old days without feeling remorse for their passing. One may regret the misdeeds of a family member, one may even feel ashamed by them, but one does not ordinarily feel guilty. One may also sincerely regret deeds that one would not renounce, choosing the lesser of two evils, as when forced to fire a competent employee or to torture a terrorist, a situation creating what Stephen De Wijze defines as 'tragic remorse' (2005: 463). Judah Rosenthal (Martin Landau) sees himself in this dilemma (for a time) when he resolves to have his mistress murdered in *Crimes and Misdemeanors*. Having learned that the crime has been committed, Judah is overwhelmed with guilt ('God have mercy on our souls', he tells his brother Jack over the phone) and punishes himself in subsequent scenes, but his remorse 'passes' with time, and the film concludes with him happily reunited with his wife and planning his daughter's wedding – an example of what might be termed the 'comic remorse' that marks so much of Woody Allen's cinema, as when Diane apologises for killing her lover and allowing her under-aged daughter to take the rap in *September* (1987): 'I'm sorry for all the fuss. We all make mistakes.'

Compared to this kind of superficial or transient regret, remorse is much the stronger emotion, carrying with it personal responsibility along with a moral imperative to undo the action and punish oneself. According to Roger Trigg, regret seems, by contrast, more like a cognitive function with 'a rather mild flavour about it', absent 'the horror we might feel at some of the things we have to do' (1971; cited in Zoch 1986: 55). In contrast to regret (including many forms of agent regret commonly called 'buyer's remorse'), 'Remorse is felt about a sin or moral wrong whereas regret is felt about what is in some ways undesirable, but not particularly morally so' (Taylor 1985: 98). Therefore, remorse always involves self-condemnation, while 'no action need follow from regret' (1985: 99). Throughout this book, remorse will be used almost interchangeably with the moral aspect of guilt, which, to be precise, must always *precede* remorse and which, according to Freud, may result not only from an overt action (agent regret) but from a self-perception of innate or deeply-rooted immoral impulses (character regret). One can imagine an individual feeling regret without guilt, as in nostalgia or the examples of necessary agent regret, but not guilt without regret. One can also distinguish the experience of *collective* guilt (such as being born into a privileged social class or being the citizen of an aggressive or discriminatory nation) without actually feeling morally responsible for one's status or the guilty agency of others in power. Woody Allen's characters, however, rarely express either guilt or regret at being Upper East Siders or Americans abroad.

Regret as a prominent theme appears in Allen's cinema for the first time in *Play It Again, Sam*, which he wrote and starred in but which was directed by Herbert Ross. The movie's comic premise is that the protagonist, Allan Felix (Woody Allen), a recently divorced, lovelorn film critic, regrets that he is not a romantic hero like his idol, Humphrey Bogart, who comes to life (played by Jerry Lacy) to provide him with dating advice. With the help of his movie phantom, Allan seems on the verge of stealing his best friend's wife Linda (Diane Keaton), a plot point that consumes him with mock guilt. In voice-over, Allan thinks: 'Dick and I have been through a lot together. He's my best friend. This is terrible. This is going to hurt him, I know it... Dick is an emotional guy. He's liable to do something, kill himself. Kill himself? You ever think what he might do to *you*?' Hardly remorseful over the injustice of his betrayal of friendship, his regret focuses not on the immorality of the deed or the effect on his victim but on the potential personal consequences. There follows a hilarious parody of an Italian movie in which he imagines the aggrieved knife-wielding Dick (Tony Roberts) attacking his cowering self. Preparing to host Linda for dinner at his apartment, Allan is reassured by his libidinous avatar Bogart, who coaches him from the adjacent supermarket aisle: 'Come on, kid, you don't have to feel guilty.'

Play It Again, Sam begins with Allan in a movie theatre watching the climactic airfield scene in *Casablanca* (1942) and ends with an ingenious parody of Bogart's famous speech, which pivots on the concept of regret. On the foggy tarmac before boarding a plane to Cleveland (!), Linda confesses that she loves Allan but then adds that she doesn't regret their romance because it has 'reaffirmed my feelings for Dick'. In the face of another rejection, Allan confirms her decision by reciting Bogart's farewell to Ingrid Bergman: 'If that plane leaves the ground and you're not on it, you'll regret it; maybe not today, maybe not tomorrow, but soon, and for the rest of your life.' Allan immediately attests to the shallowness of his noble renunciation by admitting both that he has plagiarised the speech (anticipating how Cliff plagiarises James Joyce in his love letters to Halley in *Crimes and Misdemeanors*) and that he has 'waited *my whole life* to say it'. The film's homage to *Casablanca* – the inherent nostalgia that marks its premise – expresses the futile wish that it might be otherwise: that Allan had lived in a more romantic era; that Allen had written a more enduring screenplay. Instead Allan becomes a callow impersonator and Allen a clever parodist.

As a measure of Woody Allen's development as a filmmaker, regret receives more elaborate treatment in the early triumphs of his classic period, *Annie Hall* and *Manhattan*. Alvy Singer's acknowledgement in *Annie Hall*'s opening monologue of a 'screw-up' – what might be construed as a colloquial translation of Aristotelian *hamartia*: a mistaken action or error in judgement – subtly detaches itself from personal responsibility. His rhetorical question precludes remorse by denying agency: 'Where did the screw-up come?' not 'Where did I screw up?' Within the subsequent narrative, he mounts a series of rationalisations about his break-up with Annie that culminates not in private confession but in whining in the streets ('I miss Annie!'), self-justification ('I think we both realise we're doing the mature thing', he tells her), and, in his concluding voice-overs, nostalgia. For Alvy, the film's presiding philosopher as well as its narrator, regret may yet be redeemed by the self-serving act of re-telling the story, as when he re-stages their separation in an Los Angeles health food café as a romantic reconciliation ('What do you want? It was my first play?') and closes the film by transforming regret over his parting from Annie into wistful remembrance and philosophical resignation.

In *Manhattan*, a self-consciously more 'serious' film than *Annie Hall*, Allen foregrounds aesthetics (black-and-white cinematography, opening and closing montages set to Gershwin's 'Rhapsody in Blue', formal widescreen compositions) and, for the first time in a sustained way, ethics. Despite his involvement with a 17-year-old girl, Isaac Davis (Allen) appears throughout the narrative to value moral integrity in contrast to his best friend, Yale (Michael Murphy). In the opening dialogue at Elaine's, a conversation repeated with slight variation at the beginning of *Bullets Over Broadway*, Yale begins talking about 'the essence of art', but Isaac turns the philosophical topic to the ethical question of risking one's life to save a drowning person. When Tracy (Mariel Hemingway) leaves their table, he expresses doubts about dating such a young woman ('I'm older than her father') to Yale and his wife. Isaac's uneasiness about his relationship with Tracy reflects the shame that Jean-Paul Sartre attributes to the look of the Other – particularly in the scene later in the film when he breaks off their relationship in the malt shop. 'Shame is the consciousness of being irremediably what I always was,' Sartre writes in *Being and Nothingness*, 'not a feeling of being this or that guilty object but in general of being an object; that is, of *recognizing myself* in this degraded, fixed, and dependent being which I am for the Other' (2003: 312; emphasis in original). In this public setting, momentarily separated from Tracy, Isaac projects himself as the stereotypical dirty old man that others might see in their relationship. Yale, meanwhile, reveals outside the restaurant that he is having a 'serious' affair after 'one or two very minor things' outside his marriage. Isaac expresses 'shock' at this news. Soon thereafter, he quits his well-paying job in television to write a book about 'the decay of contemporary civilisation'. When Yale's mistress, Mary (Diane Keaton), calls to invite him for a walk that ends up at the Hayden Planetarium, Isaac resists the romantic opportunity to begin seeing her

Fig. 1: Tracy's face: for Levinas, the 'pure expression of the Other'

because, as he explains to her in a subsequent scene, he would never have betrayed his friend (unlike Allan Felix, who would if he could). Moreover, once Yale breaks off the relationship and Isaac begins dating Mary, he confesses his new relationship to Tracy ('The truth is that I love somebody else'), leaving her in tears. 'Don't cry', he implores, feeling somehow exposed by her suffering gaze. Although he has apparently taken the high moral ground, Tracy reveals the selfishness of his intentions: 'You keep stating it like it's to my advantage when it's you who wants to get out of it.' Feeling unmasked but apparently not regretful because he believes he is doing the right thing, Isaac can only respond rhetorically: 'Why should I feel guilty?' The scene ends abruptly with a close-up of Tracy's sorrowful but beautiful face, the face of the Other, the face being, for Levinas, the 'pure expression' of the Other that is the site of an ethical relationship (Macready 2013: 105). A single tear that funnels down her cheek, which Isaac gently wipes away, silently serves to indict him as the close-up excludes him from the frame, isolating the girl's innocence in the midst of a midtown malt shop.

Manhattan's philosophical climax comes in the well-known science classroom scene when Isaac confronts Yale after Mary admits she is seeing him again. Against the background of a laboratory skull (perhaps an allusion to Ingmar Bergman's *mise-en-scène* during the picnic sequence in *The Seventh Seal* (1957)), Isaac lectures on morality ('You're too easy on yourself') and responds to his feckless friend's excuse ('We're just human beings. You think you're God!') by asserting his own righteous superiority and desire for self-transcendence: 'I gotta model myself on someone.' Yale, who has been trying to complete an academic book on James Joyce while indulging his distracting tastes for stylish sports cars and attractive women, represents what Herbert Fingarette has described as the 'shallowly sincere' person. He is sincere rather than merely acquisitive when he admires and ultimately buys the Porsche; he is sincere rather than simply coarse when he falls for Mary and then steals her back from Isaac. But he fails to take seriously the consequences (for his marriage, his friendship, his work) of his actions (Fingarette 1977: 51–2; cited in Taylor 1985: 114). Exposed by Isaac – and by Allen's *mise-en-scène* – he nonetheless feels no apparent shame. As the film cuts between the two debaters after the establishing shot positions Yale in the corner of the frame and hemmed in by the two storage cabinets, the editing as well as the dialogue clearly favours Isaac, giving him more close-up time as well as the last word. But despite his insistence that 'it's very important to have some sense of personal integrity', at the end of the film we might well ask whether Isaac also is 'too easy on himself'.

The closing scene has Isaac running across Manhattan to Tracy's building in an effort to win her back. Although he regrets having forced the break-up ('I made a mistake', he says, a confession that Emmet Ray recites verbatim in *Sweet and*

Figs. 2 and 3: The *mise-en-scène* corners Yale and crowds Isaac in ethical retreat

Lowdown twenty years later), he offers the apology grudgingly, adding 'What do you want me to say?' However sincere his appeal, it remains self-serving ('I don't want that thing about you that I like to change'), ignoring the opportunity for Tracy to study theatre in London. In effect, Isaac has traded places with Yale in this exchange, occupying his position on the left of the frame with the door behind him. Tracy bests every point of his appeal, reminding him of how much he hurt her ('It was not on purpose', he replies, the passive voice again unconsciously disclaiming his own intention), invoking the enduring force of true love ('Hey, don't be so mature', he can only reply to her saying that six months is not such a long separation, after previously complaining about Yale's excuses: 'What are you, six years old?'), and finally expressing a philosophy very close to what we might imagine to be Woody Allen's: 'Not everyone gets corrupted. You have to have a little faith in people.'

In the films that follow *Manhattan*, Allen continues to explore variations on the motif of regret. *Zelig*, for example, 'mockuments' a case study of what Sartre described in *Being and Nothingness* as ontological shame, the revelation in the presence of the Other that 'I have an outside that is vulnerable and exposed, a body that exceeds my own conscious experience' (2003: 282). As a consequence, in *Zelig*, the eponymous protagonist 'hides' his shame – his regret that he is not someone else – by transforming his body in an effort to become the Other instead of an object-for-the-Other. The film's pseudo-documentary form – supplemented by real-life 'talking heads' including Irving Howe, Susan Sontag and Bruno Bettelheim – subtly underscores Zelig's absent selfhood as well as his fictionality within history: he 'exists' only in fragments of old newsreels, entirely absent from the present. His peculiar neurosis, a physical manifestation of his consciousness of being gazed at by the Other and the condition that creates his celebrity as the 'Chameleon Man' of the 1920s, involves a form of shame without guilt. Although he is the object of numerous lawsuits (among other crimes, he becomes a serial polygamist) and eventually is discovered among the adoring Nazi officers at a Hitler rally, he remains, according to the voice-over narration, 'a cipher, a non-person, a performing freak' awaiting rescue from his emptiness through the loving care of his therapist, Dr. Eudora Fletcher (Mia Farrow). In the end, Zelig returns to a normal life, free from his compulsive need to conform, publicly apologetic for his past behaviour, and finally marked by only one conscious regret: that he never finished reading *Moby-Dick*. The film's closing punch line completes the process of Zelig's rehabilitation by ironically affirming his personhood. His 'one regret' riffs on Woody Allen's wish to be someone else by confessing to a failure in Zelig's education shared by nearly everyone in the movie audience. Thus, his regret redeems him from his freakishness: by admitting his error in not reading Melville's masterpiece, Zelig, the mythically innocent nincompoop, conforms at last to common humanity. He has finally become like everyone else.

'The Shallowest Man'

As the ultimate comic manifestation of regret that he is not someone else – to date, Terry in *Cassandra's Dream* remains Allen's sole incarnation of tragic remorse – Zelig embodies the depthlessness of a cartoon, magically malleable yet unconscious of his own agency. Against charges of polygamy and treason, he is acquitted by his obvious lunacy. Throughout Allen's cinema, his characters offer excuses that range from the hilarious, as in Monk's apology for beating his wife ('It's not me, it's the whiskey'), to the appalling, as in Judah's rationalisation for killing his mistress ('What am I supposed to do, let her destroy my life?'). His characters may feel momentarily guilty, like Jack admitting his affair with a young personal trainer (*Husbands and Wives*), or at least responsible, like Jasmine lamenting not continuing her education, but their regret inevitably proves neither persistent nor profound. Thus, Jack concludes his confession with 'What's the big deal?' In the end, Allen's protagonists generally follow Peter's advice in *Scoop*: 'Let's move on with our lives.'

Getting on in life in Allen's cinema nearly always means not thinking too deeply about things. This principle is best represented by the nameless handsome young couple Alvy approaches on a Manhattan side street in *Annie Hall*. Ruminating about the cause of his recent break-up with Annie and filled with angst, he asks them to account for their apparently happy relationship. The beautiful woman replies, 'Uh, I'm very shallow and empty and I have no ideas and nothing interesting to say', to which her partner immediately adds, 'And I'm exactly the same way.' Alvy thanks them and walks away, perhaps thinking, by way of prolepsis across more than three decades of Allen's films, *whatever works*. The consequence of thinking, the cost of caring, inevitably leads to regret. Alvy spends the duration of his narrative trying to come to terms with the disconcerting truth about losing Annie, ultimately exonerating himself through the sentimental montage and fatalistic punch line ('We need the eggs') that conclude the film. Other Allen protagonists avoid confronting regret on bogus philosophical grounds, like the unproduced playwright Sheldon Flender in *Bullets Over Broadway* ('You gotta do what you do'), or offer patently insincere apologies, like Val in *Hollywood Ending* (2002): 'If I die tell Ellie I'm sorry I said all those things to her.' But if not, he quickly adds, 'tell her she's a jerk' for marrying

Hal. In Sartre's terms, they are the agents of Bad Faith. In T. S. Eliot's phrase, they are 'The Hollow Men'.

One of Allen's earliest, most direct expositions of this complacent character type occurs in the hilarious, absurd story 'The Shallowest Man', first published in the *Kenyon Review* and later anthologised in *Side Effects* (1980). The author employs the same narrative frame he applied a few years later in *Broadway Danny Rose*: several men sitting in a delicatessen swap stories about their acquaintances until Koppelman begins relating the tale of 'Lenny Mendel's record-breaking superficiality' (1980: 103). Lenny is one of a group of regular poker players whose long-standing game is disturbed by the terminal illness of one of their number, Meyer Iskowitz. Hospitalised in a cancer ward, Meyer is visited by all the players except Lenny, who procrastinates and rationalises until he is finally shamed – without guilt ('What do they think I am, a man of leisure? I've just been made associate producer. I've got a million things on my mind' (1980: 102)) – into seeing the dying man. 'The truth is, when he finally got up enough courage to make a ten-minute visit to the hospital it was more out of needing to have a self-image he could live with rather than out of any compassion for Iskowitz' (1980: 103). Only character regret, the thought that 'others will know me for what I am – a self-centered louse' (ibid.), compels Lenny to visit Sloan-Kettering. There he meets and falls in love with Meyer's buxom young nurse, Miss Hill, which leads him to embark on a series of daily visits, inveigling conversations and inappropriate gifts ('Mendel did stop short of bringing Iskowitz a pair of antique earrings although he saw some he knew Miss Hill would adore' (1980: 108)). Allen's shaggy-dog story concludes with Meyer's death, whereupon two weeks later, 'Mendel started dating her. They had an affair that lasted a year and then went their separate ways' (1980: 110). The dénouement involves the various listeners interpreting the moral until one of them, Bursky, concludes, 'Who cares what the point of the story is? If it even has a point. It was an entertaining anecdote. Let's order' (1980: 111). Let's move on with our lives…

From the perspective of this chapter's survey of Allen's 'philosophy' of regret, the story makes several points; in fact, despite its casual design and relative obscurity among Allen's writings, 'The Shallowest Man' might serve as a touchstone for understanding some of his best films. Mendel's insensitivity to the suffering of others, his self-serving rationalisations, his feeble excuses for bad behaviour define him as the comic double of the progressively darker characters that mark Allen's mature work. Perhaps his nearest incarnation in film in terms of comic proportions remains Monk (Danny Aiello), Cecilia's worthless husband in *The Purple Rose of*

Cairo. Alternating between neglect and abuse of his long-suffering wife, Monk offers only a caricature of contrition ('I never just hit you, I always warn you first') for his loutish conduct. The exaggeration of their obliviousness to any sense of responsibility allows for Mendel's and Monk's outlandish misconduct to appear funny rather than monstrous, a form of ethical incompetence that produces the kind of over-the-top humour commonly described as 'so bad it's good'. The same superficiality in smaller proportion and with greater verisimilitude exposes Yale, Doug (*Alice*), and Harry Block (*Deconstructing Harry*) as unlikable and Judah, Chris (*Match Point*) and Abe (*Irrational Man*) as despicable.

In addition to expressing the author's interest in a certain modern character type possibly derived from T. S. Eliot's poem 'The Hollow Men' (1925), the story also points to Allen's long-professed ambivalence about his own talent and commitment as an artist, a topic explored at length in Chapter Four. The shaggy-dog story nature of Koppelman's tale, its ultimate pointlessness, addresses the limitations of art – especially comedy – to resolve social and ontological problems. In 'The Shallowest Man', the problem is death – the most profound source of human regret. Allen has testified to his misgivings about the enduring value of art and his own limitations as an artist in countless interviews. His remarks on comedy, for example, reinforce Bursky's dismissal of Koppelman's amusing story: 'Comedy is less valuable than serious stuff. It has less of an impact, and I think for good reason. When comedy approaches a problem, it kids it but it doesn't resolve it' (Lax 2009: 66). As for his own creative genius, Allen is equally equivocal, if not downright self-deprecatory: 'It's just not in me to make a great film; I don't have the depth of vision to do it' (Lax 2009: 251). His phrase is telling; elsewhere he says it explicitly: 'I'm basically a shallow person' (Lax 1991: 285). Commenting on his preference for one-shot takes in his later films, he admits, 'People said this is a style, but it's not a style, it's just laziness. I don't have the patience' (Harland and Peters; cited in Bailey 2001: 277). Among the shallow men, Allen seems to be saying through his story, we must not ignore the shallowness of the artist, particularly the comedian, and especially myself.

Finally, if we read 'The Shallowest Man' retrospectively, as we may now feel compelled to view *Manhattan* and *Deconstructing Harry* in light of the revelations about Allen's personal life following the Farrow lawsuits and the continuing accusations of sexual abuse that periodically make headlines and inform gossip, we can see the story's protagonist as something like a self-caricature. Following the professional success of *Annie Hall*, his nightclub performances, and his television appearances and recordings, but also in the wake of several failed personal relationships, Allen may have conceived of Lenny Mendel in 1980 (a television producer by trade) as a comic projection of his own feeling of puerility: his regret at being capable only of parodying the great Russian novels as he had in *Love and Death*, his remorse over certain people – parents, ex-wives, former lovers, business associates – left behind, and his guilt over not experiencing those losses more deeply. If his own repeated statements can be believed, however, in both his private and professional life, Allen does not seem, contrary to Christopher J. Knight's description of him, 'a man and artist wracked by guilt' (2013: 83). Consequently, this autobiographical interpretation may well be a speculative over-reading of what is, after all, a mere sketch, 'an entertaining anecdote'; still, the personal implications of 'The Shallowest Man' return more fully developed in *Deconstructing Harry* and one of Allen's most under-valued films, *Sweet and Lowdown*, which remains the epitome to date of his ruminations on shallowness and regret.

Sweet and Lowdown

The most recent major scholarly work about Allen's cinema, *A Companion to Woody Allen*, contains twenty-seven essays but only two brief references to *Sweet and Lowdown*. Despite Academy Award-nominated performances by Sean Penn and Samantha Morton and generally positive reviews, the film did poorly at the box office (taking in barely $4 million in domestic theatre receipts) and, like its protagonist, the fictitious jazz guitarist Emmet Ray (Penn), essentially disappeared from public view – almost certainly a victim of Allen's damaged reputation at the time. To date, only Peter J. Bailey and Derek Parker Royal have given it extended scholarly scrutiny. Nevertheless, *Sweet and Lowdown* should be judged with *Broadway Danny Rose* as a small gem among Allen's more ambitious masterworks, like its predecessor a fable for adults but with an inverted story arc. While Danny Rose rises in the eyes of the comedians at the Carnegie Deli from *schmuck* to secular saint, Emmet Ray declines from genius in his own eyes to the lonely wreck of a shallow man. Only the six aficionados who serve as talking heads throughout the mockumentary (Woody Allen being the first and last of them to comment) remain to testify to his musical brilliance.

As in *Annie Hall*, the narrative begins with Woody Allen addressing the camera (the only jazz expert without an identifying caption) introducing the twentieth century's second-greatest guitarist. 'Why Emmet Ray?' Allen asks, as if responding to a question at a film festival press conference. 'Because he was interesting. To me,

Emmet Ray was a fascinating character ... and he was funny, or if funny is not the right word, sort of pathetic in a way. He was flamboyant, and he was boorish, and obnoxious.' The pseudo-biopic that follows recounts the life of the legendary jazz musician, a rather ludicrous schemer and narcissist who transcends his cynical, conniving and reckless lifestyle only when he plays his instrument. Allen skillfully conveys this transfiguration during Emmet's first performance ('Parlez-Moi d'Amour', the song reprised in key scenes of *Midnight in Paris*) with a close-up of Penn's face beatified by the music followed by a pan down to his fingers on the frets, the continuity of the shot creating the illusion that the actor – not the guitarist Howard Alden in the sound studio – is actually playing the music. Like the concluding close-up of Cecilia (Mia Farrow) smiling through her tears as Fred Astaire sings 'Heaven' off-screen in *The Purple Rose of Cairo*, in its own modest way, the panning shot early in *Sweet and Lowdown* combines musical and cinematic virtuosity.

Emmet repeatedly calls himself an artist to justify his freedom from conventional human responsibility, like Flender in *Bullets Over Broadway* declaring, 'The artist creates his own moral universe'. Emmet remains disdainful of everyone except his idol, Django Reinhardt, the great (and real) French-Gypsy guitarist of the 1930s and 1940s, whose mere presence invariably causes him to faint. The crass characterisation of Emmet throughout nearly the entire film combines Mendel's insensitivity with Monk's loutishness, redeemed only by glimpses of generosity towards his girlfriend, Hattie (Samantha Morton), and mercurial displays of his incredible talent ('a gift from God', he calls it). Upon first meeting him, his (future) ex-wife Blanche (Uma Thurman) remarks, 'Not only are you vain and egotistical, but you have genuine crudeness'; in addition to these unappealing qualities, he is a skirt-chaser, a kleptomaniac, a gambler and a drunk. Similar vices can be found in the caricature of Monk in *The Purple Rose of Cairo*, but Allen makes the protagonist of *Sweet and Lowdown* a more nuanced character in order to allow for Emmet's eventual breakdown and the subsequent confirmation of his undeniable artistry in the film's bittersweet ending; Monk, by contrast, like the figures left on the screen in *The Purple Rose of Cairo*, remains 'minor'. For all his flaws, Emmet has a sympathetic back story (abandoned by his father, he grew up in a brothel where his mother worked) and a couple of admirable personal traits (he mixes easily with black musicians and takes genuine joy in dressing Hattie in fine clothes). Although he claims no regrets ('Not a bit. It was the right decision for me'), he describes having left Hattie $500 when he deserted her, perhaps an unrecognised admission of guilt for his callous perfidy, which Allen chooses not to dramatise on screen.

As he had in *Stardust Memories*, *Bullets Over Broadway* and *Deconstructing Harry*, Allen again explores the discrepancy between the artist and the man. Like Flender in *Bullets Over Broadway*, Emmet believes his genius entitles him to deny any deep or enduring relationship to other humans: 'I gotta be free. I'm an artist', he tells each of his girlfriends. But in Hattie, a mute laundress he is left with when his musician friend wins a coin toss for first choice between two women they pick up on the Atlantic City Boardwalk ('This is my one day off. I want a talking girl', he complains), Emmet finds a totally devoted acolyte, one who loves both the artist *and* the man. After going to bed with her at the end of their first date – 'It's like shooting fish in a barrel', he mutters as the sexually ravenous Hattie readily takes the lead in the seduction – and afterwards denying her cab fare ('I'm a little short this week'), Emmet grants her wish to hear him play. In a marvelous split-screen composition that compounds the effect of his earlier performance, he plays 'I'm Forever Blowing Bubbles' while a backlit close-up reveals Hattie's rapturous aesthetic response. The camera slowly tracks in on Hattie's expression, excluding Emmet, the source of her pleasure, from the right side of the screen. 'Her face alone, in the moments of pure ecstasy Emmet's music instils in her, lifts her beyond the pedestrian circumstances of which she is product and victim into an almost extrahuman prettiness' (Bailey 2001: 272). Although he doesn't fully recognise it, in this scene Emmet has discovered (as Zelig found in Dr. Fletcher) both the love of a good woman and his ideal audience. Even the insensitive egotist recognises the pleasure Hattie has experienced, as his boasting about his sexual prowess shifts to his own musical genius: 'You might be mute', he tells Hattie, 'but you're not deaf.'

Fig. 4: The split screen illuminates Hattie's rapture

After careening from job to job and woman to woman, after abandoning Hattie and being two-timed by Blanche, Emmet returns to Atlantic City for a recording session and surprises Hattie as she eats her lunch on the Boardwalk. For the only time, he offers her an apology, however self-justifying: 'I'm sorry I cut out on you like that. It was time to move on. I was fair – I told you not to fall in love with me.' Although he acknowledges some regret at causing her unhappiness at the time, Emmet feels no true remorse, believing that his undesirable action was necessitated by his status as an artist. In short, he feels unashamed in her presence, having experienced, in Dan Zahavi's definitive phrase, no 'global decrease of self-esteem' (2012: 316) in this moment, despite his admission to thinking about her from time to time, going so far as to confess how, according to his ex-wife, he once called out her name in his sleep ('must have been a nightmare'). When he tentatively invites her to come to New York with his band, Hattie passes him a note. Allen preserves a moment of suspense as Emmet tries to decipher her handwriting, then fills in her personal history with the guitarist's poignant one-word question: 'Happily?' Pained by the news of her new family, Emmet thinly disguises his disappointment by reverting to his mantra – 'It's just as well. You know me, I can't take entanglements' – and bidding a hasty farewell ('Take it easy') as he exits screen left. The camera remains fixed, and Allen holds the image of empty space, the blue sky meeting the seashore, for an extra beat to conclude this extraordinary scene in which the two characters never appear in the same shot once the camera pans to cover Emmet's monologue.

Sweet and Lowdown winds down rapidly from this final parting. Almost immediately, however, Emmet reaches an epiphany of regret at having rejected the woman he had earlier described as 'a genuinely sweet person', a recognition similar to what Isaac Davis discovers with the memory of Tracy's face. In drunken despair, he roughly picks up a new girl (played by Gretchen Mol), drives her to his habitual dating spot, the railroad tracks, to watch trains, and, when she ignores his invitation for 'requests', begins strumming 'Sweet Sue'. In a shift that echoes the second lobster scene from *Annie Hall* when Alvy tries to re-create the memory of an absent romantic ideal, Emmet changes the tune to 'I'm Forever Blowing Bubbles'. The camera moves to a close-up that excludes his indifferent date and surrounds the guitarist in darkness. Suddenly, sadly, the shallow man seems to collapse inwardly, confessing his profound error. 'I made a mistake!' Emmet wails in the presence of his uncomprehending companion and proceeds to smash his guitar against a telephone pole. To whom is this confession addressed? The camera's pan to the left into the black of night and away from his irrelevant companion suggests it is Hattie, present in her absence rather than the screechy woman (identified in the credits as 'Ellie' – sounds like 'Hattie') permanently excluded from the frame. In Penn's delivery of the line (different from Allen's restrained reading of Isaac's admission in *Manhattan*), there is true self-loathing and depths of despair, unlike his false bravado when he said goodbye on the Boardwalk. In contrast to Isaac, who feels regret but not remorse because his intentions in breaking up with Tracy were honourable, Emmet now recognises that his 'mistake' was wrong insofar as he abandoned Hattie rather than explaining his reasons face-to-face and that he should have acted differently, as evidenced by the money he left behind to ease his minimally developed conscience. This newly awakened moral awareness measures precisely the distinction between regret and remorse that the philosopher Gabrielle Taylor has defined between an act that produces an undesirable consequence (regret) rather than a morally abhorrent one (remorse) (1985: 98). In his act of destroying the instrument of his one claim to an honorable self, there is not only guilt but punishment. In the naked admission of his connection to the Other and remorse without excuse, Emmet experiences a moment of authentic shame, his ultimate exile from the screen a form of atonement for his mistake. The camera cranes up to a high-angle long shot of his ghostly figure dressed in an iridescent white suit crumpled beneath the streetlight – the same would-be star who tried to emerge from the background in his one Hollywood movie appearance, now exposed and vulnerable, wishing 'to hide and disappear, to become invisible, to sink into the ground' (Zahavi 2012: 313). A sound bridge conveys us to the present for the concluding expert interviews, in which the fictitious musicologist A. J. Pickman (Daniel Okrent) testifies to the greatness of Ray's

Fig. 5: The high-angle long shot in darkness marks Emmet's descent into remorse

final recordings, how Emmet the artist finally became 'every bit as good as Django Reinhardt'. Allen himself closes the film, using a cinematic expression to describe how Emmet 'seemed to just fade away' and confirming how his music at the very end was 'absolutely beautiful'.

At the risk of perpetuating Blanche's superficial brand of psychological criticism ('What are your real feelings when you're playing?' Emmet: 'That I'm underpaid'), this analysis might suggest that *Sweet and Lowdown* is not only Allen's most nuanced portrait of the shallow man's regret – one that finally devolves into remorse – but that it also might be his most self-revealing film. From this view, Django Reinhardt becomes an Ingmar Bergman for Allen, the embodiment of cinematic artistry to which the talented filmmaker can only aspire. In his eulogy to Bergman for *The New York Times*, Allen wrote, 'he was a genius and I am not a genius and genius cannot be learned or its magic passed on' (2007). Of course, we know that Woody became friends with Ingmar later in life, that he found him to be 'a regular guy' (Lax 2009: 368), and that he certainly never fainted in the Swedish master's presence, but from the time he was writing jokes for money as a teenager, Allen has maintained a modest attitude towards both his artistic abilities and his accomplishments. After having watched Bergman's *The Seventh Seal* and *Wild Strawberries* (1957), he told his film biographer, Robert B. Wiede, he thought his own career was 'pointless'. Compared to Shakespeare, Dostoyevsky or Kafka, all authors he has parodied but not challenged, as well as to auteurs like Fellini or Bergman, Allen sees himself, it seems fair to say, as something more than Allan Felix but perhaps something less (in keeping with his assessment of himself as a clarinetist) than Emmet Ray. *Sweet and Lowdown* may be understood as the artist's acknowledgement that his own body of work, while consistently good, has never reached greatness, and as his expression of the hope (to paraphrase Professor Levy's closing voice-over in *Crimes and Misdemeanors*) that he might do better in the future.

What might the film reveal about Woody Allen the man rather than the artist? We enter even more speculative territory in suggesting that, at the end of the century and the most painful decade in Allen's career, *Sweet and Lowdown* reflects a personal coming-to-terms with the events that defined the third stage of the public's perception of him. Emmet, in this view, becomes a caricature of the insensitive, arrogant deceiver perpetuated in portraits of Allen throughout the 1990s (and persistent until today), epitomised by Marion Meade's biography, *The Unruly Life of Woody Allen* (2000). Only Hattie, in her silent adulation and unaffected goodness, stands apart from the succession of frivolous women, itinerant collaborators and criminal types who comprise Emmet's occasional need for company. The simple pleasures of living and the faithful love she offers him, the loss of which is the source of Emmet's eventual remorse, Allen seems to have found with Soon-Yi Previn and refuses to renounce, whatever the price to his fame. In contrast to the defiant tone of *Deconstructing Harry*, which many reviewers regarded as his most autobiographical film, *Sweet and Lowdown* concludes on an elegiac note as Allen remarks on Emmet's 'fade' from history. This self-reflexive phrase speaks to a sense of cinema at the end of the twentieth century – the passing not just of Hollywood or the foreign art film, but of celluloid itself, a medium he clung to until finally submitting to digital filmmaking with *Café Society* (2016). Perhaps the verb 'fade' also conveys Allen's sense of his own eclipse (although he would adamantly deny it), the nostalgia he has so often applied to Manhattan, jazz and Hollywood movies now reflecting the loss of his own ideal conception of himself. Fortunately for admirers of *Match Point*, *Vicky Cristina Barcelona*, *Midnight in Paris* and *Blue Jasmine*, this *fin-de-siècle* moment of regret, if it ever indeed existed, has apparently passed, and Allen, rather than fading away, persists in pursuing the phantom of film greatness one year at a time. Admiring Bergman's lifetime achievement of sixty films, Allen would write in 2007, 'At least if I can't rise to his quality maybe I can approach his quantity' (2007). Resolute in this philosophy, he may yet produce for himself a fifth and final act.

CHAPTER TWO

Apprentice Works

'I saw [Ingmar Bergman's] *The Seventh Seal* yesterday and *Cries and Whispers* today. I see his films and wonder what I'm doing.'

– Woody Allen, 1973 (Lax 2009: 3)

Although Emmet's remorse over abandoning Hattie in *Sweet and Lowdown* can be distinguished from Isaac's regret at breaking up with Tracy in *Manhattan*, the difference hinges on a fine point: Emmet's drunken 'I made a mistake!' acknowledges a decision that produced an unfortunate outcome without actually confessing to an immoral act. That he feels some moral responsibility (unlike Isaac, who rhetorically asks, 'Why should I feel guilty?') is evidenced by the reparations he leaves her ('$500 cash by the bed') when he 'cuts out' and the apology, however qualified, he offers when he sees her for the last time: 'I was fair. I told you not to fall in love with me. It's nothing personal.' But his remains a shallow man's remorse. Emmet regrets leaving Hattie because he misses her company, not because he betrayed her trust. 'Not one time did I ever regret dumping a beautiful dame', he tells his friend Billy (Brian Markinson); he certainly does not think twice about leaving his wife Blanche, but he truly does regret losing the one good thing ('a genuinely sweet person') in his lowdown existence.

Except for the interludes when he plays his guitar or the one occasion when he reminisces in bed with Hattie about his mother, Emmet is, no less than Zelig, a nearly forgotten figure of faux history in the eyes of the experts who testify about him and a buffoon in the eyes of the film audience. The technical aspects of *Sweet and Lowdown* – the Oscar-calibre performances of Sean Penn and Samantha Morton, Zhao Fei's luminous cinematography, the diegetic and non-diegetic music track – reflect the mature talent of a sophisticated filmmaker, but for most of Emmet's scenes (as when he descends to the stage balancing on a crescent moon or shoots at rats in the local dump), the movie's protagonist exhibits the two-dimensionality of a cartoon. Whether stealing ashtrays or chasing women, Emmet remains the caricature of an artist whose only genius is revealed in the act of creation. In this respect, he takes the viewer back to Woody Allen's origins as a gag writer, stand-up comedian and apprentice director. Indeed, the story line for *Sweet and Lowdown* traces back to a screenplay he had offered United Artists in 1970 titled 'The Jazz Baby' that he subsequently shelved when the UA executives were unenthusiastic about its downbeat tone.

Most readers will know the story of how Allan Stewart Koningsberg, a shy, unpromising high school student from Brooklyn, began submitting clever jokes to popular New York newspaper columnists like Nick Kenny, Earl Wilson and Walter Winchell and took the pen name Woody Allen to conceal his slightly 'embarrassing' occupation from his friends (Schickel 2003: 89). Here, for the historians among you, is his first published joke under his pseudonym, from Wilson's *New York Post* column of 25 November 1952: 'Woody Allen figured out what OPS [Office of Price Stabilization, a government price control agency] prices are – Over People's Salaries' (Lax 1991: 69). Perhaps a wittier example is this one, also from Earl Wilson: 'Says Woody Allen: A hypocrite is a guy who writes a book on atheism, and prays it sells' (Shone 2015: 15). Almost immediately, he was taking the subway into Manhattan after school and writing gags – fifty a day – in a small office for $20, then quickly $40 per week. 'I always said that I could write before I could read', he told Stig Björkman (2004: 8), describing a natural talent that soon earned him a significant salary writing for television stars like Sid Caesar and Garry Moore and cabaret comedians like Sammy Kaye, the latter being the kind of crude entertainer briefly portrayed in *Annie Hall* who may have driven the reluctant Allen to begin performing his own material.

Now under the superb management of Jack Rollins and Charles H. Joffe, his producers for the next half century, Woody overcame his initial stage fright and began doing stand-up in several Greenwich Village nightclubs, where he was 'discovered' by the New York press and, soon thereafter, found himself playing the top spots across the country and appearing on numerous network television shows. Small in stature, marked by nervous tics and a stammering delivery, Allen on stage was his own sight gag, having 'turned his fear of performing into its own performance' (Shone 2015: 24). By 1964, when he met the movie producer Charles Feldman, who offered him $35,000 to write the script for what became *What's New Pussycat?* (1965), he had become a household name. He had also decided he wanted to become a filmmaker – despite having barely passed a film course on his way to flunking out of New York University a decade earlier.

Looking back, Allen tends to be self-deprecating about his wildly successful career as a comic. He was inspired to perform in cabarets after admiring Mort Sahl, a seemingly more cerebral monologist who dressed in street clothes and carried a copy of *The New York Times* on stage. Allen briefly channels Sahl in a moment from *Annie Hall* where he appears at a political rally for Adlai Stevenson telling a joke about dating a girl during the Eisenhower administration and trying to do to her what Eisenhower had been doing to the country for the past eight years. Compared to the political humour of Mort Sahl, Woody was, in his own estimation, 'just a tummler, a guy up there making jokes' (Lax 1991: 194). He seems to regard his 'talent to amuse' with, if not contempt, at least suspicion: 'I'm a Brooklyn-Broadway wisecracker who's been very lucky' (Lax 2009: 365). Hardly the 'genius' his fans have celebrated, Allen sees himself as 'a silly comic, a lower comic' (Lax 2009: 41) when he does not simply view his humour as what used to be called idiot savantism – an exceptional mental skill within an extremely limited field. Nevertheless, his performances on stage (as preserved in recordings and now on YouTube) reveal two important reasons for his success: the creation of an original persona and, increasingly as his stand-up career developed, a capacity for creative storytelling. Woody's persona combines the Freudian-derived neuroses of Shelley Berman, a largely unacknowledged source whose act he followed at the Blue Angel in 1960, with the false bravado of Bob Hope, whose influence he has frequently cited as dating back to his childhood movie-going. The narrative style, which he perfected in many of his later writings for the *New Yorker* and other magazines, evolved from Henny Youngman-type one-liners derived from his adolescent gag writing to a form a shaggy-dog storytelling, an elaborately detailed, digressive piece of nonsense that culminates in an anticlimactic punch line, one that reveals the pointlessness of the entire story. Like 'The Shallowest Man', the successful shaggy dog story is merely 'an amusing anecdote', a kind of extended *non sequitur* in the form of what seems to be consequential narration. The trick of the story lies in convincing the audience that something significant is at stake – an uplifting fable of redemptive friendship in the face of terminal cancer, in this case – rather than a preposterous example of insensitivity and misdirected lust. Many of Woody Allen's movies play a similar trick.

One of his most enduring monologues from this time, the early 1960s, may serve as an example of both Woody's stage persona and narrative style. 'I shot a moose once', he begins *in medias res*, provoking immediate laughter at the incongruity between his diminutive, bespectacled presence and his self-projected image as a hunter in the woods upstate from his Manhattan apartment. The three-minute story proceeds in three nearly equal parts. The first concerns his discovery that the moose has only been stunned by the bullet and is now regaining consciousness on the fender of Woody's car, making turn signals, in fact. The *schlemiel*'s ineptitude and the moose's anthropomorphism structure the rest of the story. Woody decides to avoid 'responsibility' for his mistake by taking the moose to a costume party that evening. He introduces him to the hosts – 'Hello. You know the Solomons' – simultaneously conjuring the absurd sight of a two-person moose costume and establishing the gathering's Jewish ambiance. The second section of the story centres on the moose's successful integration at the party – he mingles at the buffet table, fends off an insurance salesman, 'scores' with the female guests – until midnight, when the results of the costume contest are announced: 'First prize goes to… the Berkowitzes, a married couple dressed in a moose suit.' Furious at getting second prize, the moose 'locks antlers' with the Berkowitzes in the living room, a tableau of sublime surrealism. Seizing the opportunity to get rid of the now unconscious moose, Woody escapes with him again strapped to his fender and heads for the countryside, '*but*… I got the Berkowitzes'. The story ends with the couple waking up in the woods in a moose suit, whereupon Mr. Berkowitz is 'shot, stuffed, and mounted at the New York Athletic Club'. Allen concludes: 'And the joke's on them, because it's Restricted.' The punch line, besides being a great gag, works in two subtle ways that attest to Allen's precocious comic art: first, it formally connects the party scenes of Jewish assimilation with the elite club's policy of discrimination; secondly (and Mort Sahl would be proud), it slyly makes a political point, because at this time (around 1962) the New York Athletic Club really *was* Restricted for Jews.

With Feldman's bankroll offering an irresistible temptation, Allen eagerly plunged into writing *What's New, Pussycat?* He soon regretted it.

> I had written what I thought was a very off-beat, uncommercial film. It was not a factory-made kind of film. And the producers I turned it over to were the quintessential Hollywood machine. They undertook to execute this project with everything that everyone hates about Hollywood films. People that had no sense

of humour deciding what's funny and what's not. People putting their girlfriends in roles. People writing special roles to accommodate stars, whether those roles worked or not. The worst nightmare one could think of. (Björkman 2004: 10)

Although the consequent film was the biggest box office hit for a comedy at the time it was released in 1965, Allen dismissed it with a description that effectively combined self-deprecation and thwarted ambition: 'Left to my own devices, I could have made the film twice as funny and half as successful' (Shone 2015: 30). Embarrassed and humiliated by the experience but still confident in his ability to make people laugh, he resolved never again to lose control over his own screenplay, although it should be added that he willingly took the money and ran when offered a part in Charles Feldman's *Casino Royale* (1967), the product of a dozen other screenwriters, two years later. Charles H. Joffe prodded him through the wasteful ordeal when Woody complained about languishing unnoticed in London: 'Just shut up and be in the movie. You're trying to get into the film business' (Lax 2009: 330). Allen complied, but continued to regard the assignment 'a moronic enterprise from start to finish … a waste of celluloid and money. It was another dreadful film experience' (Björkman 2004: 13).

Allen's first official credit as a movie director came with similar regrets. Shortly before going abroad to appear in *Casino Royale*, he was invited by Henry G. Saperstein, a television producer, to write original dialogue to be dubbed into a low-budget Japanese spy thriller and re-released as *What's Up, Tiger Lily?* (1966), shamelessly capitalising on Allen's current fame and the popularity of *What's New, Pussycat?* The nominal director described the result as 'insipid … a sophomoric exercise' (Björkman 2004: 15), while Tom Shone's more recent assessment captures the project's quality more vividly: 'an act of lazy, and at times condescending, cinematic karaoke' (2015: 31). Allen sued to withdraw the film from distribution, but when *What's Up, Tiger Lily?* became a box office success he withdrew the lawsuit, again profiting financially from what he deemed an embarrassing artistic mistake. Apparently, as a hip celebrity with a Midas touch, he might regret his string of meretricious good fortune without experiencing anything like remorse, which, according to philosophers such as Gabrielle Taylor, involves an effort (as in filing a lawsuit or making a different kind of movie) to repair the damage or offset the regrettable action (1985: 99). He would feel much better about his next project, the first true 'Woody Allen film', *Take the Money and Run*, although the picture itself is another spoof that merely extends the comic premises of his stand-up routines and the silliness of his screen image.

The Limits of Parody

Like his earlier screenplays and also the short pieces he began publishing in the *New Yorker* at this time, *Take the Money and Run* relies on parody, although without a consistent satirical purpose or specific origin text in mind. Thus, its documentary style lacks both the historical context and social critique of, for example, Orson Welles' 'News on the March' in *Citizen Kane* (1941), which had managed to satirise the bombastic, syntactically challenged journalism of *Time* magazine and its movie theatre newsreels, the public and private life of William Randolph Hearst, and the rags-to-riches mythology of American capitalism, all the while brilliantly reflecting the evolution of cinematography during the film industry's first forty years. *Take the Money and Run* incorporates numerous recognisable reference points, of course – the protagonist's name, Virgil Starkwell, recalls the notorious mass murderer from 1958, Charles Starkweather; Jackson Beck's melodramatic voice-over evokes the old Movietone newsreels, while the straight-on witness interviews imitate the standard techniques of contemporary documentaries that Allen would later employ in *Zelig*, *Sweet and Lowdown* and, in a modernist context of fictional meta-commentary, *Husbands and Wives*. In addition, various scenes allude to *West Side Story* (1961; Virgil shoots out his switchblade), *The Seven Year Itch* (1955; Virgil stores his clothes in a refrigerator), *I Am a Fugitive from a Chain Gang* (1932; the road gang), *Cool Hand Luke* (1967; the prison camp and Virgil's solitary confinement), among other less direct allusions, but they comprise a pastiche in the service of laughter rather than, say, subverting the criminal justice system or commenting on the iconic images of the movies themselves. Viewed today, the film remains genuinely funny, if ultimately superficial beyond the humour, 'inconclusive about whether we should value Virgil's innocence or reject his illusions' (Pogel 1987: 38).

Allen's own confusion about the 'meaning' of his mock-heroic story of a wannabe bank robber may have been epitomised in a scene he had intended for the film's climax but was persuaded to cut by the executives at Palomar and the veteran editor Ralph Rosenblum, with whom Allen collaborated on several of his early films. The original rough cut culminated with Virgil being gunned down, lying soaked in blood and twitching his leg, a grotesque parody of the celebrated ending of Arthur Penn's *Bonnie and Clyde* (1967) – and a singularly unfunny conclusion to the film's ladder of laughs. (Allen and his co-screenwriter, his boyhood friend Mickey Rose, had earlier conceived of an ending in which the producers appear and admit that they have mistakenly shot the wrong life, having intended to make a documentary about the person living next door (Lax 1991: 67)). Although both ideas attest to Allen's uncertainty about his first directorial project, the scene that was actually shot but not used – Virgil's melodramatic demise as a movie gangster – speaks to the comedian's anxiety about reproducing a 'cartoon' version of life, comedies in which 'people don't bleed and nobody dies really' (Björkman 2004: 45). He knew that the film's jokes would work, that his *schlemiel* persona (Virgil's birthday, announced in the opening voice-over – 1 December 1935 – coincides with Woody's) would appeal to his fans, but intuitively Allen seems already to be struggling with the limitations of his own creative gift, as if the illegibility of Virgil's botched stick-up note (is it 'GUB' or 'GUN'?) mocked his very efforts at writing something worth reading.

Fortunately, *Take the Money and Run* does end with appropriate humour, although the final scene remains a bit anticlimactic. Virgil is apprehended not in a hail of gunfire but through another bumbling crime in which he tries to rob a man on the street who turns out to be an old childhood friend. After some nostalgic banter amidst reminders to keep his hands raised and turn over his wallet, the victim reveals that he is a cop, the roles reverse, and Virgil is led off to jail. The dénouement involves an interview with Virgil in prison, serving an 800-year sentence that he hopes to reduce by half in return for good behaviour. The off-screen reporter asks whether he regrets his life of crime. 'I think that crime definitely pays,' he quickly replies, 'and that, you know, it's a great job. The hours are good, you're your own boss and you travel a lot, and you get to meet interesting people, and it's a good job in general.' The humour here, of course, lies in the revelation that Virgil has learned nothing from his experience, that he can express his insights only in a string of clichés, and that the documentary's earlier psychological explanations for his criminal behaviour ('Destitute and in love, Virgil seeks to change his life with one bold stroke') do not apply to farce. He is the first of Allen's many Shallow Men, shameless as well as thoughtless, denying any regret 'in part to deny that [they] are now or have ever been losers' (Landman 1993: 9). Even as Allen took pleasure in again amusing his audience as he had been since submitting jokes to Earl Wilson before performing stand-up in Las Vegas or guest-hosting *The Tonight Show*, he yearned to transcend what he continues to view as the fecklessness of comedy, which he has frequently compared to eating at the children's table (Brode 1985: 180), in order to create 'the more serious things that I enjoy more' (Lax 2009: 42). He would have to wait nearly a decade, until *Annie Hall*, to realise his ambition.

Allen had no such misgivings about having his comic writing published in the *New Yorker*; in fact, he was thrilled. His first pieces – called, tellingly, 'casuals' by the editors and Woody himself – were, like his early films, usually parodies (literary criticism, Nazi memoirs, college catalogues, hardboiled detective fiction), often imitating his literary idols at the time, S. J. Perelman and Robert Benchley. 'Death Knocks', on the other hand, marks the first of several attempts to parody (or, in the case of the final scenes of *Interiors*, pay homage to) Ingmar Bergman. In this short closet play, a Kew Gardens dressmaker named Nat Ackerman is visited by Death, whose apparition derived from *The Seventh Seal* he fails to recognise ('What is wrong with you?' Death replies when Nat does not identify the stranger in his living room. 'You see the black costume and the whitened face?'). Nat manages to postpone his fate by winning a game of gin rummy after discovering that Death does not know how to play chess. Death exits despondently, muttering, 'I couldn't just take him and go, I had to get involved in rummy.' Instead of a stately dance against the horizon with the strict master leading the way as in *The Seventh Seal*, Allen's play ends with Death taking a pratfall down the staircase ('such a *schlep*!' Nat describes him in the last line). The dialogue is funny enough, but the humour of 'Death Knocks' depends on the reader knowing its source and recognising the incongruity between Bergman's philosophical enquiry into the nature of human existence in the face of the Plague and Allen's amusing diminution of the issues at stake.

Woody's status as an auteur as well as an author was dramatically confirmed when United Artists, apparently delighted by the modest box office payoff for *Take the Money and Run* and probably impressed by Allen's unbroken string of successes in the preceding decade, offered him an unprecedented contract to make three pictures with complete creative autonomy. The first of these was *Bananas* (1971), loosely based on a script he had been developing with Mickey Rose while idling in London during the prolonged production of *Casino Royale* and a related sketch titled 'Viva Vargas', a mock revolutionary diary he had published in the *Evergreen Review* and subsequently anthologised (along with 'Death Knocks') in *Getting Even* (1971). Now in his mid-thirties, he could no longer be called an apprentice in the movie business – he had been granted control over the content, casting and final cut for his films, a privilege he has never relinquished – but he remained a novice regarding the technical aspects of his craft and, perhaps more importantly, he continued to rely on parody and imitation for much of the humour. *Bananas* compounds the episodic style of *Take the Money and Run*, piling on the sight gags and providing numerous in-jokes in the form of allusions to *Bonnie and Clyde* and Eisenstein's *Battleship Potemkin* (1925) during the opening assassination scene (broadcast by Howard Cosell performing a self-parody of his television persona) and Chaplin's *Modern Times* (1936) when Allen's *schlemiel* protagonist, Fielding Mellish, tests products at his workplace, Execuciser Corporation. The overall cinematic source of *Bananas*, according to Tom Shone, is not difficult to trace: 'With its fictional tin-pot dictatorship of San Marcos, its cigars, its nonstop gags, and sense of anarchy – it's Allen's *Duck Soup*' (2015: 46), a favourite film that the director specifically referenced in *Crimes and Misdemeanors*, where it serves as a remedy for his character Cliff's suicidal despair.

The movie remains funny when viewed today, largely because of Allen's under-appreciated physical comedy and despite the topicality of many of the satirical barbs. Nevertheless, it is hard to agree with Maurice Yacowar's assessment in one of the first books about him that '*Bananas* is a significant advance in Allen's artistry ... its comedy has a serious social and political underpinning' (1991: 129). At Fielding's trial for 'subversive acts' following his return from San Marcos, for example, the testimony of a large African-American woman identified as J. Edgar Hoover depends for its humour on several levels of audience recognition – from the obvious anomaly of the female witness's assumed name, to the CIA director's reputation for illegal surveillance activities, to the rumours about Hoover's transvestitism – but the bit is merely a small part of the trial scene's comic business rather than a sustained satire on American injustice or foreign policy. Allen (and Yacowar) need only recall Stanley Kubrick's *Dr. Strangelove* (1964) to measure the shallowness of *Bananas*' satire; for the director, the goal is more straightforward: 'the movie is entirely free of subtext', he told Richard Schickel, 'it's just one damn thing after another' (2003: 22). Comparing this kind of plotless comedy to the Marx brothers' *Duck Soup* (1933) and *A Night at the Opera* (1935), Allen remarked in 1974, 'You have to be hilarious from the start and hilarious again and again' (Lax 2009: 70). Thus, *Bananas* ends amicably enough with Fielding marrying Nancy (Louise Lasser), the campus activist whose rejection had prompted him to visit San Marcos to observe the revolution first hand, and Howard Cosell returning to provide play-by-play coverage of the nuptial consummation. No regrets; for the first time, the Woody Allen character gets the girl.

An auteur by virtue of his contract as well as his celebrity as screenwriter and star, Allen nonetheless depended on the considerable contributions of Ralph Rosenblum for editorial advice on most of his films through to *Interiors*. Rosenblum was largely responsible for saving the funniest material from the first two films and famously changed the balance and tone of *Annie Hall* by suggesting that Allen shift the emphasis from his own character's anhedonia to Annie's maturing personality. The other great collaborator during these years was, of course, Diane Keaton, who had co-starred with Woody in the Broadway production of *Play It Again, Sam* and again in Herbert Ross's film adaptation. Although she had little to do except to respond to Allan Felix's witticisms and amorous advances in *Play It Again, Sam*, Keaton emerged as an equal comic partner in her first picture with Allen directing, *Sleeper* (1973).

This spoof of science fiction films (with an implicit nod to Kubrick's *A Clockwork Orange* (1971), released less than two years earlier) followed Allen's adaptation of Dr. David Reuben's bestselling self-help book, *Everything You Always Wanted to Know about Sex* (*But Were Afraid to Ask)* (1972), where, for once, the director's comic instinct betrayed him. 'I thought I was going to have a million comic ideas on sex – but it wasn't as fertile a notion as I imagined, and I had about six' (Lax 2009: 6). Viewers may recall fondly Woody's impersonation of a sperm preparing for ejaculation or Gene Wilder's deadpan performance as a physician involved in a sexual relationship with a sheep, but the six-sketch anthology – an additional sequence involving Allen as a spider and Louise Lasser as a black widow ('What makes men homosexuals?') did not make the final cut – sags for minutes at a time and lapses into tasteless, dated burlesque club humour. Nevertheless, the film was a major hit, earning $18 million at the box office and becoming his fourth-biggest earner ever when adjusted for ticket price inflation. It was as if Allen had inverted his prediction about what would have happened if he had directed *What's New, Pussycat?* He had made a movie that was half as funny as he had imagined and scored twice the profit.

Nearly as commercially successful (ranking immediately after *Everything You Always Wanted to Know...* in adjusted gross receipts), *Sleeper* marked 'a step forward for me' because 'it had a real plot' (Lax 2009: 348). In fact, it had originally been conceived as an *epic* plot: a four-hour movie covering two hundred years that included an intermission – like Kubrick's *2001: A Space Odyssey* (1968) and Coppola's *The Godfather* (1972) – with Woody living in contemporary Manhattan and then being cryogenically frozen for two centuries before resuming life in a futuristic city. Characteristically, Allen rebukes himself for failing to fulfill this 'good idea. I just didn't have the stamina to write so much. I didn't have the will to carry it off. I wasn't good enough to, to work for months on the first movie, and then when that was finished put it aside and work for months on the future part. I just didn't have it in me' (Schickel 2003: 95). Influenced by his admiration for the silent comedies of Chaplin and Keaton, he had gone so far as to imagine a future in which the citizens were prohibited from speaking, and so the second act of *Sleeper* would be entirely without dialogue. Was Allen being 'too easy on himself' by not following through on his original conception? Hard to say, but his interviews all make clear that he dismisses the project as beyond his physical talents and creative energy, even though United Artists 'loved the idea' (Björkman 2004: 67). The script he ultimately wrote with new collaborator Marshall Brickman combined a zany science fiction spoof involving his alien avatar from the past, Miles Monroe, performing feats of physical comedy (in a jet pack, as a robot in white face) that now serve as reminders of how much Allen had absorbed from those early comedies and a charming romance in which Miles pairs with co-star Diane Keaton as Luna, who joins him in fleeing from their dystopian society. The first half of *Sleeper* looks back to Allen's earlier, gag-filled movies, dependent on the *schlemiel*'s witty responses (as when he comments on a series of 'artifacts' from 1973) to his hapless fate (as when Miles realises upon wakening that he has been victimised by 'a cosmic screwing'). Once Keaton enters, however, the film looks forward to the more romantic (as opposed to sexual) storylines and more broadly philosophical satire of the Woody Allen films to come ('political revolutions don't work', Miles tells Luna near the end of *Sleeper*, in contrast to the news he learns at the beginning that nuclear war had been set off by a man named Albert Shanker, the now largely forgotten head of New York's teachers' union).

Two lines, neither of them particularly humorous, stand out. The first occurs when Miles responds to Luna's complaint about his constant joking. 'I'm always joking,' he admits. 'It's a defence mechanism.' In context, during their flirtatious repartee, Miles' observation seems almost a *non sequitur*; it makes sense only in light of Woody Allen's existentialist philosophy, in which joking provides a rejoinder to the meaninglessness – the 'cosmic screwing' – inflicted on mankind in a godless universe. Is it also a confession of the director's regret over the compulsive nature of his inadequate artistic gift? In *Sleeper*, Miles' throwaway line serves as the set-up for the film's truly funny closing punch line. Now safe from the minions of state authority, Luna prompts Miles to declare his love. After chiding him for rejecting science, political revolution and God, she asks him, 'What do you believe in?' 'Sex and death,' he replies. 'Two things that come once in a lifetime, but at least after death you're not nauseous.' They kiss, and the credits roll, with any thought about the efficacy of science or revolution subsumed by laughter and the strains of Woody Allen playing Dixieland jazz on the soundtrack.

The second line is Miles' comeback when Luna blushingly suggests that she thinks he really loves her: 'Of course I love you. This is what this is all about.' By prolepsis Miles tries out the poignant response Isaac offers to Tracy at the end of *Manhattan*. In both cases, Allen's character conveys a measure of exasperation as well as sincerity, as if Luna (or Tracy, abandoned for months and on her way to London) were stupid not to recognise his romantic intention. And Miles goes on, extending the argument in the manner of Bob Hope rather than Allan Felix channeling Humphrey Bogart: 'And you love me, I know that. And I don't blame you, honey.' When Ike finally acknowledges his love to Tracy, however begrudgingly, he at least follows by trying to tell her *why* ('Hey … you look good … I just don't want that thing about you that I like to change'). Playing more for laughs in the earlier film, Allen delivers a line that reveals (again) his character's vanity ('I don't blame you, honey') and defensiveness (because 'you love me'). In contrast to the ambiguous ending of *Manhattan*, Miles' declaration of love is so purely funny *because* it is so shallow.

Love and Death

Love and Death continued Allen's progress as a filmmaker, by virtue of both the enhanced visual quality and new philosophical concerns (however mocked) that would define his more mature works. Allen attributed the 'big improvement' (Lax 2009: 200) in the look of the film to the contributions of his new cinematographer, the Belgian Ghislan Cloquet, who had shot such prestigious European art films as Alain Resnais' *Night and Fog* (1955) and Robert Bresson's *Au hazard Balthazar* (1966). The sweeping widescreen battlefield scenes, for example, or the concluding long shot, a long take of Woody's character, Boris, dancing with Death along a tree-lined river add an epic or lyrical dimension that deepens the broad comedy. The title itself points to the abstract issues – specifically, the ephemerality of love and the morality of murder – that Allen will revisit in some of his best films. In *Love and Death*, however, these concerns are still played for laughs, and the characters fail to transcend their status as cartoons. '*Sleeper* and *Love and Death* are fine for what they are,' the director told Stig Björkman. 'It's just that I quarrel with what they are' (2005: 347). In his own eyes, despite several hits to fortify his confidence, Allen remained a novice.

James M. Wallace has observed how the pleasure of reading Allen's stories derives 'from the self-congratulations we most likely feel upon recognizing a more obscure reference or connecting a complicated set of allusions' (2004: 72) – what Annie Hall calls 'getting the references' after watching Alvy's stand-up routine. The following dialogue between Boris Grushenko (Allen) and his father (Zvee Scooler) near the end of *Love and Death*, for example, would make little sense to someone unaware of Dostoyevsky's novels:

Father: Remember that nice boy next store, Raskolnikov? He killed two ladies!
Boris: No! What a nasty story!
Father: Bobick told me. He heard it from one of the Karamazov brothers.
Boris: My God, he must have been possessed!
Father: Well, he was a raw youth.
Boris: If you ask me, he was an idiot.
Father: And he acted insulted and injured.
Boris: I hear he was a gambler.
Father: Funny, he could have been your double.
Boris: Really, how novel!

A slightly more bibliographically informed viewer than one who only recognises titles would also appreciate the irony of the film's ending, which had been foreshadowed in the opening voice-over when Boris complains about being condemned to death for a crime he never committed. Unlike Dostoyevsky himself, who was saved from the firing squad by the Czar's last-minute reprieve, Boris goes to his death confidently joking with his executioners ('No blindfolds. That's for losers. I like to see where the bullet hits') after an angel visits his cell to reassure him that he will be spared. But Boris, no less than Miles Monroe, is victim of 'a cosmic screwing'. He soon reappears as a ghost explaining to his wife Sonia (Diane Keaton) how 'I got screwed! Some vision came and told me I'd be pardoned, and they shot me.' The film's closing sequence mimics the famous ending of *The Seventh Seal*: the *schlemiel* dancing merrily with Death, who is dressed in an ill-fitting white sheet. Death's unimposing figure as silent second banana to Boris's wisecracking complaint about death being worse than the chicken at Tretsky's restaurant undermines the solemnity of the occasion, while the thought of the angel's dirty trick (whether imagined by Boris or calculated by God) subtly subverts Dostoyevsky's theme of spiritual salvation at the end of *Crime and Punishment*.

Love and Death continuously employs such parodic moments to burlesque its own widescreen pretensions. For Woody Allen, the seriousness of the philosophical issue he had in mind – 'the tragedy of life, the fact that in the end you're screwed by death' (Schickel 2003: 105) – gets subordinated to silly jokes and *kvetching*, just as Prokofiev's original score for Eisenstein's *Alexander Nevsky* (1938) becomes relegated here to accompanying a period farce. Two of the earliest books about Allen's film comedy, Maurice Yacowar's *Loser Take All* (1979) and Nancy Pogel's *Woody Allen* (1987), identify several other prominent moments where the comedy of *Love and*

Figs. 6 and 7: Death in Bergman's *The Seventh Seal* transmogrified into a second banana in *Love and Death*

Death depends in part on recognising the incongruity between the classic original and the film's parody:

- The opening shot of billowing clouds and Prokofiev's orchestral music, which mocks the portentous beginning of *The Seventh Seal*;
- The associative cut from soldiers engaging in battle to a flock of sheep, which echoes both Eisenstein's *Strike* (1924) and Chaplin's *Modern Times*;
- The three-shot montage of the stone lions (the last of which collapses in post-coital exhaustion), which parodies Eisenstein's revolutionary metaphor in *Battleship Potemkin*;

- The extended speeches about 'Wheat', which spoof the long apostrophes to the grain in Tolstoy's *Anna Karenina*;
- Boris's observation about how different the battlefield looks when viewed from the perspective of the generals, which echoes Prince Andrey in *War and Peace*;
- The formally composed close-up of Sonia and her cousin Natasha (Jessica Harper) – one in profile, the other facing the camera – which alludes to Bergman's *Persona* (1966).

The cumulative effect of these references, aside from flattering culturally literate viewers, is to undercut the presumed profundity of high art as well as to underscore the *nebbish* protagonist's outsider status. Essentially, Allen is still playing the jester role he assumed in the first episode of *Everything You Always Wanted to Know About Sex*, entertaining the royalty without belonging to the court. If *Sleeper* can be described as his Groucho movie, *Love and Death* is his homage to Bob Hope, an influence he has readily acknowledged. 'Yeah, I was doing him all over the place', he told Eric Lax about the scene in which Boris arranges a rendezvous with Countess Alexandrovna (Olga Georges-Picot), a scene that clearly borrows its repartee from *Monsieur Beaucaire* (1946).

Similarly, the duel scene in which Boris tries to choose both pistols and then hides behind the back of the cuckolded Count instead of facing him at ten paces copies Bob Hope's antics in *Never Say Die* (1939). In the same interview, Allen actually regrets that Hope himself was not playing his role – 'it would be a better movie' (Lax 2009: 352). Herein lies the parodist's dilemma: the necessity of imitating your betters. As Allen told Richard Schickel, 'I think that I do Bob Hope all the time, I'm just nowhere near as good ... I mean it's, it's just shameless how I steal from him' (2003: 82). Harold Bloom famously described this difficulty for the young artist who must overcome the accomplishments of the previous generation as 'the anxiety of influence' (1997). The pop singer Dobie Gray expressed the problem succinctly in a hit song from 1964, 'The "In" Crowd': 'Other guys imitate us/But the original is still the greatest.' (The citation perhaps is not as farfetched as it seems, since Allen employed the Ramsey Lewis version of the same song on the soundtracks of *Mighty Aphrodite* (1995) and *Irrational Man*.) After all, it is one thing to regret not being Fyodor Dostoyevsky or Ingmar Bergman; it's another to regret not being Bob Hope.

As announced in the initial monologue, the plot of *Love and Death*, anticipating the narrative structure of *Annie Hall*, retrospectively tells the story of how the undersized, cowardly Boris came to the 'incredible' fate of being executed for a crime he didn't commit – assassinating not Napoleon, but his double. In the film's second act, this 'young coward all of St. Petersburg has been talking about' accidently becomes a war hero through his own 'terrible mistake' of being shot from a cannon and destroying the tent of some French generals. Now happily married to Sonia and far from the battlefield, he resolves to become a great poet. 'I should have been a pair of ragged claws/Scuttling across the floors of silent seas', he writes, before tossing away the lines from T. S. Eliot's 'The Love Song of J. Alfred Prufrock' as 'too sentimental'. No doubt this may be reading too much into what is simply another clever allusion, but it is tempting to interpret this moment in *Love and Death* as reflecting Allen's self-assessment of his own 'predicament' as a filmmaker in 1975: doomed to parody the artists he most admires and being amply rewarded for his superficial talent. The joke here is that Eliot's famous poem is anything but sentimental, but, for Allen, the fact remains that he can only invoke it for laughs rather than creating something original and profound himself. He is not Tolstoy, not Dostoyevsky, not Eliot; nor was meant to be.

As parody, *Love and Death* directs its humour at specific works, but the film also more generally burlesques the abstract realms of religion and philosophy, topics that interest Allen but that he satirises with evident relish. As a consequence, Sonia's predilection for 'deep conversations' devolves into a hilarious disputation about love and suffering in response to Natasha's confusion, and Boris's question as he contemplates murder degenerates into gags about homosexuals and a ludicrous syllogism (concluding that 'All men are Socrates. That means all men are homosexuals'). This soliloquy, with Boris directly addressing the camera, concludes with a characteristic return to the quotidian: 'I'm just wracked with guilt and I'm consumed with remorse, and stricken with suffering for the human race. Not only that, but I'm developing a herpe on my lip here that is really killing me.' Thus, guilt gives way to the concerns of the body, as it had when Boris consoles himself awaiting execution by savouring the French prison food. Sonia learns the same lesson when she seeks Father Andre (Leib Lensky), a (very long-)bearded religious sage drawn from Father Zossima in *The Brothers Karamazov* (Pogel 1987: 73), whose muddled advice for alleviating Boris's thoughts of suicide ends by recommending a paedophiliac orgy. 'See, that's the thing about philosophy,' Allen writes in 'My Apology', his parodied Socratic dialogue from this period, 'it's not all that functional once you get out of class' (1980: 38). Later in Allen's cinema, Professor Levy will apparently illustrate this sad conclusion when he suddenly commits suicide in *Crimes and Misdemeanors*. Forty years after *Love and*

Death in a very different kind of film, Allen would still be questioning the value of philosophy in *Irrational Man*.

Despite the mock heroic treatment of the great nineteenth-century Russian novelists and the movie characters' abstract gibberish that passes for philosophy, *Love and Death* makes no invidious comparisons, its creator self-consciously aware of the discrepancy in cultural capital between Socrates and Kant (Sophia and Boris debate the moral imperative of murdering Napoleon), Tolstoy and Dostoyevsky, Eisenstein and Bergman, on the one hand, and Hollywood film comedy on the other. At the culmination of his apprenticeship, Allen might still regret the shallowness of his achievement, but his ambition to do better – in many interviews he remarks in wonderment about his self-confidence – never sways. Fully conscious of the masterpieces created by his literary and cinematic models, he begins a new phase of artistic development that casts off the anxiety of influence and leads to an astonishing period of originality and critical acceptance. As Janet Landman reminds us about what generally is thought to be a negative self-assessment, 'genuine regret signifies that you have standards of excellence … you still care about – a good thing in itself' (1993: 26). In the films that follow *Love and Death*, Allen will turn away from parody and reflect upon the regrets – the *shallow* regrets – of his characters.

CHAPTER THREE

The Relationship Films

'If you take very good care of your styptic pencil and dry it after every shave, it will last longer than most relationships that you're in.'

Anything Else

'There's only one kind of love that lasts – unrequited love. It lasts forever.'

Shadows and Fog

In *Husbands and Wives* the Woody Allen character, a writer named Gabe, meets the parents of his talented, seductive young college student, Rain (Juliette Lewis). Honoured to have the admired author in their home and searching for praise, Rain's mother (Blythe Danner) confides how she wishes Gabe would return to writing those 'funny sad stories' she had so enjoyed. This comment virtually echoes the famous compliment paid to the filmmaker Sandy Bates (Allen) by the aliens from outer space in *Stardust Memories*: 'We like your movies, especially the early funny ones.' Both backhanded tributes imperfectly conceal the audience's implicit regret regarding the artist's present serious work, their disappointment in his more recent creative trajectory. The distinction added by Rain's mother – the addition of 'sad' to 'funny' – reflects the shift in Woody Allen's critical reputation in the decade that separates *Stardust Memories* (in which the extraterrestrial visitors could only be alluding to Allen's *Interiors*, the aberrant and humourless melodrama made two years earlier) from *Husbands and Wives*, a period that includes two more chamber pieces (*September* and *Another Woman*) plus a movie about an unpunished murder (*Crimes and Misdemeanors*) and several melancholy 'comedies' (*Broadway Danny Rose*, *The Purple Rose of Cairo*, *Alice*). What contributes to the sadness in all these films is their depiction of fragile or inauthentic personal relationships, their preoccupation throughout Allen's 'classic' period (1977–1992) with misunderstanding, delusion, unfaithfulness, separation, divorce and, as a consequence, disillusionment, nostalgia or, occasionally, premonitory recovery.

Annie Hall

The first of these relationship films, widely regarded as also Allen's greatest, remains, of course, *Annie Hall*. 'It was a major turning point for me,' the director told Stig Björkman. 'I had the courage to abandon … just clowning around and the safety of complete broad comedy' (2005: 75; ellipsis in original). Neither Alvy nor Annie is a cartoon, a point made explicit when, in one scene, they are rendered as animated figures who caricature their more complicated selves. Like *Love and Death*, *Annie Hall* is retrospectively narrated by the protagonist, which means when Alvy begins by directly addressing the camera – by re-telling two old jokes that serve as epigraphs for his autobiographical story and then instigating the first cut to the diegesis, the Coney Island of his childhood – thereby taking control of the film's verbal and visual content, he already knows the story's outcome: 'Annie and I broke up.' In short, the narrating-I (whom the audience initially takes to be Woody Allen in the opening shot) already knows what will happen to the relationship between himself as the experiencing-I (Alvy Singer, as they soon learn from the flashbacks) and Annie Hall. Discourse precedes story. Because the spectator knows from the outset that the love affair between Alvy and Annie, however charming and 'funny' in the tradition of American romantic comedy, will not hold, their every scene together carries a residue of sad reminiscence that emanates from Alvy's original sigh as he announces their fate. 'I still can't get my mind around that', he says about the break-up, and the rest of the story amounts to a subjective series of recollections constructed by Alvy in the narrative present while 'sifting the pieces of the relationship through my mind and examining my life and trying to figure out where did the screw-up come'. In this re-creative task he is like T. S. Eliot's Fisher King in 'The Waste Land', a modernist narrator conjuring voices and images from the past, 'mixing/Memory and desire', and arranging these fragments to shore against his ruins. Eliot concludes his poem by reciting the Sanskrit words for the Peace which Passeth Understanding; Allen concludes his film with nostalgia and an old silly joke.

As the celebrated tag line about 'needing the eggs' suggests by subordinating rational understanding to irrational desire, the second sad aspect of his narration stems from the discovery that Alvy never successfully figures out the source of the screw-up. The reasons *why* he and Annie break up never occur to him. Immediately before the scene in which he appears as a cartoon character with Annie as the Wicked Queen in *Snow White*, Alvy and Annie separate for the first time following an argument in the street. Alvy turns to address the camera as a cab whisks Annie away: 'I don't know what I did wrong', he whines, after having stalked her and her college professor and reversed his positive opinion of adult education. Oblivious to why she has 'cooled off to me', he approaches an older woman carrying groceries to ask her if he did something wrong. 'Never something you do,' the woman tells him, 'That's how people are. Love fades.' Freed from personal responsibility by this fatalistic observation, the philosophical insight of a casual bystander, Alvy immediately reverts to abstract thinking – 'Love fades. God, that's a depressing thought' – and continues questioning pedestrians in search of the key to a happy relationship, interviews that produce only audience laughs from the elderly 'psychopath' who recommends a vibrating egg and the beautiful but 'shallow and empty' couple who apparently share connubial bliss, but no insights. All Alvy ever truly learns, after Annie moves out for good near the end of the film, is that 'I miss Annie. I made a terrible mistake' – *there it is again*, the line that reverberates throughout Woody Allen's cinema of regret. But Alvy's admission (like Val's abortive message of apology to Ellie in *Hollywood Ending*) is immediately replaced by recriminations directed at Annie for moving to Los Angeles: 'Then the hell with her! If she likes that lifestyle, let her live there!'

Alvy's predicament anticipates the regret of the similarly named Alfie (Anthony Hopkins) in *You Will Meet a Tall Dark Stranger* (2010) more than three decades later in Allen's oeuvre. Both men at first experience an unacknowledged period of self-doubt. Alvy announces in his opening monologue that he has just turned forty, but he quickly dismisses any thought of 'going through a life crisis or something' by reverting to the Woody Allen persona (whom the audience at this point takes Alvy to be) to boast: 'I think I'm going to get better as I get older, you know? I think I'm going to be – the balding virile type.' Restless in a retirement community, Alfie dumps his longtime wife Helena (Gemma Jones) to take up with a much younger gold-digging prostitute. Cleaned out of a considerable fortune, Alfie comes to his senses and desperately seeks to reconcile with Helena, admitting to her: 'I made a terrible mistake. My life is so messed up, I can't tell you how messed up it is … I saw my life slipping away, and I panicked.' Like Alvy, however, Alfie expresses only regret, not remorse. Neither man offers to change, or to recompense the women for their mistakes. Instead, their narcissism prevails. After Annie rejects his proposal of marriage, Alvy reverts to complaining about the three thousand 'air miles' he has travelled to see her. 'You know what that does to my stomach?' Like New York City, as Annie tells him, he has become 'this island unto yourself' that can no longer contain her, and so, proclaiming 'it's perfectly fine out here', she again exits the screen, leaving Alvy alone in the Los Angeles health food café. Similarly, Helena gently dismisses Alfie's proposal: 'I have a new life,' she tells him. 'I've moved on.'

Annie Hall's epilogue, which combines a brilliant montage recapitulating their romance, a lush soundtrack reprising Annie's singing 'Seems Like Old Times', and Alvy's nostalgic narration and closing punch line, brings his story to its bittersweet ('funny sad') conclusion. Without this final extradiegetic intrusion – initiated by Alvy's direct address to the camera at the rehearsal of his first play – *Annie Hall* might be just another 'amusing' shaggy-dog story of the sort that *Anything Else* unfortunately turns out to be. While the *story* of the dénouement depicts reunion ('kicking around old times'), reconciliation ('what a terrific person she was and how much fun it was just knowing her') and even a note of self-vindication (seeing her at *The Sorrow and the Pity*, 'which I counted as a personal triumph'), the *discourse* – the *cinematic* discourse – conveys a different message, one of distance (as in the long shot from across the street of the two couples standing in front of the Thalia theatre) and separation. The extradiegetic repetition of Annie singing the melancholy 'Seems Like Old Times', whose nostalgic lyrics draw their sadness from the word 'seems', the song being heard representing Alvy's *memory* of Annie's presence now absent from wherever he is narrating the monologue (presumably the stage rehearsal hall). Moreover, when we see Annie and Alvy together for the last time on the corner of 63rd Street, they are separated from us by window glass – twice: initially with the camera outside the coffee shop, then inside as they part on the street – that prevents any eavesdropping on their conversation. In the first of these long shots, they are also separated from each other. Alvy remains seated on the left side of the frame, his access to Annie symbolically cut off by a prominent window border that he briefly reaches across before receding to his place left of the vertical divide. Finally, we view their farewell from the empty space they had occupied inside the restaurant, and, for a third time, Annie exits the screen, leaving Alvy alone in the street.

The closing montage and Alvy's voice-over narration serve both to validate his experience of knowing Annie and to exonerate him from personal blame for the

Fig. 8: Vertical composition undermines Alvy's fond memory of his reunion with Annie

relationship's demise. For the first time but hardly the last in an Allen film, the tone of voice and images are decidedly nostalgic, a sentimentalised recollection of the past that filters out memories of Alvy imposing control over the relationship. For example, the montage includes an intimate bedroom scene of the couple cuddling (the unheard dialogue had involved Annie asking whether 'you think we should go to that party in Southampton?') but excludes the subsequent superimposition shot of Annie withdrawing to smoke grass, leaving Alvy to make love to her body ('Now that's what I call *removed*', he complains); similarly cut is the crucial moment when Alvy reminds her of 'the thing' they have to do rather than join Tony Lacey's party after Annie sings 'Seems Like Old Times' for the first time. As Landman reminds us in her account of nostalgia, 'to reflect on the real, unsentimentalized past is to open oneself up to regret, feeling sorry about past mistakes, misfortunes, and missed opportunities' (1993: 6). In his effort to control the sorrow of the experiencing-I standing alone on the corner of 63rd Street, the narrating-I resorts to nostalgia, the antidote for regret because it precludes personal agency and moral responsibility.

Annie Hall remains Allen's greatest critical and commercial success (based on adjusted gross receipts), one that has clearly stood the test of time. It beat out *Star Wars* (1977) for the Academy Award as Best Picture of 1977; it was rated the fourth-best comedy of all time by the American Film Institute and recently was voted the funniest screenplay ever by the Writers Guild of America. By all but abandoning slapstick humour and gradually limiting the sight gags (save for one celebrated sneeze and one brief impersonation of a Hasidic Jew), by resisting parody (despite at least fifty cultural references interspersed in the dialogue), Allen had created an original work of art that earned him his place at the adults' table. For the first time, he had directed a film in which regret was reflected in the screenplay rather than as his own disappointed response to what he had achieved on the screen.

In *Annie Hall*, Alvy Singer's imperfectly repressed regret over what might have been – the lost opportunity to redeem his previous two failed marriages by remaining with Annie – motivates his initial compulsion to re-tell the story. Alvy's narration, culminating in a Catskills-styled joke, tries wistfully to illustrate a romantic comedy about how 'Love fades', but the punch line more precisely concludes with the clichéd idea that 'Tis better to have loved and lost than never to have loved at all'. Woody Allen's film, on the other hand, narrates a more complex Romantic – capital R – myth about mutability (and the melancholy that attends it), aspiration and the limits of personal control, and the necessity of illusion. Alvy's moment of regret, his acknowledgment of having made 'a terrible mistake', proves shallow in the end, a momentary panic that is immediately replaced by anger and, ultimately in the epilogue, by nostalgia. The presumptive sequel to *Annie Hall* would seem to be *Manhattan*, where Isaac comes to a clear recognition of what scholars on the topic call *agent regret* – accepting blame for something he did rather than simply lamenting what might have been – and immediately races uptown (left to right on the screen) to try to retrieve Tracy through his act of contrition. Although his realisation and subsequent self-abnegation represent a growth from Alvy's self-absorbed *kvetching*, Isaac's apology, which denies any former intention to hurt Tracy (and thus *moral* responsibility) and remains focused on what he fears losing rather than what she might gain, does not rise to the level of remorse. Moreover, the motivation for Isaac's narration of *Manhattan* has little to do with regret and everything to do with creating a work of art, the book he is completing for Viking Press. For a more precise comparison to *Annie Hall*'s retrospective narration motivated by unacknowledged regret and a fuller treatment of the potentially positive repercussions of remorse, a far less esteemed film from Allen's so-called classic period deserves renewed attention.

Another Woman

Another Woman begins with the protagonist formally introducing herself:

> If someone had asked me when I reached my fifties to assess my life, I would have said that I had achieved a decent measure of fulfillment, both personally and professionally. Beyond that, I would say I don't choose to delve. Not that I was afraid to reveal some dark side of my character, but I always feel if something seems to be working, leave it alone. My name is Marion Post, I am director of

undergraduate studies in philosophy at a very fine women's college, although right now I am on leave of absence to begin writing a book.

The monologue begins as voice-over narration, with the speaker somewhere beyond the frame, which reveals only an empty hallway apartment in which an unseen clock seems to be ticking. Marion (Gena Rowlands) soon appears and walks toward the camera, pausing to adjust her earrings in front of a mirror, putting on her glasses while her voiced narration describes her family as the camera pans across their framed photographs. She then leaves to go to the room she has sub-leased as a private office. 'A new book is always a demanding project,' she concludes her introduction, 'and it requires that I really shut myself off from everything but the work.' In her formalist analysis of the narrator's role in *Another Woman*, María del Mar Asensio Aróstegui deftly illustrates how Marion is retrospectively telling the story, using the past tense until the very end of her narrative, from a different place and time than is shown in the opening shot, namely her writing studio (2006: 259). As a result, like Alvy Singer, Marion 'knows perfectly well from the very beginning how her story is going to end'; this particular form of narration 'generates ambiguity and irony by spreading inconsistent and incomplete clues' (2006: 260, 257) throughout the film, thereby complicating the veracity of the developing narrative, in particular Marion's achievement of 'a decent measure of fulfillment' (2006: 257).

As Alvy had complacently acknowledged turning forty, Marion displays no anxiety about reaching a watershed period in her life ('my fifties'), but her qualifying phrase, 'Beyond that', raises a doubt that she immediately seeks to quell: 'if something *seems* to be working, leave it alone'. The formality of her language, her button-down wardrobe (shades of beige – the favoured colour of Eve (Geraldine Page), the controlling matriarch in *Interiors*) plus her turtleneck blouse, scarf, tightly-wound hair and vocal restraint all suggest a repressed self that Marion's story will ultimately expose, a 'dark side' she denies here. Even as she innocuously describes the figures in the family photographs, beginning with her husband ('a very accomplished physician, a cardiologist'), she neglects to reveal some pertinent information concerning both the 'second marriage for both of us' – that she began an affair with Ken (Ian Holm) while he was still married; that her first husband had committed suicide after their divorce – and the relationship with her married brother, which, we soon learn, has become strained. Although the experiencing-I, the Marion seen leaving her apartment, does not yet realise it, the narrating-I, the Marion speaking in voice-over about her experiences, is relating a story filled with regret over relationships that have been lost, denied, perverted and destroyed. At the end of the film, she will continue to wonder whether these memories signify 'something you've had or something you've lost'.

The cracks in Marion's defences show up almost immediately. At the fiftieth birthday party for a social friend, an erotic fissure in her marriage appears during a tense exchange in which Marion responds to another couple's sexual disclosure by asking her husband whether he had ever thought about making love on the kitchen floor, to which Ken replies, 'I don't think of you as the hardwood floor type'. The following morning begins with another icy conversation, this time with her sister-in-law Lynn (Frances Conroy), who is divorcing her brother Paul (Harris Yulin) and needs to borrow money. Marion is impatient because Lynn has been stuck in traffic and arrives late, delaying her return to the office to write. She reacts with astonishment when Lynn suggests that Paul 'hates' her, to which she coldly replies, 'I'm sorry, I don't accept that', and begins searching for a cab so that she can end the conversation. Throughout this two-minute scene, shot in one take on the sidewalk in front of her building, Marion remains set off from Lynn (to whom she replies when accused of not 'approving' of her sister-in-law, 'I hardly know you') by a gold canopy pole directly behind them – a composition that resembles the imperfect reunion at the Manhattan coffee shop in *Annie Hall*. As in that case, the scene concludes with Marion commenting from a different time and place, trying, as Alvy does, to reconcile her conflicted emotions: 'The encounter with my sister-in-law had left me a little angry, but I refused to let it interfere with my work.' The scene cuts to a dimly-lit, sepia-toned long shot of Marion at her writing table, clearly not enunciating this voice-over narration. Although she calls her meeting with Lynn an 'encounter', it is, in Martin Buber's terms, more precisely an 'experience', as distinguished from, in existentialist terms, a *relation*. 'Those who experience do not participate in the world,' Buber writes in *I and Thou*, first published in 1923. 'For the experience is "in them" and not between them and the world' (1996: 56). From this point forward in her story, Marion's struggle will be to discover and begin to resolve her estrangement, to transcend her self-contained experience of the world (I-It) in order to stand in reciprocal relation to others (I-You) (1996: 54–8).

It seems surprising that so few scholars (with the exception of Sander H. Lee) have suggested Martin Buber's influence on Allen's cinema since *I and Thou* provides an alternative to Freudian narcissism and Sartrean existentialism in delineating reasons for the shallow and impermanent relationships that characterise his work. Buber's philosophy, perhaps *passé* in the twenty-first century or subsumed by

Levinasian ethics, gained intellectual credence during Allen's early years and surely was a part of his self-education, even though he does not frequently cite him in interviews. Nevertheless, Buber's apothegm in the First Part of *I and Thou* – 'Relation is reciprocity' – defines the source for the 'screw-up' in Alvy's experience of losing Annie as well as Marion's two unsuccessful marriages and tense relations with her family and her former friend Claire (Sandy Dennis), and nearly all the broken, hostile or simply uneasy relationships in so many of Allen's films. The 'depressing thought' that 'loves fades', which defines not only the theme of *Annie Hall* but the soured relationships in such esteemed works as *Manhattan*, *Hannah and Her Sisters*, *Vicky Christina Barcelona* and *Blue Jasmine*, closely corresponds to 'the sublime melancholy of our lot that every You must become an It in our world' that Buber describes in *I and Thou*; 'The You becomes an object among objects, possibly the noblest one and yet one of them, assigned its measure and boundary' (1996: 68).

Marion's identity crisis in *Another Woman*, her discovery of the judgemental, unfeeling person she has become, begins with her eavesdropping on a psychiatric therapy session that can be heard through the ventilation duct in her writing space. She becomes intrigued, then obsessed by the confessions of another woman (Mia Farrow), who is unhappily married and pregnant. Starting with the opening image of casually viewing herself in a mirror, Marion enters into an unexpected, traumatic re-visioning of her life initiated by the haunting testimony of the troubled woman in analysis, her psychological double. The turning point in her self-examination appears as an extended dream sequence triggered by the presence of the absent therapy patient (signalled by a close-up of the ventilation grate). Marion dreams about her father (John Houseman), who declares, 'Now that my life is drawing to a close, I have only regrets', and then concludes with an admission that clearly emanates from Marion's unconscious: 'Even though I have achieved some eminence in my field, I asked too little of myself.' As the dream continues, Marion observes the rehearsal of a play about her life that reveals repressed moments from her past – the recent quarrel with Ken, their unspoken hostility now openly expressed; a romantic encounter with Larry Lewis (Gene Hackman), whom she had spurned for the sake of propriety (being already engaged to Ken, his friend at the time); her first husband, Sam (Philip Bosco), her former teacher who died a likely suicide ('suffocation', he mentions, was the official cause) fifteen years after their divorce. As they part in the dream, Larry, now happily married, says he must return to his wife and refers to his daughter. The shot cuts to a close-up of the other woman, the psychiatric patient, perhaps symbolically the daughter Marion never had. As Jill Gordon observes in her essay about the film, 'All of the dialogue by all of the characters who populate her dream comes from Marion's own psyche. All the pointed remarks about regret, passion, self-deception, and repression are Marion talking to herself, and are thus the beginning of her transformation to better self-knowledge' (2004: 236–7). The dream, which extends for ten full minutes and ceases only when Marion pleads 'no more', marks a critical turn not only in Marion's journey towards self-knowledge but in Woody Allen's cinema of regret. For the first time, a protagonist's regret – although expressed subconsciously at this point – deepens into something like remorse.

Although the voice narrating the story remains composed, unlike her voice within the dream that begs for it to end, Marion resumes her waking life feeling profoundly disturbed by her suddenly exposed past and the apparent emptiness of her present – her marriage and her work, in particular. In the film's final movement, her regret threatens to overwhelm her as she becomes aware that, to quote Steffie (Diane Wiest) in *September*, the film that immediately preceded *Another Woman*, she is 'not who I thought I was'. From regret over simply the state of things (how the passion has drained from her marriage), or agent regret over mistakes she has made (resisting Larry, judging Paul and, as is revealed in the closing section, aborting Sam's child without consulting him), Marion begins to experience what Amelie Rorty has described as *character regret* – regret for what she *is*, or rather, has become (in Landman 1993: 70). In this gradual awareness of her personal responsibility – a consciousness that motivates her act of re-telling the story rather than her diegetic behaviour as the experiencing-I in the present or the flashbacks and dream sequence – Marion begins to relate to the fullness of remorse, with its consequent desire to undo the wrongs of the past. Recalling her mother's book of Rilke's poetry and the tears that stained the pages of his poem, 'Archaic Torso of Apollo', Marion recites the closing lines: 'for here there is no place/That does not see you. You must change your life.' Lee (Kenneth Branagh), the protagonist of *Celebrity* (1998), experiences precisely the same need for personal rehabilitation ('I gotta change my life before it's too late') when he attends his high school reunion, although the movie's end suggests that he has remained among the Shallow Men.

The day after her self-revelatory dream, Marion picks a fight with Ken that centres on their lack of passion, which in turn triggers memories of her first marriage. The following day, while wandering through an antique store searching for an anniversary gift, she encounters the unnamed pregnant patient, weeping in front of a reproduction of Gustav Klimt's painting 'Hope'. She tries to comfort the young woman, displaying genuine empathy for the first time, and, intrigued by her presence, takes her to lunch, where she drinks too much wine and (as Marion later overhears in the woman's re-telling to her therapist) reveals her own unhappiness. As this last session continues, the woman describes how Marion 'has pretended for so long that everything's fine, but you can see clearly how lost she is'. She then relates how Marion discovered Ken at a nearby table conducting an affair with their mutual friend Lydia (Blythe Danner), the woman who had confided in the pleasure of having sex on the floor. *Another Woman* fairly quickly concludes after Marion confronts her feckless husband, but not before she attempts to reconnect with her brother (who, ironically, has reconciled with Lynn) – 'I really do want a clean start', she tells him – and tries to reassure Laura (Martha Plimpton), Ken's daughter, that their relationship will endure the break-up ('I really value your friendship', she tells Laura, perhaps the symbolic incarnation of her unborn child). Significantly, in Buber's terms, both conversations end with intimate touching, the I truly encountering the You. After Marion seeks out the psychiatrist and learns that the mysterious patient had recently 'terminated her treatment' and a final flashback triggered by reading a passage from Larry Lewis's novel about a character rumoured to be based on her (reprising a scene that had appeared in her dream), Marion concludes her narration in a tone that recalls the ending of *Annie Hall*. She speaks of a 'strange mixture of wistfulness and hope'. Only in the closing credits is it revealed that the Mia Farrow character, the ghostly presence who at different moments represents Marion's double, her unborn daughter and her potential redeemer, is named Hope.

Despite their formalist similarities as retrospective first-person narrations with a complex chronology of flashbacks culminating in a bittersweet coda, *Another Woman* leaves a very different impression than *Annie Hall*, and not simply because the earlier picture is a romantic comedy and this one a drama without a single joke. Alvy avoids responsibility for his missteps in the past; Marion acknowledges hers. Alvy celebrates the past now lost; Marion sadly admits to Sam in her dream, 'we both paid a price' for their mistakes. Janet Landman writes, 'Though there is no redemption in the mere act of acknowledging regret, there is no redemption without it' (1993: 34). While Alvy concludes his narrative with resignation, Marion closes her story committed to personal change 'full of energy' as she renews relationships nearly lost, seeking to undo her mistakes. Her last words suggest the renewed hope of the closing line of 'The Waste Land' ('*Shantih shantih shantih*'), as she calmly describes how, 'For the first time in a long time, I felt at peace.'

Joanna Rapf has noted how 'the importance of growing and changing, of avoiding structure, stasis, and sterility, are key concepts in Allen's mature films' (2013: 266).

As Alvy puts it to Annie on the plane ride back from Los Angeles, 'A relationship, I think, is like a shark, you know? It has to constantly move forward or it dies. And I think what we got on our hands is a dead shark.' It is Annie, of course, who has changed, leaving Alvy alone in New York. When she asks him what he is doing, Alvy can only reply, 'The usual, you know'. The saddest characters in all of Allen's cinema are three women – and it is undoubtedly telling that they are women – who, for different reasons, remain isolated in their fixed identities, incapable of changing their lives: Eve (Geraldine Page) in *Interiors*, Cecilia (Mia Farrow) in *The Purple Rose of Cairo*, and Jasmine (Kate Blanchett) in *Blue Jasmine*, doomed to suicide, fantasy and madness.

Alice

Although *Another Woman* does not dramatise the full consequences of Marion's awakening and transformation – a foreshortened ending that disappointed several critics – the film does at least underscore the necessity for personal change that Alvy Singer, as the first in a succession of Allen protagonists, had effectively denied. During this classic period (1977–1992) dominated by 'relationship' narratives, Marion's closest counterpart might be the eponymous protagonist of *Alice*, despite that film's reversion to the sight gags and magic tricks of old-fashioned farce, so different in tone from *Another Woman*'s unrelieved melodrama. Allen himself has acknowledged the connection, describing *Alice* as 'the comedy version of *Another Woman*' (Björkman 2004: 228). Plagued by psychosomatic symptoms of her repressed ideals and ambitions, Alice (Mia Farrow) visits Dr. Yang (Keye Luke), a Chinatown acupuncturist. Under hypnosis, she tells him that 'I want to be more' than a financially secure wife and mother. Although she is less educated and accomplished than Marion – like the equally well-taken-care-of wife Jasmine in *Blue Jasmine*, she explicitly regrets not completing college – Alice shares their wealthy Upper Manhattan lifestyle. Like Marion at an earlier age, she is tempted by the possibility of adultery and haunted by the memory of a romantic infatuation long ago lost. While Marion's dramatised dream of the past had incorporated memories of her disillusioned father and the possibility of a fulfilling romantic relationship she had foolishly denied, Alice's herbally induced vision conjures the ghost of her former boyfriend Ed (Alec Baldwin) – 'You do have some regrets?', he asks her – and, through the supernatural intervention of her Muse in a creative writing class, the spirit of her mother, a minor actress who gave up her career for the security of marriage ('You were so charming and so misguided', Alice tells her). As Marion had re-visited her brother to repair their separation, Alice tries to draw closer to her older sister Dorothy (Blythe Danner) after a prolonged absence. Both women are married to insensitive, ultimately unfaithful husbands whose adultery they each discover at the emotional end of their respective tethers. Marion knows her marriage is finished when Ken repeats the response she had heard him make when confronted by his first wife's bitter recriminations: 'I accept your condemnation.' This formulaic expression actually precludes personal responsibility ('*If* I've done anything wrong, forgive me', he says to Marion's protest that the passion had gone out of their marriage, in full awareness of the unacknowledged affair with their friend she has yet to discover). Far from an apology, Ken's patronising 'acceptance' lacks any sense of shame or guilt, or any impulse to alter his behaviour. Alice's self-absorbed stockbroker husband, Doug (William Hurt), employs the same false solicitousness as Ken with regard to his wife. Although less of a caricature than the comically brutish husband in *The Purple Rose of Cairo*, Doug's gesture of concern as his wife sets out from their apartment on her abortive romantic rendezvous (as Cecilia had left to meet Tom Baxter) precisely echoes Monk: 'I worry about you.' In both instances, the husbands mean *I take you for granted*.

Just as Marion eventually encounters the person she first sees in her mirror, Alice slowly confronts the unrealised woman she has become. At the end of her first consultation with Dr. Yang, she confesses, 'I'm at a crossroads. I'm lost, lost.' After imbibing Dr. Yang's herbal potion, she comes on to Joe (Joe Mantegna), a single father whom she meets at her children's school. Their flirtation, guided by the ghost of Ed playing the Bogart role in *Play It Again, Sam*, fulfills her thwarted romantic desires until Joe also drinks Dr. Yang's invisibility potion and discovers by eavesdropping on her therapy session that his ex-wife Vicki (Judy Davis) regrets their break-up, whereupon he returns to his marriage.

Remembering her Catholic girlhood during an opium dream earlier in the film, Alice had asked herself, 'When I was young, I wanted to be a saint... Why did that part of me go?' In a self-transformative act after Joe breaks off their affair that surprises everyone, she decides to go to Calcutta to work with Mother Teresa, leaving Doug in total shock. 'You'll be back!' he shouts at her, another line stolen from Monk when Cecilia sets out for Hollywood near the end of *The Purple Rose of Cairo*. With financial resources Cecilia lacks (presumably provided by a team of Manhattan divorce lawyers), Alice truly does leave, and in the film's closing montage she returns to New York a 'changed woman', apparently content with her more modest life raising her children alone in a smaller apartment – and without regret. The choice of Mother Teresa in India marks a step beyond seeking to repair the broken relationships that Marion has uncovered. In the Third Part of *I and Thou*, Buber addresses how the lines of personal relationships (I-You) extend to the eternal You, which is God, the quintessence of all relationship. '"World here, God there" – that is It-talk; and "God in the world" – that, too, is It-talk; but leaving out nothing, leaving nothing behind, to comprehend all – all the world – in comprehending the You, giving the world its due and truth, to have nothing besides God but to grasp everything in him, that is the perfect relationship' (1996: 127). *Alice* is a comedy, of course – and a slight one, at that – but Alice's restless desire for encounter with an infinite, eternal You remains a fundamental, if thwarted expression in Allen's cinema of relationships. In Buber's account, it is the only alternative to the 'false drive for self-affirmation, which impels man to flee from the unreliable, unsolid, unlasting, unpredictable, dangerous world of relation into the having of things' (1996: 126).

Alice concludes with an apparently happy ending – the closing image depicts Alice pushing her two children on park swings – but Allen remains sceptical about the efficacy of her transformation: 'She's not going to be happy as the years go by as change happens. Her children are going to grow up and leave her and go out in the world. She's going to get older… And when that life changes, at some point she's going to be faced with a very, very bleak end and she's going to say, "Look, I will take anything now. I will be happy to go back to my husband"' (Björkman 2004: 231). In her creator's eyes, even her redemptive path of self-reconstruction – the closest equivalent to a conversion experience in all of Allen's cinema (ignoring Benny's ludicrous conversion to Catholicism as he awaits the electric chair and the promise of an afterlife in *Café Society*) – comprises but a shallow phase, a 'transient' (*Vicky Christina Barcelona*) part of her life.

Hannah and Her Sisters

Allen has been equally sceptical about the happy ending of one of his most successful and revered films, *Hannah and Her Sisters*, which, as he told Eric Lax in the same language heard at the beginning of *Annie Hall*, 'I feel I screwed up very badly', especially with the ending, 'the part that killed me' (2007: 359). Note the switch away from Alvy Singer's passive voice ('where did the screw-up come?'): speaking in his own voice as the film's auteur, Allen can accept responsibility for his creative failure. He elaborates on his regret in an interview with Richard Schickel:

> I, myself, found the biggest weakness with a film like *Hannah and Her Sisters* was the ending of the picture. The original ending was supposed to be that Michael Caine has been in love with Hannah's sister all the time, and Hannah's sister gets tired of waiting around for him, and she marries some other guy. And he is despondent, but goes back with Hannah to live his life out with Hannah in a way that is a second chance, and he'll always long for the sister, and see her at little family parties, but never be able to have a relationship with her again, and always be stuck with his second choice for life. (2003: 139)

In this original conception of the screenplay, in short, Elliot (Michael Caine) would have shared the marital fate of both Marion and Alice before discovering their husbands' affairs, consigned to live with a professionally stable and secure spouse in the absence of their romantic ideal. Had he not had his epiphany about Tracy, Isaac might have settled for the same kind of marriage with Mary (after Yale's inevitable return to his wife) in *Manhattan*.

Much to his personal disappointment – and almost certainly to the delight of movie critics and his fans – Allen compromised his pessimistic (he would say 'realistic') conclusion by portraying Elliot as grateful to return to Hannah (Mia Farrow) and, in a magical coda, tacking on a final scene in which Hannah's sister Holly (Diane Wiest), now surprisingly married to the presumably infertile Mickey (Allen), tells him that she is pregnant. 'When I put that picture together,' Allen continues with Schickel, 'and that ending was as I just described it, it was such a downer. It was like the picture ... just fell off the table. And so I had to put a more upbeat ending on the picture, because I had not justified that level of a sort of Chekovian sorrow' (ibid.; ellipsis in original). Instead, the finished film adheres to a comic worldview from which Elliot's regret over his adultery is but a brief interruption on the road to his eventual redemption (Landman 1993: 60). The director's cop-out clearly worked. The leading American reviewers of the day – Vincent Canby (as expected), Roger Ebert, Gene Siskel, Richard Corliss, Rex Reed, Pauline Kael (not always Allen's champion) – lauded *Hannah and Her Sisters*, which went on to win three Academy Awards and still ranks as one of Allen's biggest financial hits.

Still, the director's criticism of his own work lingers, especially when we re-consider the prior fragility of the familial and marital relationships that the film seems to consecrate in the last of the three Thanksgiving scenes that provide its narrative scaffolding. For a certified masterpiece that has retrospectively been praised by one of Allen's most astute and articulate contemporary observers as the product of 'a benevolent paterfamilias who treats each of his characters with the tenderness and bluntness one reserves for a blood relative. The film is, in every respect, family' (Shone 2015: 145), *Hannah and Her Sisters* surveys an extraordinary number of dysfunctional relationships. Set aside Hannah's two sisters, Holly and Lee (Barbara Hershey), both of whom can barely conceal their resentment of Hannah, their parents' favoured child. Holly has survived a bad marriage and struggles with a cocaine habit; Lee is 'suffocating', as she puts it, in a 'tutorial relationship' (Walker 2006: 96) with an older artist, Frederick (Max von Sydow), and is herself a recovering alcoholic. Holly fails every theatrical audition (intensifying her jealousy of Hannah, a successful actress when not raising four children) and dissolves her promising catering business when her partner wins the affection of an architect they both admired. Lee is flattered by her brother-in-law's attention ('I still feel a little buzz from his flirting', she thinks after the opening Thanksgiving dinner) and rather easily slips into an affair with him. She has no career of her own and no apparent direction in life ('I don't even know what I want', she acknowledges to Frederick when they break up, an admission that aligns her with both Marion, who confesses as much to her brother late in *Another Woman*, and Cristina (Scarlett Johansson), certain only of what she does not want, as the narrator reports in the last lines of *Vicky Cristina Barcelona*. Forget, too, their parents, Norma and Evan (Maureen O'Sullivan and Lloyd Nolan), disappointed stage performers ('Both of them just full of promise and hopes that never materialised', as Hannah observes) whose marriage has been marked by continual rivalry, bickering, mutual infidelities and Norma's periodic drunken binges, apparently held together only by Evan's sentimental memories and Hannah's steadfast interventions. In the tradition of romantic comedy, as in Allen's own *A Midsummer Night's Sex Comedy*, the proper relationships are ultimately established (or re-established) to comprise the film's happy ending, but the marriage of Elliot and Hannah merits a closer look.

Frederick may be a misanthrope, but he might be right when he describes Hannah's husband as a 'glorified accountant'; in his amorous pursuit of Lee, at least, Elliot seems little more than a culturally sophisticated version of Allen's prototypical self-absorbed urbanite in his story 'The Shallowest Man', a direct descendant of Yale in *Manhattan* – or, to indulge in a bit of autobiographical speculation, a projection of Woody Allen's own erotic attraction to Mia Farrow's sister (Farrow 1997: 226). *Hannah and Her Sisters* begins with a trumpet solo on the soundtrack playing 'You Made Me Love You' (next line: 'I didn't want to do it'), a title card that reads 'God, she's beautiful', a close-up of Lee gazing at the camera followed by a tracking shot as she moves from room to room, accompanied by Elliot's interior monologue:

Fig. 9: The tracking shot follows Elliot's besotted gaze at Lee

> She's got the prettiest eyes, and she looks so sexy in that sweater. I just want to be alone with her and hold her and kiss her and tell her how much I love her and take care of her. Stop it, you idiot. She's your wife's sister. But I can't help it. I'm consumed by her. I think about her at the office. Oh, Lee. What am I going to do? I hear myself mooning over you, and it's disgusting. Before, when she squeezed past me in the doorway, and I smelled the perfume on the back of her neck, Jesus, I thought I was gonna swoon! Easy. You're a dignified financial advisor. It doesn't look good for you to swoon.

Carlo Di Palma's camera perfectly simulates the male gaze, sexually objectifying Lee as she appears to Elliot: in Buber's terms, as an 'It', a *thing* to be loved. The conventional moral restraints against seducing his sister-in-law immediately are subsumed by his denial of agent regret ('I can't help it'), his helplessness to oppose the 'unpredictable' and 'resilient' (as Mickey will later describe it) demands of the heart. When self-reproach fails, Elliot resorts to the Sartrean definition of shame, exposure in the eyes of another ('It doesn't look good for you to swoon') that stands at odds with his professional self-presentation ('a dignified financial advisor'). As Levinas describes shame, Elliot's is 'an existence that seeks excuses' (2002: 65), one that refuses at this point to take responsibility for Hannah's happiness. His rationalisations and prevarications persist until the final Thanksgiving sequence, preventing him from taking action by encountering Hannah with the truth even after he has begun an affair with Lee. Hours after his first intimate rendezvous with her sister at the St. Regis Hotel, Elliot recalls the 'totally fulfilling experience' but immediately lapses into sentimental feelings for Hannah, reading in bed beside him. 'There's something lovely and real about Hannah. She gives me a very deep feeling of being part of something. She's a wonderful woman, and I betrayed her. She came into my empty life and changed it, and I paid her back by banging her sister in a hotel room. God, I'm despicable. What a cruel thing to do... It can't ever happen again. I'm not that kind of man, and I value Hannah too much.' Elliot's shallow remorse, his acknowledgment of agency ('I paid her back by banging her sister') and acceptance of guilt ('God, I'm despicable'), give way in the same breath to denial of character regret ('I'm not that kind of man') and, moments later, to renewed sexual infatuation when Lee surreptitiously calls him to say goodnight.

As he continues to contemplate his romantic options, Elliot reverts to the standard economics decision theory of a 'glorified accountant', ignoring the 'sunk cost' of his affair and calculating his potential future gains and losses (Landman 1993: 7). 'I'd rather hurt Lee a little,' he thinks, 'than destroy Hannah.' Although Elliot undoubtedly experiences lingering distress and even guilt over his infidelity (unlike Judah in *Crimes and Misdemeanors*, who basks in the flattering admiration of his lover and never considers breaking off the relationship until he is threatened with exposure by his mistress), he never quite accepts his own moral responsibility beyond an occasional insincere self-reproach. Instead, he seems to regard his dilemma as analogous to Gabrielle Taylor's description of *necessary* regret that does not entail undoing the regrettable action. Taylor cites the example of firing a competent and valuable employee for the greater benefit of the company (1985: 99). Herein lie two crucial distinctions between regret and the related but more profound emotion of remorse: regret does not necessarily involve moral responsibility nor the desire to take back the regrettable act. Thus, Elliot carries on the affair for at least a year without reaching a decision. He tells his psychoanalyst, 'I can't seem to take action. I'm like Hamlet unable to kill his uncle. I want Lee, but I can't harm Hannah.' But he is 'not Prince Hamlet, nor was meant to be' (T. S. Eliot, 'The Love Song of J. Alfred Prufrock'). He is instead an ordinary man in mid-life crisis – a glorified accountant – who is saved from the shame of exposure and the remorse of divorce by luck rather than his own agency. Still seeking a tutor, Lee falls in love with and marries her instructor at Columbia University, leaving Elliot relieved and content to be with Hannah, 'who as you once said', he muses in voice-over as he gazes at Lee, 'I love much more than I realised.'

And what of Hannah, the sole person in the ensemble cast who is entirely without regret (she remains on good terms with Mickey, her first husband, and never discovers Elliot's infidelity)? While Elliot is probably right when he cryptically tells her while still deeply involved in the affair, 'I don't deserve you', Hannah is not immune to the self-possessed and judgemental qualities that undermined Marion's relationships in *Another Woman*. In a flashback in which she appears devastated by the diagnosis of Mickey's infertility, she responds to his immediate humiliation by accusing him of 'ruining himself' through 'excessive masturbation'. Although she generously supports Holly's loan request to start up a catering business in the opening scene, she cannot resist (twice) reminding her sister of her cocaine habit. Sometime later, she hesitates when Holly announces she is doing a singing audition, provoking her to complain, 'Boy, you really know how to cut me down', and when Holly asks her to subsidise six months of writing, Hannah again agrees, but not before suggesting a safer salaried position at the Museum of Broadcasting. 'You really think I'm a loser, don't you?', Holly testily responds. Just as Marion had reacted critically to her brother Paul's attempts to write, Hannah becomes openly angry when Holly shows her a script that suggests the fissures in her marriage to Elliot. Significantly, insofar as it illustrates Hannah's exercise of familial control, Holly abandons this first play in favour of a second script that Mickey unreservedly applauds. For her, it is Mickey's approval, and not Hannah's, that marks an end to the bad and a beginning of the good. As for Hannah, she is neither as cold as Eve nor as judgemental as Marion, neither as foolish as her husband nor as peripatetic as her sisters, but in Allen's cinema of regret, their confusion remains significant, while her order is not.

Hannah and Her Sisters concludes with all three sisters happily married (even Norma and Lloyd seem to be getting along) and with that celebrated punch line of Holly's announcing her pregnancy. Two ingredients seem necessary for Allen to contrive such an unqualified happy ending: luck and the expression of regret. In *Whatever Works* (2009), a far less rich film, the misanthropic protagonist Boris (Larry David) tries to commit suicide by jumping out of his apartment window but is saved when he lands on a woman walking her dog, sending her to the hospital. When he visits the unfortunate victim, the habitually unrepentant Boris apologises and seeks to make amends: 'I'm really very sorry,' he tells her, 'Is there anything I can do to make this up to you?' The film ends with Boris cheerfully describing how he 'totally lucked out' with his new girlfriend, his accidental saviour, and philosophising about the importance of chance. In *Hannah and Her Sisters*, the surprising marriage of Holly and Mickey, who had barely survived each other's company on a date years earlier, depends upon their chance meeting in a record store ('Lucky I ran into you' reads the title card introducing this sequence). After Mickey has complimented her work and confessed to his own failed suicide attempt, Holly shifts the conversation during their autumn stroll through Central Park to take responsibility for their bad date years ago: 'I've always regretted the way I behaved that evening we went out … I just thought I'd tell you because I really made a fool of myself.' Mickey immediately shares the blame, and the next time we see them they are married, and Holly is (miraculously) pregnant.

Husbands and Wives

If Woody Allen had compromised his vision of distressed and fragile relationships in *Hannah and Her Sisters* – he recently described his decision to let Elliot return to his wife unscathed as having 'sold out' (Jones 2011) – he sought to correct the artistic error in *Husbands and Wives*, made six years later. '*Husbands and Wives* would be Allen's unsparing repudiation of the familial values equivocally treated in *Hannah [and Her Sisters]*' (Bailey 2001: 117). The cinematic style, for one thing, is totally unprecedented in Allen's oeuvre. In contrast to the smooth tracking shots through Hannah's apartment during the opening scene and the 360-degree pan that serves to reinforce their bond even as the sisters quarrel during lunch at the Art Deco restaurant in *Hannah and Her Sisters*, the jittery hand-held camera, zooms, jump cuts, zip pans, erratic editing and decentred compositions that mark the first ten minutes of *Husbands and Wives* reinforce a tension that the narrative about broken marriages never relieves. As the opening credits roll, the film's central question, sung in a melancholy minor key recorded by Leo Reisman's Orchestra in 1930 – not the later jaunty version that was a hit for Ella Fitzgerald – asks 'What is This Thing Called Love?' None of the characters, either within the diegetic dialogue or in the fifteen cutaway interviews interspersed throughout the story, can offer a more hopeful or honest answer than Sally (Judy Davis), who defines love as 'a buffer against loneliness' after she returns to her estranged husband … and so the same vintage recording plays again over the closing credits.

Husbands and Wives has become a kind of Rorschach test for audiences ever since its release in 1992 immediately following the acrimonious public break-up of Allen and Mia Farrow, a circumstance that remains impossible to ignore when watching the slow dissolution of Gabe and Judy's (Allen and Farrow) marriage. That Allen had written the screenplay two years before Farrow discovered his affair with Soon-Yi Previn hardly mitigates the bleakness of their onscreen relationship or the ferocity of Farrow's quiet performance – in a re-shoot after she found the infamous Polaroids of her adopted daughter – when Judy declares, 'It's over, and we both know it.' After acknowledging his longstanding attraction to 'kamikaze women' and thus his flirtation (without consummation beyond a 'professional' kiss on her 21st birthday) with his creative writing student, Rain, Gabe can only offer the off-screen interviewer (Jeffrey Kurland, the director's longtime costume designer) an equivocal explanation for his behaviour: 'My heart does not know from logic,' even as he admits, 'Everything about it was wrong.' Not long after the film was released, Woody Allen used a spookily similar expression, oft-quoted since, to describe his love affair with Soon-Yi: 'The heart wants what it wants.'

The other characters fare no better in changing their lives or forming more enduring relationships. Gabe, who had claimed that 'change equals death' moments before Judy pronounces an end to their marriage, becomes no fewer than the fourth member of what Rain calls 'the midlife crisis set' to be seduced by her precocious charms. Her tendency to categorise her relationships and to see them as part of the ongoing drama of her life – to regard people as *things*, in Buber's terms – becomes compulsive (to comic effect) in Judy's desire to cut off the dicks of all men, as she tells her hapless date before they leave for a performance of *Don Giovanni* following her separation from Jack and, later, in her mental division of her acquaintances into hedgehogs and foxes after failing to reach orgasm with her new lover, Michael (Liam Neeson). Her husband Jack (Sydney Pollack) is a bit like Elliot in *Hannah and Her Sisters*, temporarily lost in a hopeless midlife affair with an aerobics instructor; he is the film's Shallowest Man, oblivious to the young woman's intellectual limitations or his own fatuousness. 'What's the big deal? So I did a couple of things wrong. I yelled. I misbehaved', he admits while trying to return to his wife. 'Does it have to be irreversible?' He happily rejoins his marriage despite the couple's 'unresolved sexual problems' and remains apparently content with 'whatever works', a phrase to be heard again in much later Allen films including *Whatever Works* and *Café Society*. Judy, described in an interview with her first husband (Benno Schmidt) as a 'passive aggressive' type who 'always gets what she wants', ends the narrative married to her third husband, Michael, a lifelong bachelor on the rebound from his affair with Sally, who echoes Elliot's praise of Hannah: 'I don't deserve you.' A regretful, weary Gabe ('I really blew it'), now declaring himself 'out of the race' for a new relationship, concludes one of Allen's most despairing films, an ending perhaps matched only by *Blue Jasmine*, with a plaintive rhetorical reply to the interviewer: 'Can I go now?', he asks. 'Is this over?' The screen goes black, and so the drama's opening *'sturm und drang'*, as Jack had described Judy and Gabe's reaction to the news of their separation, ends *not with a bang but a whimper* (T. S. Eliot, 'The Hollow Men').

Chapter Four
The Murder Quartet

'It's important to feel guilty. Otherwise, you know, you're capable of terrible things.'

Broadway Danny Rose

In their opening scene together in *Love and Death*, Sonia engages her cousin Boris in the first of their several philosophical discussions: 'Let's say that there is no God, and each man is free to do exactly as he chooses,' she proposes. 'Well, what prevents you from murdering someone?' Her thought experiment quickly descends into parodic dialogue, but the question lingers in Woody Allen's cinema of regret. If murder is the ultimate 'mistake' and regret can be essentially defined, in Rudiger Bittner's terms, as the 'painful feeling about something we did which we think was bad' (1992: 262) – as *agent regret* – then committing murder should produce in his characters the strongest feelings of remorse (regret inflected with moral self-reproach). Allen tests this hypothesis in four films spanning twenty-five years – *Crimes and Misdemeanors*, *Match Point*, *Cassandra's Dream* and *Irrational Man* – only to reveal, with the exception of a single character, the shallowness of regret, the transience of guilt and the absence of shame.

Allen has deployed murder as a plot element in other films but without the ethical element raised and then dismissed within Sonia and Boris's devolution into philosophical jargon. In *Love and Death*, for example, Boris's fate turns on his failed attempt to assassinate Napoleon in a scene that concludes with the unexpected intrusion of another man who kills the Emperor's double while Boris hesitates, contemplating the morality of the crime. A serial killer on the loose serves to establish the Kafkaesque ambiance of *Shadows and Fog*, but 'The Strangler' is never apprehended nor his motives explained. When confronted by a paranoiac mob of his fellow townspeople, Allen's hapless character Kleinman can only whine by way of self-defence, 'Nobody is guilty.' Murder is a generic element in *Manhattan Murder Mystery*, but the focus remains on the amateur detective couple's solution of the crime rather than the killer's psychology or his criminal motives. The film's climax, with its *tour de force* allusion to Orson Welles' *The Lady from Shanghai* (1947), emphasises the cinematic presentation – literally, within a movie theatre, as *Shadows and Fog* had concluded within a magician's tent – at the expense of any revelation of the murderer's ethical character or psychological motives. As Vittorio Hösle has noted, 'In *Manhattan Murder Mystery* the tension between the comic atmosphere [produced by the would-be sleuths] and the murder is lessened by the inclusion of films in the film, an inclusion that has an impact on the action but at the same time diminishes the credibility of the "real" killings within the film' (2007: 27). Similarly, when the vocally challenged Olivia (Jennifer Tilly) gets bumped off by the mob hitman-turned-playwright Cheech (Chazz Palminteri) in *Bullets Over Broadway*, audiences are more likely to smile at the killer's expression of relief ('Thank God I don't have to hear her voice any more') than to question his morality, as the callow director, David Shayne (John Cusack), will do in a subsequent scene. David's self-righteous outrage, which hinges on the difference between art and life and will be examined in the next chapter, lacks weight in part because of the cartoonish cinematic presentation of Olivia's demise (repeating an earlier rubout at the same waterfront location accompanied by 'Up a Lazy River' on the soundtrack) and the caricature created by Tilly's hilarious performance. *Bullets Over Broadway* remains pure comedy; the accumulated corpses – like those that scatter the battlefield in *Love and Death* – do not really count.

In the 'Murder Quartet', however, Allen treats homicide seriously, even philosophically. In each case, the murder itself is meticulously planned, allowing the murderer sufficient time to contemplate the moral consequences. Three of the crimes hinge on the idea of a 'perfect' murder, following the blueprint established in Hitchcock's *Strangers on a Train* (1951) by which the killer is a person unknown to his victim, while in *Match Point* the crime is staged so as to look like the intended target was merely an unfortunate eyewitness. In both *Crimes and Misdemeanors* and *Match Point*, the killers feel genuinely sorry, at least for a while, for the harm they have caused, but this sense of regret never reaches the point of wishing they had done differently or that they could undo their acts. They accept – indeed, they *live with* – the aftermath of their crimes; according to Gabrielle Taylor's understanding of the distinction between regret and remorse, they never become truly repentant. 'Remorse,' Taylor writes, 'never implies acceptance. It is impossible to feel remorse and yet believe that *overall* it was right to act as one did' (1985: 99; emphasis added). In Terry (Colin Farrell), the protagonist of *Cassandra's Dream*, Allen presents the single murderer among his works who experiences not simply regret but the entire gamut of self-condemning emotions – remorse, guilt and shame. At the opposite extreme stands Abe (Joaquin Phoenix), the existentialist philosophy professor who murders for a 'righteous' cause in *Irrational Man*, a killer who experiences neither regret nor remorse following his crime but rather exhilaration at his exhibition of Sartrean freedom.

Crimes and Misdemeanors

Among these four films, *Crimes and Misdemeanors* has received by far the greatest scholarly attention; in fact, it is almost certainly the most written about of all of Allen's works. In the special issue of the journal *Film & Philosophy* devoted to Woody Allen published in 2000, for example, more than half of the eleven articles are devoted to this film; even in Bailey and Girgus's recent anthology, *A Companion to Woody Allen*, which is presented as being as focusing on the works after *Husbands and Wives* and the tabloid scandals, references to *Crimes and Misdemeanors* appear in the index as frequently as do any other film. Philosophers dwell on the existentialist ethics that are debated in three separate scenes (Judah's internal dialogue with his patient, Rabbi Ben (Sam Waterston), during the stormy night before the crime, the flashback to his family's Passover Seder, and his conversation with Cliff at the wedding) or explain the film's elaboration of Plato's depiction of the Ring of Gyges in *The Republic*. Literary scholars analyse the parallels to Dostoyevsky's *Crime and Punishment* or *The Brothers Karamazov* to suggest the Bakhtinian dialogism or intertextuality that characterise Allen's oeuvre. Professors of religious studies or cultural studies privilege *Crimes and Misdemeanors*, along with *Deconstructing Harry*, as they define the influences of the director's Jewish background. Allen himself has expressed his ambitions for the film in fairly modest terms. 'First off, I wanted to make a movie that was serious and also comic,' he told Richard Schickel. 'I just wanted to illustrate in an entertaining way that there's no God, that we're alone in the universe, and that there is nobody out there to punish you, that there's not going to be any kind of Hollywood ending to your life in any way, that your morality is strictly up to you' (2003: 149).

Perhaps because the narrative structure of *Crimes and Misdemeanors* combines a serious plot (Judah's responsibility for the murder of his mistress) with a comic subplot (Cliff's troubled marriage and his courtship of Halley (Mia Farrow)) – the only film among the Murder Quartet to do so – some commentators have been led to contrast Judah's perfidy with Cliff's 'moral integrity' and to suggest that Judah has been somehow positively transformed 'by the crucible of despair' (Vigliotti 2000: 159). As the proximity of *Annie Hall* may have affected interpretations of *Manhattan*, the success of *Hannah and Her Sisters*, released three years earlier, might account for the frequent conflation of Mickey's character in *Hannah and Her Sisters* with the less reliable character of Cliff and the tendency of some viewers to regard Judah as a more menacing but no less fortunate adulterer than Elliot, restored to his secure domestic place in the film's happy ending, his guilty secrets safely, if unjustly, concealed. Certainly, Allen's professed theme in *Crimes and Misdemeanors* – that 'you can commit a crime and get away with it because the universe is godless' (Lax 2007: 358) – has remained clear to nearly all commentators on the film. What seems less obvious, however, is that this consequence has less to do with the absence or withdrawal of God from the modern world or the incompetence of the criminal justice system than with the murderer's capacity to rationalise his behaviour and cope with his own superficial sense of guilt.

Crimes and Misdemeanors begins at a testimonial dinner in honour of Judah Rosenthal. The camera zooms in on this proud, blushing figure of civic responsibility, handsome in his tuxedo, cultured in his demeanour, mellifluous in his speech, as he prepares to address a country club filled with admirers. As Mark W. Roche has reminded us, citing Genesis, the name 'Judah' means 'praised' or 'object of praise' (2006: 272). Before the master of ceremonies can complete his flattering introduction, however, the narrative flashes back to earlier that same afternoon to depict Judah nervously reading a handwritten letter he has – 'by a miracle', as he later puts it – intercepted before it reached his wife. The voice of his mistress, Delores Paley (Anjelica Huston), recites the threatening message that Judah has managed temporarily to silence: 'I wish to cause no suffering, but … the situation has got to be confronted in some fashion. I want what's best for everyone.' Judah immediately burns the letter in the fireplace, his face aglow from the proximity of the flames, and the story returns to a slightly low-angled shot of him standing at the podium, his persona intact for the seated audience in the dining hall but his moral stature already compromised for the movie audience. Allen's composition subtly reflects the fate that shadows his impeccable façade. Directly behind him, Judah is confined within

Fig. 10: The 'object of praise' at his testimonial dinner, Judah remains ensnared by darkness

two vertical window frames that constrict his space in a manner similar to the coffee shop shot at the end of *Annie Hall* described earlier. Outside in the darkness an ominous tangle of leafless branches appears to close off his escape. While his speech is graceful and self-assured, the movie spectator comprehends the oblique confession expressed by his reference to his religious father's reminder that 'the eyes of God' always watch out for our sins, a memory which Judah now lightheartedly accounts, for his medical specialty is as an ophthalmologist.

Presumably the next day, Judah confronts Delores in her cramped Manhattan apartment, having arrived using his key before she returns from neighbourhood grocery shopping. Despite her obvious agitation and suicidal thoughts ('I'll jump out the window, I swear,' she tells him, a line that echoes much later in another character's actual suicide note), Judah dismisses her recriminations and argues only for himself: 'Do you want to destroy my life, my family?' Driving to work soon after, he recalls meeting her, an airline attendant, on a business trip to Boston, a flirtation that turns into a two-year affair. Through a brief flashback from Delores' perspective, he is seen running on the beach at sunset, flattered by her comments about being in 'such wonderful shape' and instructing her in the difference between Schubert and Schumann. Summoned again to her place, he adamantly denies making promises to her, costing her business and romantic 'opportunities', and when these protestations fail, he calculatingly softens his approach, caressing her hand and offering to 'reimburse' her. Delores responds angrily, not only refusing to be bribed but accusing Judah of embezzling philanthropic funds to cover his investment losses. The quarrel escalates with Judah rising in outage to assert his innocence – 'My conscience is completely clear... Moving around funds is not stealing' – and then, in essence, begging for mercy: 'Think what you're doing to me, *please*!'

Having failed to placate his mistress by offering to improve her current financial status or invoking their past romantic relationship, Judah confronts his two remaining options. He can accept Rabbi Ben's suggestion to confess his indiscretion to his wife Miriam (Claire Bloom) and 'hope for forgiveness' or he can call upon his reprobate brother Jack (Jerry Orbach), who offers to 'straighten her out'. 'She can be gotten rid of', Jack tells him, reassuring Judah that 'you won't be involved'. Despite his performance of moral outrage ('She's not an insect. You can't just step on her'), Judah has already begun to disregard Delores as a person for whom he has any responsibility. Having called her 'Del' when he appealed to her affections for the final time, he never again uses her name. She has become, instead, in Buber's terms, an 'It', 'another woman', as he bluntly describes her to Ben, as anonymous as the unnamed character Mia Farrow plays in Allen's earlier film, and 'a helluva problem', as Jack calls her. Summoned by Delores to a gas station close to his suburban home and threatened again with exposure, Judah can offer his hysterical mistress nothing other than suggesting that she see a therapist, thereby avoiding any further encounters. That evening, as lightning flashes and thunder sounds, he engages in ethical dialogue with the imagined vision of Ben imploring him 'to confess to wrong and hope for understanding' in acknowledgment of a universal 'moral structure with real meaning'. As in the classroom discussion between Isaac and Yale in *Manhattan*, the colloquy is not visually balanced. Allen uses an extremely shallow focus to reveal Ben as an insubstantial spectre standing in the dark living room behind Judah, whose face in the foreground is again demonically lit by the embers from the fireplace.

Throughout this intense internal monologue – the audience understands through the ghostly voice-over at the beginning of the scene and the shallow focus that Ben is not actually there in the living room – Judah cannot acknowledge his mistakes or encounter Miriam face to face. His narcissism prohibits confession. 'Miriam won't forgive me,' he says. 'She'll be broken. She worships me.' Moreover, he will not expose himself to shame ('we'd be humiliated before our friends'). Musing on what Ben refers to as his 'financial improprieties', Judah acknowledges only that his dealings might have been 'questionable'. Ben joins him on the sofa to continue asserting reverence for the Law, but even in the intimate two-shot (Ben slightly behind) Judah alone remains in sharp focus as his resolve hardens. 'I will not be destroyed by this neurotic woman,' he concludes, objectifying Delores' personhood. 'Is what she's doing to me just? Is this what I deserve?' Allen cuts to a close-up of the telephone, then pans up to Judah calling Jack 'to move ahead with what we discussed'. By refusing to feel guilty throughout this compelling scene, Judah acts out the moral consequences as defined by Broadway Danny Rose: he does a terrible thing.

Judah reacts with genuine shock when Jack calls during a dinner party to convey the good news: 'Everything came out fine. It's over and done with, no problems, so you can forget about it.' Although he prays for God's mercy as he hangs up the phone, Judah is not so overwhelmed with remorse that he cannot immediately feign an excuse to leave his guests. 'I've made a terrible mistake,' he tells them – *there's that line again*, only ironic this time, as Judah explains that he has left behind important papers at the office that he must immediately retrieve, the same excuse that Chris will improvise to get away from *his* family in *Match Point*. Accompanied by Schubert's String Quartet in G major on the soundtrack, which had been heard earlier when the anonymous hitman stalked Delores, Judah returns to the scene of the crime to retrieve some incriminating evidence. Allen orchestrates this set piece brilliantly. Judah pauses for a moment across the street from Delores' apartment building just long enough for a long shot to register the sign on the adjacent storefront, 'Jack's Hairstyling', subliminally reminding the audience of his brother's agency in committing the murder. Immediately upon entering, Judah discovers the corpse on the floor as Allen slowly pans from a close-up of his stricken expression down his body and across to Delores' lifeless but placid face, her eyes wide open, unlike the last time he saw her that rainy night in the car when she was crying behind her dark glasses. The Schubert quartet reaches a crescendo, and the camera pans up again to Judah's tormented face as he sits next to her. The camera movement here, visually connecting murderer and victim and insisting upon their relationship, perfectly reflects what Emmanuel Levinas described as 'the infinite ethical demand of the other' (Girgus 2010: 4). Judah, on the other hand, will not look her way again as he rummages for her diary and a framed photograph before sneaking away in the night. Instead, while still in the apartment, he enacts the first of several ultimately facile acts of penance as he conjures the memory of his religious father lecturing him about the penetrating 'eyes of God', the very image he had deployed to great effect in his speech at the testimonial dinner.

Scenes of anguish follow for Judah – sleepless nights, a sentimental journey to his boyhood home where he recalls the family debate over morality at the Passover Seder, a Raskolnikov impulse to confess that he describes to his unrepentant brother, another return to the crime scene (again, like Raskolnikov), bouts of excessive drinking

– although he remains steady enough to handle a police investigator's enquiry with his customary aplomb. For all the studies of the influences of Dostoyevsky's *Crime and Punishment* that the title of Allen's film along with its plot have invited, *Crimes and Misdemeanors* remains 'Dostoyevsky Light' in the sense that Judah is a relatively unreflective protagonist. As William C. Pamerleau properly points out, 'Raskolnikov is guilty of hubris for the sake of his ideals; Judah is guilty of nihilism for the sake of comfort' (2000: 103) in order to preserve, as another comparative analysis with Dostoyevsky puts it, 'his shallow and banal way of life' (LeBlanc 2000: 92). According to the schematic formula offered by Marcia Baron, he has, during this period of self-reproach, acknowledged his general *regret* ('If only it had been otherwise') as well as his *agency* ('And it happened through me'), but he never reaches the level of *remorse* ('And I should have averted it') (1988: 267–8). As another philosopher, Bernard Williams, puts the case in his study of *Moral Luck*, Judah's regret for being responsible for Delores' death 'does not necessarily involve the wish, all things taken together, that one had acted otherwise' (1982: 33). Most obviously of all, Judah's *punishment* is light.

Recalling Hösle's observation about the effect of the self-reflexive inclusion of films within the film in *Manhattan Murder Mystery* brings to mind how the insertion of several cutaways to classic Hollywood movies as well as to the raw footage from Cliff's documentary in progress might also serve to lighten the moral shock of Delores' murder. The movie theatre scenes of Cliff with his niece provide both a simplified commentary on the melodramatic events (Betty Hutton sings an over-the-top version of 'Murder He Says' in *Happy Go Lucky* (1943), for example) and an affectionate, likable side to his otherwise morose character. The cutting room scenes that show parts of his film about Professor Louis Levy (Martin Bergmann) similarly allow Cliff's flirtation with Halley to develop, encouraging the audience to root for him. Finally, there is his aborted commission to shoot a hagiography about his pompous brother-in-law Lester (Alan Alda), which also allows us to sympathise with the beleaguered Cliff. In each case, the reminders that we are watching a movie subtly undermine the horror and verisimilitude of Judah's crime – at the same time making *Crimes and Misdemeanors* a more philosophical film. After a clichéd montage sequence of slowly passing time in Alcatraz from the black-and-white movie *The Last Gangster* (1937) returns to a long shot in colour of the Waldorf Astoria and the caption 'FOUR MONTHS LATER', the closing sequence of *Crimes and Misdemeanors* brings together all of the film's major characters for the marriage of Ben's daughter.

In the penultimate scene, Judah, wearing the same tuxedo and looking as self-contented as he did at the country club, wanders away from the festivities and meets sad sack Cliff, who, having just learned that Halley is now engaged to Lester, says he is 'planning the perfect murder'. Apparently feeling no pain, the mildly drunk Judah offers Cliff a 'movie story with a strange twist' and proceeds to recount the outline of his own 'awful deed'. In Judah's autobiographical scenario, the evil doer is 'plagued by deep rooted guilt' for a time, but then 'mysteriously, the crisis is lifted' and he is returned, unpunished, to his 'world of wealth and privilege'. Cliff resists the superficiality of the guilty man's restoration, asking, 'Yes, but can he really go back?' Allen pans to a perfectly balanced two-shot as Judah replies that all men carry sins. 'Oh, once in a while he has a bad moment, but it passes.' Cliff objects that 'then his worst beliefs are realised' and doubts that 'many guys could live with something like that on their conscience', which prompts Judah – repeating Lester's comment to his sister, Cliff's soon-to-be ex-wife, moments earlier in a cutaway from Judah's intimate conversation with Cliff – to assert a 'real world' ethical standard: 'People carry awful deeds around with them', he argues with some annoyance. 'What do you expect them to do, turn themselves in?' Annoyance turns to disdain when Cliff suggests an alternative ending in which the guilty man assumes responsibility 'in the absence of a god', thereby raising the story to tragedy. With a smile that puts an end to the moral debate, Judah tells Cliff that 'if you want a happy ending you should go to see a Hollywood movie'. Miriam appears on the scene, the couple compliment each other on their good looks, and they go off together arm-in-arm planning their own daughter's wedding. Having served slightly more than four months of penance for his crime, an unrepentant Judah happily heads home.

The existentialist philosophy that Allen explicitly intended to express in this celebrated scene – 'we live in a world where there's nobody to punish you, if you don't punish yourself. Judah is someone who does what's expedient for him when he has to. And he gets away with it!' (Björkman 1993: 212) – has seemed clear to most commentators on the film, but there have been some exceptions in addition to Vigliotti's aforementioned account of Judah's positive transformation from guilty despair. Sander Lee, for example, has argued that Judah has not escaped punishment: 'Given what we have seen of his character, it is more likely that his high spirits at the film's end are temporary, and that, in the long run, he will secretly torment himself for the rest of his life' (1997: 287–8). Interestingly, Allen himself felt strongly enough about this (mis)interpretation to depart from his usual practice and directly reply to Lee in a written interview cited in the appendix of his book: 'You are wrong about

Judah; he feels no guilt and the extremely rare times the events occur to him, his mild uneasiness (which sometimes doesn't come at all) is negligible' (1997: 374). For Allen, it is the superficiality of Judah's regret, amounting to a temporary 'mild uneasiness', that matters more than the injustice that prevails.

The sub-plot in *Crimes and Misdemeanors*, Cliff's failed marriage prompting his flirtation with Halley and Lester's ultimate triumph in winning her heart, has further frustrated audiences seeking some justice that might validate the hopefulness associated with the final wedding scene. Thus, many critics have lamented the unhappiness of 'a virtuous artist' like Cliff and the success of 'a corrupt hack' like Lester (LeBlanc 2000: 92). But Cliff is neither a paragon of virtue nor of art. He actively pursues an adulterous affair with Halley, to whom he writes a love letter plagiarised from James Joyce. More to the point, he is a second-rate filmmaker, jealous of his brother-in-law's success. Aside from his career highlight of an honourable mention at a minor documentary festival and the testimony of his wife that his films 'come to nothing', the two examples Allen shows us of Cliff's work hardly inspire admiration. His ongoing project on Louis Levy consists almost entirely of head shots of the professor talking to the camera, amounting to little more than filmed lectures, and his comic editing of the documentary about Lester, involving inserts to Mussolini and Francis the Talking Mule, are more sophomoric than clever – reminiscent of the editing of *What's Up, Tiger Lily?*, they reflect the cheap shots of a shallow, resentful man. Lester, on the other hand, proves to be a man of some substance despite his apparently self-aggrandising style. He might seem obnoxious when he surrounds himself with gorgeous young television actresses, puts down Cliff ('a poor loser agrees to do the story of a great man's life'), or pontificates about the art of comedy, but the facts remain that he does not cheat on his new wife (and apparently was single when flirting with Hallie and the others), hires his brother-in-law as an act of charity to help out his sister, and has won multiple Emmys for shows that are being taught in colleges. When Halley recalls the first line of an Emily Dickinson poem ('Because I could not stop for Death') and Cliff chimes in with the familiar second line ('He kindly stopped for me'), Lester effortlessly recites the rest of poem. Most importantly, he has paid for the wedding at the Waldorf. When an aggrieved Cliff attacks Halley for falling for him, she replies with conviction: 'He's not what you think. He's wonderful. He's warm and caring and romantic… He's *endearing*.'

In an ironic sense, Lester's glib definition, 'Comedy equals tragedy plus time', is vindicated by *Crimes and Misdemeanors*, as the film ends with the beneficent image of Ben, now totally blind, dancing with his newly married daughter as the orchestra plays 'I'll Be Seeing You'. Allen juxtaposes this sentimental moment with a montage of prior events and the voice-over of Professor Levy expounding on what philosopher Sander Lee cites as 'one of the best short descriptions of existential beliefs I have ever heard or read':

> We are all faced throughout our lives with agonizing decisions, moral choices. Some are on a grand scale, most of these choices are on lesser points, but, we define ourselves by the choices we have made. We are, in fact, the sum total of our choices. We wince and fail so unpredictably, so unfairly, human happiness does not seem to have been included in the design of creation. (2001: 57)

Zachary T. Ingle cites the same passage, quoting its optimistic conclusion as well to illustrate how Levy's 'final message' confirms 'a life of meaning and mortality':

> It is only we, with our capacity to love, that give meaning to the indifferent universe. And yet, most human beings seem to have the ability to keep trying, and even to find joy, from simple things like their family, their work, and from the hope that future generations might understand more. (2015: 127)

But this is *not* the professor's final message. Professor Levy, the audience now knows, was a Holocaust survivor who suddenly and inexplicably committed suicide four decades later, thereby putting an end to Cliff's current artistic dream. His absurd farewell note, 'I went out the window', rhymes with Delores' melodramatic threat, only as a realised existential choice – an accomplished act. The philosopher's name is intriguing: many educated viewers will associate Levy with the author Primo Levi, an Auschwitz survivor and apparent suicide – Allen has acknowledged the connection, although he claims it was unconscious (Lee 1997: 374) – but the emphasis in this invocation of the professor's recorded philosophy speaks more directly to Levinas's ethics of responsibility for the Other (including 'family' and 'future generations'). As Professor Levy's off-camera voice speaks of 'moral choices', the retrospective montage, in contrast to the nostalgic flashbacks that conclude *Annie Hall*, replays several unpleasant moments – arguments, mismatched couples, dark plots – until the reprise brightens as the new bride and groom approach the altar, at which point Levy intones his optimistic conclusion. This ending is sentimental, knowingly so, as Allen reflexively demonstrates the audience's immersion in the spectacle on which film art depends. Peter Bailey is certainly correct in defining how this closing montage 'utterly fails to exact the neat resolution that such endings traditionally generate largely because the articulation of values superimposed upon it is constantly contradicted by the content of the images that voice-over projects' (2001: 139). In short, Allen has assumed Judah's view of reality by refusing to construct a Hollywood ending based on a simplistic philosophy, as he had in *Annie Hall* ('We need the eggs') and several other entertaining films. 'And yet' (as Professor Levy might phrase it), the very last image in *Crimes and Misdemeanors* does preserve a kind of life-affirming idea: the dance ends with Ben and his daughter perfectly centred in the frame, basking in the warm glow of the low lighting and the wedding guests' applause (Judah and Miriam having already departed) – a display the film's audience, watching in the moment, likely shares. Levy's professed philosophy of hope, however inadequate when applied to Judah or contradictory when applied to his own suicide, serves as an artificial benediction on the occasion, the necessary illusion (like cinema itself) that brings joy to the spectators in the Waldorf's ballroom as well as those in the movie theatre.

Match Point

Although Judah rejects Cliff's 'movie idea' on existentialist grounds (in the absence of God, man must make his own moral choices and live with the consequences of their 'awful deeds'), Allen finds the inverted Job story – a guilty man prospers despite his irreverence – sufficiently intriguing to make *Match Point*, the film that in 2005 restored his critical and, to a lesser degree, commercial reputation. Chris Wilton (Jonathan Rhys Meyers), a self-described 'poor boy from Ireland come to London' seeking his fortune after a mediocre career on the professional tennis tour, succeeds in marrying wealth and, like Judah, settles into a protected life of culture and privilege. He too is threatened by his nagging mistress, Nola (Scarlett Johansson), living in a small London flat, pregnant and unwilling to endure a third abortion. Her motive for responding differently this time to the mistake of conceiving out of wedlock seems less a matter of moral regret than simply mercenary, given Chris's social status. Unlike Judah, whom Jack accused of not wanting to get his hands dirty, Chris commits the murder himself, staging the crime as a burglary of Nola's neighbour, Mrs Eastby (Margaret Tyzack), and killing them both. Despite his revulsion at the scene of the crime – Allen again avoids showing the gruesome details of the violence – Chris, like Judah, immediately assumes a veneer of calm when he joins his wife at the theatre to establish his alibi. The shallowness of Judah's 'deep rooted guilt', as he had described it in his movie scenario, can be measured by its circumscribed duration – about *four months*; similarly, the limits of Chris's regret can be measured by his forced confession to the lesser crime of adultery in a Shepherd's Bush police station and the sophistic rationalisations he offers on a single dark night of the soul.

The aftermath of the crime in *Match Point* follows a similar course as in *Crimes and Misdemeanors*, although Chris, uninhibited by any warnings about 'the eyes of God' from a religious upbringing, quickly recovers from the agony of actually committing cold-blooded murder. Like Judah, he is questioned by the police, but in the face of indisputable evidence from Nola's diary, he admits to the extramarital affair without even the pretence of regret. Caught in a lie about when he last saw Nola, like the talented tennis player he is, he volleys moral responsibility back to the interrogators: 'You can't blame me for trying to hide the fact that I had an affair with her, but you people have to protect me here… God, have a heart! My wife is going to have a baby. This will devastate her.' Chris's claim to be protecting his wife rather than himself precisely repeats what Judah had argued to Ben about shielding Miriam from shame. The lead investigator, Detective Banner (James Nesbitt), gives him a pass on his confession of marital unfaithfulness: 'We're not making any moral judgements. Just investigating a crime.'

'Remorse is memory awake', reads the first line of an Emily Dickinson poem, and so, like Judah (and the insomniac Terry in *Cassandra's Dream*), Chris must confront his guilt in the very next scene when he is visited in the middle of the night by the ghosts of his two victims. Steely in his resolve, he faces down their accusations. 'It wasn't easy,' Chris tells Nola, 'but you can learn to push the guilt under the rug. You have to.' This admission of guilt seems crucial because it implies regret as well. According to Janet Landman, 'it seems impossible to imagine experiencing guilt without regret ["It wasn't easy"], but quite possible to imagine experiencing regret without guilt' (1993: 56). Chris speaks of guilt that is immediately *repressed*, however, almost as if it were now more or less a legal concept rather than a psychological experience. Perhaps this objectification of the crime defines him as a sociopath. Mrs. Eastby joins the moral inquisition, reminding him of her own fate as 'an innocent bystander'. Chris replies in the restrained voice of a philosophy professor: 'The innocent are sometimes slain to make way for a grander scheme. You were collateral damage.' She scores a point with her reply – 'So was your unborn child' – and Allen pans from Chris's face to Mrs. Eastby (after having cut between Chris and Nola) to underscore the human connection he has severed that she has insisted upon. As the camera pans back to Chris, he returns her accusation by quoting Sophocles on the 'boon' of never having been born – a line Allen has recycled from *Deconstructing Harry*. In response to his remorselessness, Nola warns him: 'Prepare to pay the price.' Still in a philosophical mood – at the beginning of the film Chris had been reading Dostoyevsky's *Crime and Punishment* (a favourite of Abe as well in *Irrational Man*) – he reverts to the idea of a 'moral structure' that had informed Judah's father's and Rabbi Ben's view of the world – 'It would be fitting if I were apprehended and punished. At least there would be some small sign of justice, some small hope for the possibility of meaning' – only to regret that the real world remains otherwise.

Both Christopher J. Knight and John Douglas Macready interpret this scene, the moral climax of *Match Point* as Judah's dialogue with Cliff had been in *Crimes and Misdemeanors*, to reflect something like Cliff's alternative ending: the criminal truly cannot get away with it. Knight argues that 'Wilton, following the murders, is, like Macbeth, haunted by his victims' ghosts' (2013: 85); Macready suggests that 'the presences of Mrs. Eastby, Nola, and their unborn child hang like an anvil on Chris's soul' (2013: 111). But the close-up of Chris as he rallies against his demons reminds us of his tennis skills ('very steady, cool under pressure… never beat yourself', as his old friend on tour had described him). To the extent that he gets the last word in each exchange, he wins every point. Moreover, these ghosts, unlike Banquo, never reappear. Where he had performed the role of the contrite philanderer back in the police station, covering his face and brushing back tears, now he is dry-eyed and prepared with a ready rationale for his phantom accusers. Robert H. Polhemus more precisely interprets the shameless man's response: 'Far from remorseful honesty, it's

Fig. 11: Chris in rueful contemplation of 'luck'

a self-deceiver's way of escaping from a vicious self into the softer abstractions of ethics and literature' (2013: 126). In the film's closing close-up, Chris stands aside from the rest of his family as they toast his newborn, legitimate son. Like Judah, he is now safe from prosecution (as in *Crimes and Misdemeanors*, luck has provided an anonymous, rootless surrogate to whom the police assign blame for the crime) and restored to his prosperous existence. Macready describes 'the camera lingering on Chris's face, full of guilt and despair' (2013: 112), but perhaps the close-up is more ambiguous than that, like Isaac's at the very end of *Manhattan*. Granted, he has temporarily withdrawn from the celebration, but his expression seems closer to rueful rather than guilty as he contemplates his brother-in-law's toast to the baby's 'luck' instead of greatness. This may be a 'bad moment' for Chris, but one that seems destined soon to pass.

Cassandra's Dream

Cassandra's Dream represents the third permutation of Allen's thought experiment in which a murderer goes unpunished by the law, 'the only one in which a perpetrator is psychologically tormented by remorse over what he has done' (Hutchings 2013: 372). In insisting on the crucial distinction between agent regret and remorse, Marcia Baron points to the moral element (the *ought*, as philosophers sometimes term it): 'Remorse involves not just a judgment that it would have been much better if one had acted otherwise, and not just (in addition to this judgment) recognition of the connection between his character and the catastrophe. It involves a judgment that one could have acted otherwise and, more important, that one *should* have' (1988: 267). In *Cassandra's Dream*, the compulsive gambler Terry is not as lucky as Chris Wilton – perhaps because he only recognises 'Cassandra' as the name of a dog that paid off a 60-to-1 bet at the beginning of the film, not the gloomy and unheeded prophetess of Greek tragedy (who appears in Allen's *Mighty Aphrodite*). Like the protagonist of 'true tragedy' that Cliff had proposed to Judah at the end of *Crimes and Misdemeanors*, Terry cannot live with the terrible thing he has done. It is as if Allen had allowed brother Jack from the earlier film a larger role or split the internal conflict Judah undergoes into two separate persons: Terry, whose conscience argues that murder is 'just wrong', and his brother Ian (Ewan McGregor), whose desire for a better life overcomes his initial revulsion at the idea. Ian's rationale for murder repeats the formula proposed in *Crimes and Misdemeanors*: 'You push a button and it's over.'

Needing money for different reasons, the brothers become hitmen for their revered Uncle Howard (Tom Wilkinson), a global entrepreneur of 'organised medicine' who is visiting his sister's family while stopping in London on a business trip to Asia. After the brothers ask Howard for separate loans to cover Terry's gambling debts and front Ian's investment opportunity, Howard reveals that he has become involved in 'a little situation' that requires their help. He is being threatened with exposure for embezzlement by a business associate, Martin Burns (Philip Davis), who therefore 'has to be got rid of'. Allen underscores Howard's melodramatic proposal with an ominous clash of thunder in the English garden where the three men confer, just as he had on the night when Judah decided to dispatch Delores. 'I want it taken care of while I'm away,' Howard says. 'I don't want to know about it. I just want it over and done with when I get back. Quick. Simple. No witnesses. And then just let it fade into history.' Both brothers are initially appalled, but Terry's immediate response, arms tightly crossed, marks a sharp difference from the more conciliatory Ian: 'I cannot kill someone.'

Allen's characterisation of Uncle Howard makes an interesting comparison with his portrait of Diane (Elaine Stritch), Lane's mother, in *September*. Financially secure, charismatic and buoyant, both older relatives have deflected their own murderous intent on to their vulnerable dependents. As Howard has commissioned the boys to silence Martin Burns, Diane once allowed her 14-year-old daughter to take the rap when, after leaving Lane's father 'for a gangster who used to beat her up all the time', Diane was the one who actually shot her lover (a scenario Allen probably adapted from the notorious 1958 case of Lana Turner's 14-year-old daughter fatally stabbing her mother's lover, the gangster Johnny Stompanato, during a quarrel). Twice in *September*, Diane tells Lane to let go of the past – 'What's done is done' – just as Howard advises the boys to allow their crime to 'fade into history'. Similar to how Howard had excused Terry's confession about his gambling – 'Everyone makes mistakes. We'll deal with it' – before rationalising his own corruption and appealing to 'family loyalty', Diane exonerates her own 'superficial existence', as Lane had described it: 'Sorry for all the fuss. We all make mistakes.' Allen follows this admission at the film's emotional climax with a prolonged fade, allowing the audience time to contemplate Diane's formulaic expression of regret.

In all four films comprising the Murder Quartet, Allen does not dwell on the violence itself, leaving the killings to take place off screen in *Crimes and Misdemeanors* and *Irrational Man* and not showing the victims in *Match Point* and *Cassandra's Dream*, where he pans left across a verdant hedge at the moment Terry pulls out his homemade zip gun and shoots Burns, as if the camera were ashamed to look upon the site of the brothers' disgraceful act. Even before he commits the crime, Terry is tortured by the moral transgression he has been asked to perform. 'What if there is a God?' he asks his brother. 'We're crossing the line, Ian. There's no going back.' Having crossed that line, Terry quickly descends into morbidity and self-destructive behaviour, seeking oblivion in pills and alcohol and, like Judah, threatening his brother with his need to confess. His predicament mirrors the dilemma of shame as described by the philosopher Lisa Guenther: 'when it really takes hold of me, I cannot even stand myself' (2011: 24). For Terry, regret for having made a mistake has soured into the shame of a character who no longer matters to himself. Emmanuel Levinas, going beyond Sartre's understanding of shame as the consequence of being gazed at or imagining the gaze of the Other, defines such personal shame in *On Escape* as 'precisely the fact of being riveted to oneself, the radical impossibility of fleeing oneself to hide from oneself, the unalterably binding presence of the I to itself' (2003: 64). Thus Terry speaks of suicide, to which his brother can only callously reply, 'Go and commit suicide, and leave Howard and me out of it.' When Ian informs their uncle of Terry's threat to confess to the police, Howard repeats the remorseless calculation he had made regarding Burns, 'I just don't see any alternative…', and so the film rushes to its tragic finale. Aboard their fateful sailing ship, 'Cassandra's Dream', the brothers confront their guilt, Ian reluctantly regretting their decision – 'We made a mistake', he finally admits – but refusing punishment ('but it's over'). Having reconsidered Howard's responsibility ('Maybe Uncle Howard deserves to go to jail'), Terry, by contrast, requires retribution in the wages of remorse: 'restitution, suffering, repentance, atonement, and punishment' (De Wijze 2005: 464). In desperation, Ian tries to follow his plan to poison Terry's beer but then smashes the bottle, they fight and Ian is accidentally killed, at which point the film cuts to the shore where the police outline their hypothesis of a murder-suicide. True to Greek tragedy, both brothers die; true to American tragedy (as in *Crimes and Misdemeanors*), Uncle Howard, absent from the brief epilogue, escapes unpunished.

Irrational Man

Uniquely among these four films, *Irrational Man* employs retrospective voice-over from its two protagonists, the burnt out visiting philosophy professor, Abe Lucas (Joaquin Phoenix), and his infatuated student, Jill (Emma Stone), although only she has access to the end of the story. The plot differs in that the murder is conceived as a deliberate moral choice – Abe kills a biased family court judge in order to give a mother a fair chance to keep her children in a custody case (a scenario that awakens memories of Allen's custody battle with Mia Farrow) – after which the killer experiences not a moment of regret. Unlike the insomniacs who kill in the earlier films, Abe 'slept the sleep of the just' even before he actually commits the crime. The day after he successfully poisons Judge Spangler, he tells Jill, who had been with Abe when they overheard the distraught mother's description of her situation, 'We have nothing to feel guilty about', and so he invites her for a romantic dinner as a 'wicked celebration'. Even after Jill discovers that Abe is a murderer, he tells her, 'I consider myself a moral man', and, as the film nears its violent climax, he reflects in voice-over how 'I still felt justified in what I'd done' and 'had no intention of giving myself up'. In *Irrational Man*, Allen shifts the emphasis to the consequences of *absent* rather than merely shallow regret.

Abe takes enormous pride in his decision to act on his existentialist freedom – 'It was at this moment', he says of his choice to help the distressed woman, 'that my life came together' – but his moral stance remains flawed on two accounts. First, he is not truly motivated by responsibility for the anonymous woman going to court (whose face, with his own back turned, he never sees; who remains, for him, a relationship defined as 'It' – the subject of a thought experiment – rather than 'You') but by a selfish need to alleviate his own ontological impotence, which takes both intellectual and sexual form. The effect of his crime on the mother for whom he killed remains dependent on chance, namely the appointment of a new judge who might see her case more favourably, but its effect on Abe is immediate and decisive: 'My zest for life had returned.' Secondly, his thinking is shallow. He does not take into account either the full dimensions of the judge's life, its ethical reality, or what Chris Wilton would call the 'collateral damage' of his action. The plot twists decisively (it remains unclear what Jill will decide three weeks after hearing his confession) when the newspapers report the arrest of an innocent man suspected of the murder, forcing Jill's hand and prompting him to plot her death. What a colleague had said early on in the film about Abe's philosophy papers ultimately proves also true for his character: 'It's the triumph of style. The substance just doesn't stand up to scrutiny.'

This critique poses a problem for interpretation: is Abe's intellectual superficiality deliberately written into his character or a product of the autodidact screenwriter's own limitations? Allen's praise for William Barrett's 'classic' book *Irrational Man* – 'because he has that knack of popularizing a subject so a mental cretin like me can get it' (Lax 2009: 86) – provides fodder for either side of the argument. Certainly

Jill is impressed ('He was so damn interesting'; 'He's so brilliant'; 'He was truly an original thinker'), but the philosophy that Abe actually expounds is both second-rate and second-hand, as when he name drops about the categorical imperative ('Kant would argue…') and feminism ('Simone de Beauvoir pointed out, and correctly…') or concludes a class lesson with, 'Much of philosophy *is* verbal masturbation.' Without fully realising the implications of her assessment (narrating from a time after the conclusion of the story), Jill describes early on how 'he could always cloud the issue with words'. From her perspective, the story she re-tells is a *bildungsroman* – an account of her initiation into the terrifying dichotomy posed in Abe's first lecture between abstract philosophy and 'real, nasty, ugly life'. Her narration amounts to a confession of her own naiveté, of having been seduced by 'the romantic concept of being in love with your college professor', as Abe puts it, and, in the process, having concealed the identity of a monstrous murderer and nearly becoming his second victim. Only the intervention of chance, in the form of a flashlight that he had won for her betting on a carnival wheel ('We're all at the mercy of chance', he pontificates), saves her in the end when Abe trips on it while struggling with her and falls down an open elevator shaft. Jill is left to reflect in the film's closing long shot by the sea on her 'painful lesson, the kind Abe used to say you can't get from any textbook'. But what *is* that lesson? Abe has repeated a number of philosophical apothegms – 'Anxiety is the dizziness of freedom', 'Luck rules the universe' – that hardly seem to encompass the situational ethics of his righteous murder, leaving Jill presumably to contemplate other banal lessons such as the commandment against murder or the rule about not falling in love with your teacher. Another, perhaps more instructive insight appears in Jill's very first words of narration: 'I think Abe was crazy from the beginning.' Finally, there is Halley's commentary after the suicide of Professor Levy in *Crimes and Misdemeanors*: 'No matter how elaborate a philosophic system you work out, in the end it's going to be incomplete.' The same might be said about the inadequacy of art when compared with life, a topic Woody Allen has continuously explored in a wide range of films.

Chapter Five
The Reflexive Films

'I'm not overly humble. I had grandiose plans for myself when I started out. And I have not lived up to them. I've done some things that are perfectly nice. But I had a much grander conception of where I should end up in the artistic firmament. What has made it doubly poignant for me is that I was never denied the opportunity. The only thing standing between me and greatness is me.'

– Woody Allen

Woody Allen's confession of artistic mediocrity during his appearance at the 92nd Street Y in New York in 2002 (Evanier 2015: 10–11) repeats a self-assessment he has been sounding in interviews and films at least as far back as *Interiors*. He has always insisted that he is not simply *kvetching* or being falsely modest – he remains grateful for his singular talent to amuse, which has enabled him to fulfill his childhood dream of an affluent Manhattan lifestyle – but rather expressing his 'objective feeling … that I haven't achieved anything significant artistically' (Lax 1991: 365). Along with this regret about his own creative shortcomings, Allen has consistently avowed distrust about the efficacy of art itself as well as ambivalence about his audience. He is quoted by his first biographer, Lee Guthrie, as saying, 'I'm one of those people that believes there's no social value in art, not just comedy, but no social value in art at all, anyplace, anytime' (1978: 144). In films like *Interiors*, *September*, *Alice* and *Bullets Over Broadway*, he has depicted the plight of would-be artists coming to terms with the limitations of their talent;

in works like *Stardust Memories*, *Deconstructing Harry*, *Sweet and Lowdown* and *You Will Meet a Tall Dark Stranger*, he has exposed the narcissism, cruelty and corruption that often underlies the artist's success. And in movies like *The Purple Rose of Cairo*, *Celebrity* and *Magic in the Moonlight* (2014), he has shown audiences to be gullible, sycophantic and obsessed. No wonder Peter J. Bailey has entitled his comprehensive study of the director's sceptical view of his own life's work *The Reluctant Film Art of Woody Allen*.

Allen's misgivings about his merits as an artist involve both character regret about what might be called his creative IQ, largely determined by chance ('Talent is luck', Isaac says in *Manhattan*), and agent regret about his own working methods, the shallowness not merely of his intellect but of his professional practice. The self-critique follows three lines: that he is gifted but not a genius; that his gifts are in the service of comedy rather than tragedy; that his vaunted self-discipline as an auteur imperfectly conceals a lack of artistic rigour. Whether these self-deprecatory claims are warranted is a matter for the individual viewer to discern – and judgement clearly can vary from one picture to another. Certainly, he seems to have 'mailed it in' when creating *Crisis in Six Scenes* for Amazon Prime. Acknowledging the failure of 'what may be the worst film I've made', *Curse of the Jade Scorpion* (2001), Allen admits, 'It kills me to have a cast so gifted and not be able to come through for them... So for me personally I have great regrets and embarrassment because people trusted me, and took their jobs for no money' (Lax 2009: 54). His only consistent self-defence in surveying his oeuvre has been that he never compromised his own ideal conception of a project. About his early dramas, *Interiors*, *September* and *Another Woman*, for example, he told Eric Lax, 'The impulse was honorable, the attempt was honorable, I did the best I could' (2009: 356).

In measuring his lifetime achievement, Allen regards himself as working in the shadow of his artistic idol, Ingmar Bergman, 'the finest filmmaker of my lifetime' (Allen 2007). Bergman's great films of the 1950s, especially *The Seventh Seal*, *Wild Strawberries* and *The Magician* (1958), set a standard of dramatic profundity and cinematic brilliance to which Allen, like Isaac modeling himself on God in *Manhattan* or Emmet seeking to emulate the virtuosity of Django Reinhardt in *Sweet and Lowdown*, has steadfastly aspired. The influence of *The Seventh Seal* pervades Allen's writings and films, beginning with 'Death Knocks' and *Love and Death*. Many critics have noted the similar introspective road trips that mark the narratives in *Wild Strawberries* and *Deconstructing Harry*, and recently María Elena de las Carreras-Kuntz has shown how *The Magician* shares the same premise as

Magic in the Moonlight: 'a rational man is obsessed with unmasking someone who makes claims outside the material world' (2015: 218). In addition, several other Allen films bear more than a trace of the master's inventiveness: the period farce *A Midsummer Night's Sex Comedy* follows closely the style of Bergman's *Smiles of a Summer Night* (1955); the cutaways to actors commenting on their roles in *Husbands and Wives* borrows from a similar alienation effect in *The Passion of Anna* (1969); Judah's phone ringing in the middle of the night and no one answering on the other end alludes to the similar ominous and unresponsive calls in the midst of personal crisis in *Shame* (1968).

Contrasting himself to Bergman, Allen often reverts to the distinction between talent and genius. In his thoughtful, carefully crafted eulogy published in *The New York Times*, he wrote of the director who had become his friend in later life, 'he was a genius and I am not a genius and genius cannot be learned or its magic passed on' (2007). While denying his own genius, Allen also remains uncomfortable even calling himself an artist, preferring to 'see myself as a working filmmaker who chose to go the route of working all the time rather than making my films into some special red carpet event every three years' (Lax 2009: 97), a work ethic that he ascribes to following Bergman's prolific career in theatre and cinema. Regarding his prodigious gift for writing jokes, he can only allow himself a modicum of credit for a good fortune he has not earned. 'It's typical of people who have a natural talent for any form of human activity to undervalue it,' he told Richard Schickel; 'Whether it is writing jokes or sonnets, what looks hard to the rest of us comes easy for them, and they feel they shouldn't take much – or maybe any – credit for it' (2003: 23). Allen's use of third-person pronouns here is telling, demonstrating resistance even to including himself among the talented jokesters. The real dilemma with this modest self-assessment, however, lies in his longstanding desire to write *sonnets* instead of jokes.

The history of literature in the Western world might have been much different if Aristotle's treatise on comedy had survived along with his analysis of tragedy in the *Poetics*. Perhaps then, Allen's 'early funny ones' would have been regarded as his masterpieces while *Anything Else* and *Whatever Works* were counted as gems from his late period. Allen himself shares his culture's bias in favour of dramatic storytelling over humorous entertainment, despite his paradoxical belief that 'comedy is harder to do than serious stuff'. He continues the comparison in conversation with Eric Lax: 'When comedy approaches a problem, it kids it but it doesn't resolve it ... there's something immature, something second-rate in terms of satisfaction when comedy is compared to drama' (2009: 66). Later in the same book, he compiles an 'insomniac list' of his favorite films, fifteen American and fifteen European and Japanese pictures. Not a single comedy makes the list. He then appends ten of his favorite comedies, none of them his own. He reports rebuking himself for 'wasting my time' with a trivial piece like *Scoop* instead of following up *Match Point* (a rarity among Woody Allen's films insofar as he himself likes it) with 'another meaty thing' (Lax 2009: 185), which leaves open the question of what motivated him to make *Whatever Works* and *To Rome with Love* not long thereafter. His avowed aesthetic goal, most obviously set forth in *Melinda and Melinda* and perhaps most successfully realised in *Crimes and Misdemeanors*, has been to integrate comedy and tragedy, an impulse first exercised in *Love and Death*, but Allen remains acutely aware of his own insufficient character for the task: 'I'm more the guy that's home with the beer in his undershirt watching the ball game on television … than I am poring over, you know, the Russian novelists' (Schickel 2003: 153).

Despite his Prussian work habits and early reputation for re-shooting scenes and dismissing unsuitable actors, Allen maintains that his fault as an artist resides within himself: not simply his narrow thematic and sociological range or lack of philosophical and psychological complexity but more pragmatically his compromises on the set, his need to stay on schedule and within his budget, his willingness to quit instead of shooting one more take in order to be home in time for dinner. 'I don't have the concentration or the dedication that you really need to be a great artist' (Weide 2011). Unlike his conception of a true artist, he told John Lahr in a memorable self-description, 'I'm an imperfectionist' (1996). For Allen, making pictures is work, not art. 'For me, it's like stamping out cookies. I finish a film and I go on to the next one' (Björkman 2004: 96). Or, to choose a different metaphor, filmmaking is more like therapy. 'It's like a patient in an institution who they give basket weaving to, or finger painting, because it makes him feel better. The actual work of making the film is great for me, because I get to create a fake situation and live in that situation and act the character … I control the reality for that period of time, and live amongst beautiful women and guys who are brilliant' (Schickel 2003: 145–6). More recently, in press conferences promoting his latest films at international festivals, Allen repeatedly describes his work as a 'distraction' from the hopeless problems of existence. Generally, the audiences at these events think he is kidding and chuckle in response.

If Allen has regrets about his own insufficiency as an artist, he has similar scepticism about the value of not just his art, but art of even the highest order (Shakespeare and Picasso being his go-to references in interviews). He sees a persistent motif running throughout his cinematic oeuvre as the discrepancy between the illusions –

often synonymous with magic – of art, which remains transient as well as deceptive, and the horrors of existence in the face of the permanent certainty of death. Allen has frequently described this thematic preoccupation as 'a pervasive feeling of the greatness of idealized life or fantasy versus the unpleasantness of reality' (Björkman 2004: 51). Human experience, as Allen perceives it, can be encapsulated in the old Catskills resort joke that begins *Annie Hall*: 'Boy, the food here is really terrible … and such small portions.' Against this implacable fate, the certainty of one's own death (not to mention the fact that 'the universe is expanding'), art can only simplify the reality or distract us from the truth. Although he has never cited William Faulkner as an influence or a personal favourite, Allen shares that author's implicitly regretful insight in *Light in August*: 'how false the most profound book turns out to be when applied to life' (1990: 481). The value of art for Allen lies in the *inspiration* – 'getting the idea' (Björkman 2004: 268) – and *working*, the momentarily absorbing process of refining a line or blocking a scene, rather than the promise of immortality that the artwork itself might offer. 'I don't want to achieve immortality through my work,' Allen has famously quipped. 'I want to achieve it through not dying.' As life makes a profound book seem trivial, so death overcomes 'the most profound artist', who can be redeemed only by keeping faith in 'the artist's Catholicism', the idea that one lives on through one's work, 'which I don't believe in, at all' (Schickel 2003: 134, 135). Compounding Allen's misgivings about the artist and the work of art, he has variously portrayed audiences in his films as celebrity worshipers or creatures of habit, although in interviews he has generally treated them with greater courtesy, claiming, for example, responsibility for leaving his audience behind after *Interiors* and *Stardust Memories* rather than blaming them for obtuseness or disloyalty (Lahr 2006: 146). In *Stardust Memories*, in particular, all of the issues that permeate Allen's reflexive films – the blurred distinctions between illusion and reality or the artist and the man, the self-absorption and immorality of the artist, the ephemeral nature of art and the voyeurism of the audience – generate the modernist stream of images, leaving the spectators within its diegetic film festival alternately delighted, contemptuous or confused. Among all of his films, it remains the one about which critical opinion remains the most divided.

Stardust Memories

Following the substantial critical success of *Annie Hall* and *Manhattan* and the widespread rejection of *Interiors*, the entirely serious film that comes between them,

Allen ruminates for the first time on all three elements comprising the matrix of artistic endeavour: the artist, the audience and the creative work itself. As was true for *Manhattan* and would be again in *Another Woman*, the film being watched represents the completion of the fictional writer/filmmaker's – Isaac, Marion, Sandy Bates (Woody Allen) – work in progress. All three films are 'philosophical' in the sense not of making arguments but of 'thinking' about what it means to be in the world, contemplating the consequences of individual existential choices rather than staking out universal claims. In *Irrational Man*, Abe Lucas speaks for several established philosophical positions – from Kant, Kierkegaard, de Beauvoir, Sartre – but the 'voice' of Allen's film disavows (in Jill's opening and closing narrations) his choices as grotesque interpretations of their sources or symptoms of moral insanity. *Stardust Memories*, on the other hand, undertakes the more ambitious project of inviting philosophical enquiry (rather than lecturing about philosophy) through what Tom McClelland calls a 'Socratic voice' that, 'without stating any philosophical conclusions … can cleverly stimulate an audience into achieving their own insights' (2011: 20). McClelland goes on to suggest that film can make a contribution to the philosophy *of* film 'precisely when *the fact that the audience is watching a film* is integral to its achievement' (2011: 27; emphasis in original). Shot in black and white by Gordon Willis in a style that clearly evokes the European art cinema – specifically, by virtue of its surrealistic imagery and plot about a filmmaker struggling to complete his latest movie, Fellini's *8½* (1963) – *Stardust Memories* remains more ambiguous than anything Allen has created before or since, but it is not opaque. Two critical assumptions help to provide a coherent framework for discerning its reflexive themes: first, contrary to the view of prominent American reviewers like Judith Crist (who appears in the film) and Pauline Kael, that Woody Allen should not be identified with Sandy, the character he plays; second, that the events following the maid's serving rabbit for dinner all take place in Sandy's mind, subconscious recollections mixed with anxious projections and imagined movie scenarios.

The opening sequence of Allen's *Stardust Memories* constitutes a draft of the closing scene of Bates's film. Sandy is trapped in a claustrophobic train filled with bleak, anguished passengers, while on a parallel track a train filled with revellers, including a glamorous woman holding a trophy who blows him a kiss through the window, pulls away from the station. Maurice Yacowar identifies Sandy's train, with its close-ups of grim faced sufferers and off-screen sound of an ominously ticking clock, with 'the meditative Bergman' and the party train with 'the frolicsome Fellini' (1991: 226). Sandy is Allen's portrait of the artist, not necessarily a self-portrait but a projection (in both senses of the word) of his own insecurities about the task of filling the blank screen that his character contemplates at the conclusion of *Stardust Memories*. Sandy's movie – not Allen's – ends with the reconciliatory embrace he shares with Isobel (Marie-Christine Barrault) in the train, while Allen's concludes minutes later when his character leaves the empty theatre. There is a further distinction to be made between the *role* Sandy plays in his own film and the fictional auteur who has imagined him there. The character (Sandy) regrets being on the train to hell; the filmmaker (Bates) wants him there – and not in the 'Jazz Heaven' proposed by his producers – wants, in other words, to make serious films that have 'meaning'. Allen, on the other hand, conflicted between being 'the crowd pleaser and the artist fighting for the upper hand' (Shone 2015: 110), attempts to synthesise his comic gift with his aspirational artistry, his stated professional goal since *Love and Death*.

Because *Stardust Memories* constructs such a complex metafictional narrative – remember, the film was produced before the advent of home video recorders and DVD players that allowed for convenient multiple viewings – conclusions about the film's portrait of the artist must remain tenuous, but two 'thoughts' abide, both occurring very late. The first comes in Sandy's dialogue with the Martian (identified in the screenplay as 'Og'), whose authority rests in the fact that he is a 'superintelligent being' with 'an IQ of sixteen hundred'. To his questions about why humans suffer or whether God exists, Og tells Sandy, 'These are the wrong questions.' In addition to seconding the compliment of an enthusiastic festival fan – 'We enjoy your films. Particularly the early funny ones' – the spaceman firmly responds to Sandy's question about whether he should quit making movies and instead try to alleviate the world's problems. 'You're also not Superman, you're a comedian,' Og tells him. 'You want to do mankind a real service? Tell funnier jokes.' The artist's first commitment, Allen expresses here, is to fulfill his or her creative gift, and then to try to transcend that talent, precisely the difficult project he has undertaken in making *Stardust Memories*.

The second idea about the artist emanates from the final image of the blank movie screen that Sandy contemplates before leaving the theatre. It is the artist's summons to work. Bertrand Tavernier used a similar symbol, an artist's easel, to conclude his film about an elderly Impressionist painter in *A Sunday in the Country* (1984). Unlike Sandy Bates, Tavernier's hero, Monsieur Ladmiral (Louis Ducreux), is a minor figure among more celebrated artists, talented but not renowned, and nearing the end of his life. The blank canvas/screen links him to Sandy, however, by challenging the artist to fill the emptiness, to pursue the fugitive masterpiece and thereby, as Herman

Melville described it in his poem, 'To wrestle with the angel – Art'. In his fourth decade since making *Stardust Memories*, Woody Allen has steadfastly followed this vocation.

Once identifying Sandy with the filmmaker, contemporary reviewers frequently excoriated Allen for the vicious portrait of his audience, in effect criticising him for biting the hand that had fed him. As usual, the director denies any such autobiographical interpretation (Schickel 2003: 119; Björkman 2004: 121–2), but the negative, or at least condescending, portrait of audiences persists in numerous later films, most notably *Deconstructing Harry*, *Celebrity* and *Sweet and Lowdown*, tellingly a trio made in the same decade as the Farrow scandal. Rather than personal acts of revenge (in the case of *Stardust Memories* for rejecting *Interiors*), however, Allen's depiction of the audience more generally reflects what another New York Jewish writer of dark humour, Nathanael West, once called the 'natural antipathy felt by the performer for his audience' (1957: 25). For Allen, this antagonism largely reflects the phenomenon of celebrity, the impositions on the artist's personal life that are forced by a demanding clique of admirers. 'The audience worships the celebrity and on the one hand cuts the celebrity much more slack than the celebrity deserves, merits, or earns,' Allen has said; 'On the other hand, the audience loves it when the celebrity is denigrated... They idolize them and they're also dangerous' (Lax 2009: 53). In *Stardust Memories*, released just months before the assassination of John Lennon by a crazed fan, Sandy encounters a succession of 'film culture' groupies at the festival in his honour: flatterers and would-be lovers (one sneaks into his room to offer him 'empty sex' while her husband waits in their van), pedants (one has written 'a definitive cinematic study of Gummo Marx'), philanthropic volunteers (one seeks an old truss for a charity auction), journalists (one is writing a piece on 'The Shallow Indifference of Wealthy Celebrities'), promoters (one pitches a comedy 'based on that whole Guyana mass suicide thing', another 'a spoof on jockeys') and countless autograph seekers (one asks him to write 'To Phyllis Weinstein, you unfaithful, lying bitch'). This last request precedes the hostility that culminates in a fan (like John Hinckley with Lennon) proclaiming Sandy his hero and then, apparently, shooting him.

What else might West's memorable phrase about the antagonism between the artist and the audience tell us about Woody Allen's reflexive films? The author of *Miss Lonelyhearts* and *The Day of the Locust* (the first important American novel about Hollywood, which concludes with a mob riot at a movie premiere) depicted in both novels a shared compulsion – the artist's instinct to perform and to please, the audience's need to be enlightened and entertained – that Allen also dramatises in his works about art. The relationship between artist and audience projected in *Stardust Memories* appears as mutually degrading. In striving to find meaning that can be expressed in a comprehensible as well as pleasing form, Sandy must compromise his vision ('It's the good sentimental', he says to Isobel's critique of his movie's closing kiss) to satisfy his fans, exactly as Allen thought he had in adding the happy ending to *Hannah and Her Sisters*. Inevitably, he fails to resolve the dilemma Alvy had spelled out at the end of *Annie Hall* regarding the simple romantic resolution in his first play: 'You know how you're always trying to get things to come out perfect in art because it's real difficult in life.' The audience, on the other hand, voyeurs to the artist's exhibitions, must remain both deceived and distanced from the illusions they require, needing art's magic, as the illusionist Armstead declares in the closing words of *Shadows and Fog*, 'like they need the air'. West's novels dramatise how their repressed resentment gets expressed by mistaking the artist for the man (*Miss Lonelyhearts*) and violently attacking both the artist (Miss Lonelyhearts is assassinated by a loyal reader) and the art (the movie riot in *The Day of the Locust*). In Allen's films, the relationship never reaches West's apocalyptic intensity – *Deconstructing Harry* is his harshest portrait of the transaction between artist and audience – but the tension between the crowd's demands and the filmmaker's vision certainly creates the dialogic discourse of *Stardust Memories*, whatever more precise interpretation might emerge.

Allen extends his critical examination to the work of art itself, which, if it is serious, risks being solipsistic or simply incomprehensible rather than granting pleasure or distraction for its audience. For the studio executives in the screening room, Sandy's opening rough cut that brings the two trains to a seaside garbage dump represents the same 'self-indulgent' filmmaking that the Columbia film professor ascribed to Fellini in *Annie Hall*. 'He's pretentious. His filming style is too fancy. His insights are shallow and morbid,' one of Sandy's producers complains. 'They try to document their private suffering and fob it off as art.' An equally appalled fan voices a similar complaint from the auditorium after the scene of Sandy's perfect moment of happiness with Dorrie (Charlotte Rampling): 'Why do all comedians turn out to be sentimental bores?' Only the purely funny scenes from his early comedies draw the festival crowd's unabashed applause.

This climactic scene, a paradigm of pure cinematic subjectivity, crystallises the ambiguity of the film as a whole. Sandy imagines receiving a 'posthumous' award at the festival and recalls for the audience how, 'just before I died', he thought of a

Fig. 12: The long take at the climax of *Stardust Memories*: a paradigm of cinematic subjectivity

single memory that gave his life meaning. In a single shot that runs for a full minute, the camera shows Dorrie (Charlotte Rampling) sprawled on his apartment floor reading the Sunday newspaper and then gazing tranquilly at Sandy offscreen while Louis Armstrong's 'Stardust' plays on the soundtrack. Sandy describes how 'that simple little moment of contact moved me in a very, very profound way'. What this moment means for Sandy is clear enough; what it might signify for Woody Allen remains uncertain. On the one hand, the shot embodies the idea of human happiness, not only in its carefully composed synthesis of spectacle and music (recalling Aristotle's *Poetics*) but in its duration, which preserves the sense of perfection that is so fleeting in life. On the other, both the very unnaturalness of the long take, which remains fixed until the end of Armstrong's song about 'love's refrain', and the audience's knowledge of 'a love affair that ended unhappily' with Dorrie suffering a mental breakdown and currently living with her husband in Hawaii, subtly underscore the very *artifice* of the image. The crowd in the Stardust movie theatre responds accordingly. 'Cop out artist!', a man yells out; 'That was so beautiful', responds a woman in the crowd. Confronted with these contradictory responses, Allen's audience must decide for themselves. 'The intellectual strength of *Stardust Memories* lies in this remorseless self-interrogation' (Ames 2013: 224). Are we to view this moment as equivalent to Bergman's golden shot of the three sisters in their white parasols sitting together in the double swing near the end of *Cries and Whispers* (1972), a memory that Agnes (Harriet Andersson), the dying sister, records in her diary: 'This is happiness. I cannot wish for anything better'? Or is it a deliberately overplayed expression of the art work's irrepressible need to please, like the rescue of Vogler's troupe at the end of *The Magician* – or like the *deus ex machina* that brings Linda (Mira Sorvino) a husband at the end of *Mighty Aphrodite* and Boris a wife at the end of *Whatever Works*?

As Peter Bailey demonstrates in his lucid analysis of this difficult film (2001: 85–99), *Stardust Memories* concludes on the same note of ambivalence that complicates the presentation of Sandy's idealised memory of Dorrie. *Sandy's* film ends romantically with his appeal to Isobel on the train that affirms their relationship and promises a happy ending, but *Allen's* audience is immediately disenchanted by the revelation that they have been watching a film within the film and by the actors' jaded comments leaving the theatre, oblivious to the emotional reverberations of the screen fiction. While Dorrie had commented within the film about Sandy's osculatory proficiency – perhaps projecting Sandy's own self-congratulation – Marie-Christine Barault now shares with the other two actresses their mutual disgust at his irritating French kissing. The romance of the art work gives way to the disillusionment of reality. 'Nowhere in Allen's movies is there a more unequivocal dramatization of … the impotence and inefficacy of art' (2001: 95). But this critique applies only to the film within the film – Bates's film – while Allen's *Stardust Memories* (still among his personal favourites) remains equivocal about the possibilities for art to serve a grander purpose than distraction.

Deconstructing Harry

In the calculatingly self-referential *Deconstructing Harry*, Allen reprises many of *Stardust Memory*'s reflexive themes within a similar plot about a 'blocked' writer whose memories, dreams and fictions intrude upon two days in his frenetic life. This time the portrait of the artist, Harry Block (Allen), which almost certainly reflects the negative publicity that continued to haunt the filmmaker after the Farrow scandal, remains remorseless in the face of accusations from Harry's angry ex-wives, his estranged half-sister and his murderous former sister-in-law, who says he 'takes everyone's suffering and turns it into literary gold'. Allen invites his audience to identify him with the role he plays: not content with portraying a writer with three ex-wives (assuming the public counts Mia, or perhaps Diane Keaton, among Woody's former spouses), a lifetime of psychiatry and a string of successful comic works, he piles on details such as preying on young women (including Mariel

Hemingway in a cameo role as a reminder of the post-break-up gossip about their off-screen relationship during the making of *Manhattan*), soliciting prostitutes (an Asian in one of his stories and an African-American for Harry himself, doubling down on Allen's reputation for ignoring or stereotyping cultural diversity), and kidnapping his son (evoking the charges of child abuse from Mia), plus Harry's prescription drug and alcohol habit. By Harry's own self-description, 'I'm the worst person in the world… Maybe Hitler, Goebbels, Göring – but I'm fourth.' While Sandy Bates is merely aesthetically and romantically confused in *Stardust Memories*, Harry remains personally despicable, 'a pill popping alcoholic beaver-banging excuse for a father' in the words of one of his exes. The film's explicit theme, announced in the final moments of *Deconstructing Harry* and also central to *Sweet and Lowdown*, reveals 'a guy who can't function well in life but can only function in art'. The final image picks up where *Stardust Memories* left off: Harry inserts the blank paper into his typewriter and begins composing notes for a new novel. In this way, his writing 'had saved his life', as it had at the beginning of *Deconstructing Harry*, when he had distracted his violent sister-in-law from actually shooting him by reading her one of his amusing short stories. In *Stardust Memories*, Sandy had imagined how art had failed to save him from a crazed shooter – in his fantasy of his own death Sandy says he would trade his Academy Award 'for one more second of life' – but in this film Harry ultimately concludes that art has saved him 'in more ways than one'.

As *Stardust Memories* had resembled Fellini's *8½*, *Deconstructing Harry* borrows from the plot of Bergman's *Wild Strawberries*: a celebrated but narcissistic man (Isak Borg, his initials linking him to the film's creator) travels back to his university (from which Harry, like Allen, had been expelled) for a ceremony in his honour. In what might be a coincidence, even the car they use to make the trip is a Volvo. During the journey, each man confronts the coldness and shallowness of his life, an alienation from humanity made all the worse by the esteem with which he is held by strangers who do not truly know him. Both Borg and Block ultimately confront the demons of their past and reach a form of reconciliation, although Bergman's protagonist enjoys a more serene and satisfying acceptance, comforted by the presence of his estranged son and daughter-in-law and the memory of his parents beckoning to him, while Harry can only dream of being applauded by his own fictional characters, exonerating him in the name of art.

In a long sequence shot punctuated by jump cuts early in the film (Allen employs jump cuts in several diegetic scenes but shoots the fictional sections in unbroken takes), Harry whines to his psychiatrist about his sexual obsessions and his current writer's block, about how 'nothing's changed' in his neurotic life. His therapist says he reminds him of the story he had written a couple of months earlier about the actor, Mel, who suddenly appeared out of focus while shooting a movie. The scene cuts to Mel (Robin Williams) discovering he has gone 'soft' and being sent home to rest and 'sharpen up', but as Harry now takes over the narration, Mel's condition grows worse, causing his wife to become nauseous at the sight of him. The next day they visit the doctor, who finds nothing wrong with him except his fuzzy appearance and prescribes glasses for his family. The psychiatrist notes how Mel's children are forced to wear the heavy black rims that Harry (and Woody Allen, of course) wears. 'You expect the world to adjust to the distortion you've become', the therapist explains. Harry resists this interpretation of his own perversity projected on his fictional alter ego, but the image of Mel's softness remains Allen's original and funny metaphor for a kind of existential shallowness, an incomplete humanity. At Adair University, just before the honouring ceremony, Harry himself goes out of focus in a panic attack about his own moral unworthiness. 'You're too easy on me', he had earlier told his infatuated young lover Faye (Elisabeth Shue), describing himself as Isaac had once portrayed Yale in *Manhattan*, but even this self-deprecation seems superficial since Harry refers merely to the draft of a story she has just commended and eventually will try to ease his depression by proposing to make her his fourth wife. Faye plays Galatea to his Pygmalion in *Deconstructing Harry*'s variation on one of the director's most characteristic (and by now deliberately maddening) motifs. Allen cuts from the philandering character (played by Richard Benjamin) in the opening fiction-within-the-film to Harry's first meeting Faye in a hotel elevator on his way to having an affair with Lucy, the homicidal sister-in-law who confronts him in the opening scene. Although he has warned her not to fall in love with him and subsequently introduces him to his writer friend Larry (Billy Crystal), whom she now plans to marry, Harry meets Faye again the day before the ceremony and tries to win her back.

From his 'distorted' perception of moral responsibility, Harry remains adamantly unrepentant in the face of accusations from former close relations (all women, it must be said) whose lives he has appropriated for his fiction. 'You're so self-engrossed you don't give a shit who you destroy', Lucy (Judy Davis) tells him before pulling out a gun, an indictment he inadvertently confirms when he calls her 'Leslie', her fictional avatar's name (played by Julia Louis-Dreyfuss), rather than 'Lucy'. Later on, he will refute his half-sister's claim that he is a self-hating Jew who has mocked her religious devotion in stories like 'Max Pincus's Dark Secret', an absurd tale about an *alter kocker* first seen at a *Star Wars*-themed barmitzvah who turns out to be an axe murderer, a confessed killer not only of his first wife and her children ('plus a neighbour'), but a cannibal as well. Harry's story, depicted in an extended cutaway, presents yet another version of Allen's 'The Shallowest Man' centering on the caricature of a self-complacent man without conscience. Confronted at the dinner table by his 'nudging' second wife of thirty years, Max readily acknowledges his past crimes: 'So what are you making a fuss? Some bury, some burn, I *ate*!' Although the story's autobiographical relevance remains subordinate to the farce, subtle details suggest how it is another projection of its author's distorted perceptions. Harry has previously mentioned how his mother died in childbirth and his father never forgave him, creating a lifelong estrangement. Within the story, which might be re-titled 'Harry Block's Revenge', Mrs. Pincus has a grown daughter and a son who is a writer; Max's cannibalism, a deconstructionalist might suggest, represents a displacement of the author's creative method of turning his own relationships into literature, an interpretation the writer himself would resist. 'I may hate myself', Harry protests in response to his sister's criticism, 'but it's not because I'm Jewish.'

In the manner of *Stardust Memories*, *Deconstructing Harry* proceeds by alternating the protagonist's present, the two days surrounding his journey to Adair (paralleling the weekend of the Sandy Bates Film Festival), with scenes from several of his stories and occasional projections from his unconscious, as when he converses directly with his characters. Allen provides no clear transitions among these episodes – the film begins inside one of these fictions that the audience takes to be real, so that when Harry transposes Lucy's name to 'Leslie', he is in effect inverting the spectator's temporary mistake of confusing a character with somebody real. Both his former sister-in-law and his psychiatrist concur on Harry's diagnosis: the artist as narcissist, an assessment Harry himself would not deny. He tells Cookie (Hazelle Goodman), the prostitute he pays to keep him company on the trip, that he is 'spiritually bankrupt' and lacking a soul. His egotism humorously shows up when he is accosted on the street by a former acquaintance named Richard (Bob Balaban), who has been suffering chest pains and is headed to the doctor for tests. Harry dismisses his symptoms but reluctantly accompanies the frightened man to the doctor's office, where he spends time in the waiting room ignoring Richard's medical complaints ('It's nothing,' he reassures Richard, 'I'm not afraid') and talking about his own deceased parents and his current unprecedented writer's block. When Richard, a thoroughly affable fellow, receives a clean bill of health, Harry invites him along on the drive the next day and then acts out his own offhanded remark as they set off from the city by snatching his son outside his school so that he can witness his father being honoured. Unfortunately, Richard silently dies from a coronary a few miles before they reach Adair, a tragedy that briefly moves Harry to grief but quickly transforms into embarrassment as his adoring admirers, like the worshipers at Sandy's festival, greet his arrival. 'My old school wants to honour me, I show up with a hooker and a dead body.' Like Sandy, he soon finds himself in jail after the police arrest him on campus for kidnapping, unlawful possession of a firearm (the gun he had taken from Lucy) and illegal drugs (the marijuana Cookie brought with her).

By this point, leading to three scenes that comprise the film's conclusion, Harry has fairly clinched his position as the world's 'fourth worst' human being. Sitting alone in his cell, he is consoled by the ghost of Richard – ghosts having served since the time of *Macbeth* and *Hamlet* as common metaphors for regret by embodying the presentness of past misdeeds or unfulfilled duties – with compliments about his art. 'You bring pleasure to a lot of people. That's good.' Here is another way in which Harry, having just envisioned an elaborate fantasy from his work-in-progress of himself condemned to Hell, is 'saved' by his art. Faye and Larry suddenly appear, fresh from their wedding the same day, to bail him out, but Harry responds with outrage rather than gratitude, considering only his own disappointment. 'In the end you chose him over me?' he asks Faye in disbelief while stubbornly withholding his blessing on their marriage. Larry argues back, conceding Harry's superiority as a writer but claiming he will be a better husband for Fay: 'You put your art into your work. I put it into my life. I can make her happy.' Harry never concedes the point, never grants the couple his blessing; instead, he simply surrenders to *his* fate to accept the reality: 'I give up! I give up!'

The second scene returns a rueful Harry to his apartment. The camera pans right, as it had to find Larry and Fay outside his jail cell moments earlier, to the honours committee from Adair inviting him back to the interrupted ceremony. Harry's reverie continues as an assembly of his fictional characters applaud his entrance, accompanied by the black-helmeted orchestra from the *Star Wars*-themed barmitzvah: the camera pans across a room filled with the figures depicted in the numerous cutaways earlier in the film, each of them – fuzzy Mel, carnivorous Max Pincus – playing out their fixed roles. Harry's angst turns to pleasure as he basks in the standing ovation, his creations applauding his *work* rather than his life. Gratified and inspired, Harry offers thanks (to his imagination, in effect), confident in his new story idea – 'a guy who can't function well in life but can only function in art' – and armed with a fresh self-defence as he begins typing: 'All people know the same truth. Our lives consist in how we choose to distort it.' Like all aphorisms, this philosophical explanation of a universal experience may be read as shallow or profound. In *Anything Else*, for example, the cranky and paranoid comedy writer David Dobel (Allen) believes that 'work gives the illusion of meaning'. At the end of *Deconstructing Harry*, it appears that only illusions give meaning to work.

Bullets Over Broadway

Like Harry, 'saved' from the chaos of his personal life by his art, Woody Allen sought refuge from the brutal custody battle with Mia Farrow by writing *Bullets Over Broadway*, according to his collaborator and friend, Douglas McGrath (2006). Compared with *Stardust Memories* or *Deconstructing Harry*, this film offers a lighter treatment of the artist's narcissism, allowing for a more pleasant cinematic experience while paradoxically choosing life over art as its ultimate theme. 'If not his best movie,' in Tom Shone's opinion, 'it has a good claim on being his most richly and repeatedly enjoyable' (2015: 192), which may help to explain why Allen successfully adapted the screenplay into a Tony-nominated Broadway musical in 2014. The narrative follows the evolution of a pretentious melodrama by the earnest but insufficiently talented young playwright David Shayne (John Cusack) from his original didactic script through casting and rehearsals, during which the play is substantially revised, to Boston try-out and Broadway hit. In addition to providing laughs from the antics of the play's four principal actors, *Bullets Over Broadway* raises serious questions about the nature of creativity and the artist's moral responsibility as embodied by three putative artists: David, the author of 'God of Our Fathers', the pretentious (and irrelevant) title of his domestic drama; Sheldon Flender (Rob Reiner), his mentor and the alleged 'genius' who has written twenty unproduced plays; and Cheech (Chazz Palminteri) – 'just "Cheech"', he replies when asked for his full name – a mob hitman who becomes the unrevealed author behind David's initially tepid script.

'I am an artist', David tells Julian (Jack Warden), his theatrical agent, in the opening line of this, 'the most formally perfect of all [Allen's] films' (Schickel 2003: 15), 'and I won't change a word of my play to pander to a commercial Broadway audience' (ibid.). Julian commends the 'ideas' but complains that the play is too 'heavy'. David argues for art over entertainment: 'Not everybody writes to distract. It's the theatre's duty not just to entertain but to transform men's souls.' He further insists on directing the play himself after having two 'powerful' scripts 'mangled' by actors changing his dialogue and directors misinterpreting everything – complaints that echo Woody Allen's experience writing *What's New Pussycat?* and *Casino Royale*. Having unequivocally asserted his artistic integrity, David will undergo a succession of compromises and concessions – aesthetic and moral – in order to realise his ambition of seeing his work on stage. In his last speech at the end of the film, however, he will not only renounce his claim to be an artist but return to his Pennsylvania home to start a new life. For now, Julian concludes the conversation by reminding the 'kid' playwright – in words that repeat Monk's warning to another naïf, his wife Cecilia, in *The Purple Rose of Cairo*, 'That's a real world out there, and it's a lot tougher than you think.' David's initiation into that corrupt reality thus follows the genre of a *künstlerroman*, the story of an artist's journey from innocence to experience.

The dialogue about art continues in the next scene, which takes place at a Greenwich Village sidewalk café. Allen had employed a similar expository setting at the outset of *Manhattan* and *Broadway Danny Rose* and would later in *Melinda and Melinda* and *Whatever Works*: a gathering of friends discuss their ideas about themes that inform the subsequent narrative. Gathered around David are several bohemian artists, his longtime girlfriend from Pittsburgh, Ellen (Mary-Louise Parker), and their aesthete guru, Flender, whom David certifies as a genius because 'both common people and intellectuals find your work completely incomprehensible'. Flender proposes a thought experiment to illustrate his theory about the preeminence of great art. In *Manhattan*, Isaac had asked his friends at Elaine's whether they would have the courage to jump off a bridge into the icy water to save a drowning stranger. Here, Flender hypothesises a burning building from which you could save only one thing, the last known copy of Shakespeare's works or 'an anonymous human being'. David agrees with Flender, who chooses the Bard and shouts above the objections of the women in the crowd, 'It's not an inanimate object. It's art! Art is life! It lives!' The remainder of *Bullets Over Broadway* will test this conclusion, although Woody Allen's scepticism about the efficacy of art either to 'transform men's souls' or immortalise the artist should already be clear. His often repeated response to Flender's philosophical dilemma definitely sides with pragmatism over aesthetics: 'It doesn't profit Shakespeare one iota that his plays have lived on after him. He would have been better off if he were alive and the plays were forgotten' (Björkman 2004: 103).

Julian finds a financial backer for the play, a mobster named Nick Valenti (Joe Viterelli), but only at the cost of casting his moll, a semi-literate logorrheic named Olive (Jennifer Tilly), in the ludicrously inappropriate role of a psychiatrist. Along with the hopelessly incompetent 'actress' (like 'singer' Susan Alexander in *Citizen Kane*, her vocation demands quotation marks) comes Cheech, who serves as her bodyguard for the jealous Nick. After meeting his new collaborators, David wakes up from a nightmare and rebukes himself for the 'compromises' he has made to produce his play ('I'm a whore!' he shouts out his tenement window), but his concession to hire an amateur like Olive seems balanced by the news that fading Broadway diva Helen Sinclair (Dianne Wiest) has agreed to play the leading role of Sylvia Posten in hopes of reviving her career. He quickly becomes infatuated with Helen's star persona, and she is quick to seduce him both professionally and amorously, transforming his hyperbolic admission of prostituting himself for his art into literal truth. As the actors gather for first rehearsals (Cheech occupying a back seat in the Belasco Theater), David begins to narrate events in voice-over, having 'decided to keep a journal' so that 'perhaps my experience will be of value to others, just as I pore over with relish the notes of my idols, Chekhov and Strindberg'. The young playwright's ego trip continues when he shares a martini with Miss Sinclair (she orders two for herself, then adds a third for him when she realises he thought he had been included) and later visits her penthouse, where they toast his play – '*our* play', David corrects her. On the balcony overlooking Broadway, she flatters him further by inviting him to write a new 'vehicle' for her, then slyly suggests he revise a scene in Act Two to enhance her character's sexuality.

David's ego takes a hit, however, when Olive refuses to speak some unpronounceable dialogue in rehearsal ('The heart is "labyrinthinine"', she intones from the script, 'a maze beset with brutal pitfalls and mean obstacles'). Cheech emerges from the darkness to critique what the playwright has just defended as 'a stylish way of relating a particular idea'. He argues that 'nobody talks like that'. He has memorised the dialogue while practicing with Olive, and 'it stinks on fuckin' hot ice!' In another false display of artistic integrity, David quits on the spot but is quickly mollified by Helen, to whom he confesses his love ('Be silent', she tells him, a prelude to her catchphrase throughout the rest of the film – 'Don't speak!'). Cheech offers a plot revision at the next rehearsal ('That's the way it would happen in real life', he claims), and to everyone's astonishment (including Ellen, who is visiting the set) his suggestion meets with universal approval – excepting David, of course, who again quits. At the midpoint of his film, Allen has established his comic premise – the unschooled hoodlum is a proletarian genius while the educated playwright is an egotistical poseur – and, as he would in *Deconstructing Harry*, questioned their relative commitments to art and to life.

Fig. 13: The extended two-shot in Cheech's 'office'

In three crucial scenes after he has apologised to 'the big Gorgonzola' for letting 'my ego get in the way of the work' and the cast has enthusiastically endorsed the rewrite he appropriated from Cheech, David seeks out his unrecognised collaborator in his 'office', a poolroom in the seedy part of the city. In the first of these, Cheech rewrites the dialogue for the third act in naturalistic language rather than David's 'poetic license', and reassures him that their secret partnership is safe ('Where I come from, nobody squeals'). The second scene, a single two-shot that consumes three and a half minutes, brings Cheech and David together at the poolroom bar, where they work side by side on the script. The camera zooms in to a tighter composition as David proposes a break; for the first time, their conversation becomes personal. After enquiring about his family and his 'line of work', David asks if Cheech had ever considered writing as a career: 'You have a huge gift.' When Cheech backs off a bit from his prior harsh criticism, David demurs: 'Well, sure, for you it's simple, you know. For someone who can draw, it all seems logical, but for someone who can't…' David recalls loving the accordion when he was young and practicing continually in order to become 'fluent' on the instrument. But there was another boy he knew growing up who also played accordion, and 'he would squeeze one single note and the sound of it would make you cry'. This is Woody Allen talking about the distinction between talent and genius – or perhaps simply talent versus appreciation. As he once told Richard Schickel, 'I can't draw, so I'm astonished at a kid who will draw a rabbit or something, I'm amazed by it. For him it's nothing, and he wonders why I can't do it… Well, I could write jokes, so there was nothing to it' (2003: 90). Or here he is, describing to John Lahr his limited proficiency on the clarinet: 'To maintain the low level that I play at, you have to practice every day' (2006: 154). Everyone dreams of being an artist. Cheech says he once wanted to be a dancer, and so the dialogue about art ends here with one of Woody Allen's most poignant and perfectly pitched lines: Cheech asks, 'You ever see George Raft dance?'

THE REFLEXIVE FILMS

The plot turns after the successful preview in Boston, despite Olive's inept performance. Cheech can no longer tolerate how she is ruining what he now calls '*my* show'. Despite 'decent' reviews from the out-of-town critics, he accosts David on the street ('Decent ain't good enough!') and demands a replacement. Content with directing a hit, David tries to mollify him, noting how 'this is something that just bothers you' and reminding Cheech of the 'concessions' they both have had to make to Valenti. When Olive misses a matinee, her understudy earns a standing ovation, the play comes alive, and Olive's fate is sealed. Back in New York, Cheech drives her to his favourite rub-out spot on the pier (accompanied by 'Up a Lazy River' on the soundtrack, the musical cue for his professional specialty) and, just before he pulls the trigger, tells her, 'Olive, I think you should know this. You're a horrible actress.' Earlier in the poolroom talking with David about killing people, he had explained his ethical standards: 'I never rubbed out a guy who didn't deserve it.' True to his own sense of morality, he walks away from his latest hit without a trace of regret, muttering, 'Thank God, I don't have to hear that voice anymore.'

The news of Olive's demise brings an outraged David back to the poolroom to confront her killer. This third set piece extends for a full two minutes in a single shot, the camera tracking the two men across the empty space. Cheech remains unmoved by moral arguments: 'Nobody's gonna ruin my play... You think it's right, some tootsie walks in and messes up a beautiful thing like this?' The dialogue on ethics continues:

> *David*: I wanted a great play as much as you did.
> *Cheech*: No, not as much.
> *David*: But you don't *kill* for it!
> *Cheech*: Yeah, who says? My father used to listen to the opera. He loved opera, but if a guy stunk...
> *David*: What, he *killed* him?
> *Cheech*: One time in Palermo...
> *David*: I'm an artist, too, I'm not a great artist like you, but you know what? First, I'm a human being. I'm a decent, moral human being.
> *Cheech*: Then what are you doin' with Helen Sinclair?

As much as any moment in Allen's cinema, this scene accomplishes his aesthetic goal of combining humour ('One time in Palermo...') with a serious point. As Peter Bailey explains, 'Cheech and Shayne basically exchange places, the mob hitman transforming himself into the temperamental artist, the committed playwright arguing for the superiority of life to art' (2001: 166). Cheech has acted out Flender's hypothetical position regarding the eternal value of art, dispatching an 'anonymous person' ('She was a tramp', he tells David) to save his masterpiece. Unhappily reminded of the moral hypocrisy in his own life, David still must decide between prostituting himself to Helen's vanity for the sake of his career or affirming his relationship with Ellen. For now, Cheech ends the philosophical debate by knocking him to the floor and again warning, 'Nobody's gonna ruin my work!'

As Harry will be 'saved' by his work, Cheech dies for it. At the Broadway opening, Valenti's thugs chase him backstage, shooting him in the midst of the third act. With his dying breath, he offers David a revision of the last line of the play – have Sylvia Posten say she is pregnant: 'It'll be a great finish.' As David gasps out his astonished approval of this final bit of dramatic brilliance, Cheech silences him with one of Woody Allen's great exit lines: 'Don't speak!' 'God of Our Fathers' opens to rave reviews, one theatrical critic singling out the uncanny sound effects at the end, the gunshots suggesting a psychological flashback to the male protagonist's military experience. David is proclaimed 'the find of the decade'.

But David goes missing from his moment of glory at the after-party. Earlier he had consulted Flender in an effort to clear his conscience about betraying Ellen for the alluring Helen ('a real artist – we speak the same language'), withholding the fact that Cheech has been secretly doctoring his play. Flender, withholding the fact that *he* has been having an affair with Ellen, responds by claiming, 'Guilt is *petit bourgeois* crap. An artist creates his own moral universe.' His incomprehensible advice regarding Ellen ironically confirms David's previous opinion of the proof of his genius: 'You gotta do what you gotta do.' In the wake of his own moral scandal, Allen himself repeatedly affirmed the opposite notion. 'Artists are just like everybody else when it comes to moral questions and questions of human behavior' (Lahr 2006: 163). In the film's dénouement, after David has confessed his infidelity to Ellen, who matter-of-factly owns up to her affair with Flender, he returns to the Village to win her back by acknowledging two crucial facts: 'One is that I love you. Two is that I'm not an artist.' Rather than feeling regret at the collapse of his lifelong ambition – or remorse for Olive's death – David says he feels 'free'. As the camera circles them in the romantically-lit street, Ellen accepts his proposal and he leads her away to married life in Pittsburgh, liberated from shame or guilt.

Chapter Six
Nostalgia

'The film I end up with bears little relation to the brilliant idea I had in the bedroom. The film may be a success with the public, but I feel that if only they knew what I had conceived in the bedroom they could really see something great. If only I could've given them *that*.'

– Woody Allen (qtd. in Shone 2015: 132)

In describing his experience of the creative process and the irretrievable loss of his original 'brilliant idea', Woody Allen inadvertently expresses the nostalgia that informs much of his work. The term 'nostalgia' is a 'nostalgically Greek' neologism (Boym 2001: 3) coined by the Swiss doctor Johannes Hofer in 1688 from *nostos* (to return home) and *algia* (pain) to delineate the melancholy yearning suffered by displaced mercenaries fighting in Europe. By the end of the nineteenth century, its meaning had shifted from a curable pathology to a chronic condition of wistful longing for an irrecoverable past. Like regret, nostalgia has both a cognitive and emotional aspect, synthesising passive feelings of loss or displacement with an active reconstruction of an experienced or imagined earlier time. Unlike regret, however, nostalgia 'more often concerns the loss of desirable entities or states, while regret as often concerns the gaining of undesirable entities or states'; it also lacks 'the connotation of having made a mistake' that regret or remorse implies (Landman 1993: 48). Compared with simple memory, nostalgia persists in judging the past as superior – more meaningful, more beautiful, more desirable – in contrast to the depleted, discomfiting present; in this sense, being nostalgic represents 'a longing for utopia, projected backwards in time' (Wilson 2005: 37). More blatantly than the testimony of memory or the re-telling of history (both of which are, to lesser or greater degree, constructions of the past), nostalgia involves the largely unreflective belief in the superiority of things *then* as compared with *now*, what Scott Alexander Howard calls the 'poverty of the present requirement' (2012). Extending this idea to its thematic consequences, Svetlana Boym suggests how 'nostalgia is rebellion against the modern idea of time, the time of history and progress. The nostalgic desires to obliterate history and turn it into private or collective mythology' (2001: xv). Allen's recollection of his own 'brilliant idea' for a movie encapsulates many of these fundamental elements. He relates a narrative of longing to return home – to his own bedroom – to recover what has been permanently lost, the original conception of a masterpiece. His tone is neither regretful nor resentful, but bittersweet, rueful. In this Platonic vision of art, the memory of the ideal remains *sweet*; the reality of its projection on the screen *lowdown*.

Nostalgia in Woody Allen's cinema of regret differs from both *agent* regret – Diane's facile confessing to mistakes (*September*) or Ray's (Woody Allen) more generous admission that 'everybody makes mistakes now and then' when reconciling with his repentant wife Frenchy (Tracey Ullman) in *Small Time Crooks* (2000), Zelig's apologising for his polygamies, Alvy, Ike, Emmet, John (Ed Begley Jr.) (*Whatever Works*), and Alfie chasing after the women they left behind – and *character* regret – Joey lamenting her lack of artistic talent (*Interiors*), Terry contemplating his terrible crime – insofar as nostalgia eliminates any sense of personal responsibility for the inevitable changes that follow the passage of time. Paradoxically, the nostalgic feeling involves equally the despair of knowing that nothing lasts forever, which, in Allen's philosophy, threatens to render life meaningless, and the antidote to that same melancholy awareness. The regret of knowing that the past is irretrievable becomes a seductive 'nice sort of sadness' (Davis 1979: 14). Thus, Alvy Singer overcomes his mid-life crisis by narrating his fond memory of Annie Hall, and Mickey Sachs recovers from the brink of suicide by watching an old movie, the Marx brothers' *Duck Soup* in *Crimes and Misdemeanors*. Nostalgia offers neither Woody Allen character a rational solution to their present existential crisis – Alvy remains forty and alone (despite the glimpsed compensatory presence of Sigourney Weaver as his movie date for *The Sorrow and the Pity*), and Mickey undergoes no religious epiphany in the movie theatre – but the memory of a happier, simpler time allows them both to feel better about themselves, alleviating their despair. As the postmodernist scholar

Linda Hutcheon suggests, 'Nostalgic distancing sanitizes as it selects, making the past feel complete, stable, coherent, safe ... in other words, making it so very unlike the present' (2000: 195).

One of the saddest moments in all of Allen's cinema, doubtlessly intensified by the audience's knowledge of the actors' personal break-up at the time, occurs near the end of *Husbands and Wives* when Gabe and Judy confront the dissolution of their marriage. As they return to their dimly-lit apartment after sharing drinks with their recently reunited married friends, they begin quarrelling (separated from each other by the editing) over their frayed relationship. Before long, the argument comes down to their different attitudes towards change. Gabe complains that Judy 'mispresented' herself when she had claimed not to want another child when they were first married.

> *Judy*: People change. I'm not the same person I was all those years ago.
> *Gabe*: Well, that's why relationships go sour.
> *Judy*: Yeah, you hate change.
> *Gabe*: Sure, I hate ... Change equals death.
> *Judy*: What kind of bullshit... That's just a bullshit line! Maybe you fool your twenty-year-old students into thinking that's some kind of insight or something, but it means nothing. Change is what life is made of. If you don't change, you don't grow. You just shrivel up.

As the tension slowly dissipates later in the evening, Gabe tries to restore his sense of equilibrium by resorting to nostalgic reminiscence, reminding Judy (now sitting next to him in a tight two-shot) of the night they had stayed up together to watch *Wild Strawberries* on cable ('a great moment for me', Gabe says, echoing Sandy's nostalgic recollection of Dorrie in *Stardust Memories*) or when they skipped the faculty dinner to walk through snowy Central Park. 'You were so beautiful in that black dress...' But Judy stops him short, 'because it's over, and we both know it'. Anxious and disoriented by 'all kinds of problems' in their marriage that have threatened his sense of stability, Gabe has resorted to nostalgic memory, what Walter Benjamin called 'pearls of crystallized experience' (qtd. in Boym 2001: 28) – like the icy walk on Fifth Avenue he remembers – to dispel his present uncertainty. Judy (who has just revealed that she has returned to therapy) sees through his psychic defence, unveiling nostalgia's selective reconstruction. 'Those memories,' she quietly tells him, 'they're just memories. They're from years gone by, they're just isolated memories. They don't tell the whole story.' As the spell is broken, Allen abruptly cuts to the exterior of their

Fig. 14: Judy dispels Gabe's nostalgic memories: 'it's over, and we both know it'

building, and the narrator announces how 'several days later, Gabe moved out of their apartment and into a hotel'. Reminded of this scene by Stig Björkman, Allen readily agrees with Gabe's view of change, although not nostalgically. He acknowledges the short-term benefits for a person in misery or poverty (or for a character like Alice, for example), but 'I'm against change. Because change equals ageing, change equals the progression of time, the destruction of the old order… Change is a fair weather friend' (2004: 230). By this harsh measure, even Marion's effort to heed Rilke's admonition and change her life at the end of *Another Woman* seems futile.

Nostalgia functions in several ways throughout Allen's cinema, informing both content and style as early as his two 1970s masterpieces, *Annie Hall* and *Manhattan*. The narration that frames *Annie Hall* speaks not only to Alvy's desire to recover the lost presence of his romantic ideal but, through its three philosophical jokes, to recapture the vanishing tradition of Catskill-style comedy that the director will nostalgically re-enact in *Broadway Danny Rose*. The famous punch line 'but we need the eggs' points to the paucity of nourishment in the present that the recalled relationship with Annie alone can appease. The montage of memories that inspires Alvy's closing tribute, accompanied on the soundtrack by the reprise of Annie singing 'Seems Like Old Times', is almost entirely positive (excepting one shot of the couple dividing their belongings), concluding with the romantic evening kiss with the Brooklyn Bridge in the background that anticipates the iconic long shot of the same actors in silhouette before a different New York bridge in *Manhattan*. In both psychological and cinematic senses, the ending of *Annie Hall* represents what

Svetlana Boym calls *restorative nostalgia* (2001: 41–9) by reconstructing the recalled scenes of the relationship as 'the whole story' – a mythic truth for Alvy as well as the film audience raised in the tradition of romantic comedy – rather than as 'isolated moments', the very editing of the recapitulated relationship providing its coherency. Test your own memory of *Annie Hall*: do you recall it as an analysis of a break-up or as a love story?

Similarly in *Manhattan*, Ike's narration begins with the nostalgic invocation of a city now (in 1979) very much different than the one he projects: 'Chapter One: He adored New York City. He idolised it out of all proportion… [T]his was still a town that existed in black and white and pulsated to the great tunes of George Gershwin.' Gordon Willis's luminous montage of urban images (including a brief shot of garbage piled in the street, a reminder like Annie's packing her things of the negative elements that have been all but entirely filtered out of the narrator's consciousness) simultaneously illustrates Isaac's romantic sensibility and – through the music of 'Rhapsody and Blue' as well as the anachronistic black and white cinematography – invites the audience to indulge their collective memory of an earlier era of Hollywood moviemaking so different, for example, from Martin Scorsese's contemporary version of the city in *Taxi Driver* (1976). Even Allen's narrator immediately realises that this first draft is 'too romantic' and proceeds to a more critical assessment of New York as 'a metaphor for the decay of contemporary culture'. The revised version, although dismissed as 'too preachy' and then 'too angry', represents what Boym calls *reflective nostalgia*, which casts doubt on the truth of the remembered past while sustaining the longing and resisting the passage of time (2001: 49–55). The introductory recitation ends with Isaac's shift from focusing on the collective memory of the city to his own personal involvement: 'New York was his town. And it always would be.'

The film's climax reminds the audience that Isaac is a writer and that the film they are watching (as with Marion in *Another Woman* and Sandy in *Stardust Memories*) represents the completed product of his work. As Isaac, now separated from both Mary and Tracy, contemplates an idea for a short story alone in his apartment, he conjures up a list of things that make life worth living – Willie Mays, Louis Armstrong, Groucho Marx – all nostalgic artifacts shared with his generation – until he comes to the more individualised recollection of 'the crabs at Sam Wo's' and, of course, *Tracy's face*. Rather than wallowing in the past or living with the regret of having spurned her, Isaac turns his restorative invocation of cultural tradition (Flaubert, Cézanne, the Jupiter Symphony) towards reflective nostalgia ('I think I blew that one', he has just told Yale's wife. 'She was so sweet'), creating a recalled portrait in which he has found meaning as well as a sense of his own identity. By recognising the limitations – perhaps the shallowness – of nostalgia as an inhibitor of personal growth, Isaac leaves the sanctuary of home and takes to the streets, much as another writer, Gil Pender, proceeds at the end of *Midnight in Paris*, in search of at least the potential for a new life.

As 'Rhapsody in Blue' rises to a crescendo over the concluding montage of the Manhattan skyline and the somehow familiar white credits on a black background begin to appear, the audience seems invited to suspend their anticipation of the final turn of the plot (will she stay or will she go?) in favour of recalling Isaac's celebration of the city's transcendent glory: 'This is really a great city. I don't care what anybody says', he says to Mary as the sun rises on the 59th Street Bridge. 'It's just really a knockout.' That enthusiastic opposition to the general opinion of the era reaffirms his initial romanticised perception of New York's enduring value in the face of the more realistic assessments of its current bankruptcy. Those film credits, particularly if the audience is (nostalgically) watching *Manhattan* in the twenty-first century after viewing many other Allen films, have become part of a nostalgia *for his cinema*, just as the fans at the Sandy Bates Film Festival yearn for their favourite's 'early funny ones'. Allen first used the Windsor typeface to introduce *Annie Hall*, recycling the font in the closing credits for *Manhattan* and in every film since. The white on black credits harken to a hallowed movie past in several ways. They recall the intertitles of the silent cinema as well as the unadorned credits of the Hollywood studio era. They also pay homage to the opening credits of Ingmar Bergman's classic films for Svensk Filmindustri, although Allen himself has denied making the connection (Björkman 2004: 76). And, 'as time goes by', they serve Woody Allen as a form of self-branding, an auteur's signature immediately inspiring, like a Proustian madeleine, remembrance of his entire oeuvre.

Music functions similarly as a continuing reminder of both Allen's artistic control over each film and his conservative taste, as amusingly exemplified in *Hannah and Her Sisters* when Mickey's first date with Holly pits her stoned delight while listening to punk rock against his reverence for Bobby Short. After a brief transitional period (*Annie Hall* and *Interiors*) without scoring or a soundtrack over the credits, Allen has consistently punctuated his films with 'my kind of music', which, he freely admits, means nothing after about 1950 (Björkman 2004: 101; Lax 2009: 317): traditional jazz, the American Song Book, classical music and opera. Whether symphonic pieces (Prokofiev for *Love and Death*, Mendelssohn for *A Midsummer Night's Sex*

Comedy) or familiar voices singing popular tunes (Fred Astaire in *The Purple Rose of Cairo*, Al Jolson in *Bullets Over Broadway*), the music over the title credits serves as a mnemonic device immediately conjuring up the lost era of his period films. Even for a contemporary story like *Match Point*, Allen chooses the scratchy recording of Enrico Caruso singing 'Una furtiva lagrima' from Donizetti's *Lucia di Lammermoor* rather than the exemplary modern version by Luciano Pavarotti to suggest the mythic dimension of his theme.

Music also occasionally serves within the movies themselves as a source of nostalgia that alleviates tension or mitigates sadness. In *Hannah and Her Sisters*, for example, the recriminations and regret that threaten the marriage of Hannah's parents when Norma gets drunk at lunch and 'becomes Joan Collins' dissipate when Evan sits at the piano and serenades his boozy wife, a moment that recalls the film's opening Thanksgiving scene when the couple happily sang a duet of 'Bewitched, Bothered, and Bewildered'. On traditional holidays that mark the milestones or when advancing age causes panic ('He's gotten sourer as he's gotten older, and I try to stay young ... at heart', Norma tells her daughter), nostalgia can 'assuage the uncertainties and identity threats engendered by problematic life transitions' (Davis 1979: 69). In a similar manner, the final image of *Crimes and Misdemeanors*, which depicts blind Rabbi Ben dancing with his daughter at her wedding as the band plays 'I'll Be Seeing You', offers ironic commentary but, more significantly, nostalgically counteracts the audience's memory of the film's miscarriage of justice by reinforcing Professor Levy's hopeful message heard over the music.

In addition to the repetitive Windsor font in the title credits and the music of an earlier era, Allen's preference for long master shots and (with a few exceptions like the earliest comedies and *Husbands and Wives*) minimal cutting within scenes also has the subliminal effect of encouraging nostalgia simply by resisting the steadily increasing editing pace of contemporary cinema that 'puts an invisible taboo on any form of reflective longing' (Boym 2001: 38). In a sense, Allen has never swayed from *Manhattan*'s way of perceiving present reality through the distorting lens of the films of his own childhood. In several works after *Play It Again, Sam*, he plays characters beguiled by watching movies – always *older* movies – that provide escape and comfort from the anxieties produced in the present, most clearly when Mickey (improbably) finds refuge in a matinée of *Duck Soup*. Moreover, movie references abound with his avatars (Alvy being assailed by 'the cast of *The Godfather*'; Larry in *Manhattan Murder Mystery* warning his suspicious wife about 'too much *Double Indemnity*'). Television remains conspicuous by its absence, and when characters do watch, like Alvy and Tracy or Gabe and Judy, it's nearly always old movies on late night cable. Even while preparing *Crisis in Six Scenes* (2016), a six-part series for Amazon Prime, Allen acknowledged his total ignorance of the past decade of successful 'long form' television programming and his consequent regret at having agreed to this latest project.

In his professed disregard for new trends in contemporary visual storytelling, his well-known conservative tastes in music, literature and filmmaking, his contempt for computer-generated special effects, celebrity culture and self-publicity, Woody Allen has risked becoming himself *dated*, hardly surprising for an artist working beyond his eightieth birthday. Given his enormous oeuvre and narrow range of subject matter, combined with his adherence to a regimen of producing a new movie every year, his films remain remarkably consistent in their concerns and yet largely free of redundancy; at the same time, they have become themselves objects of nostalgia for his increasingly aging (American) audience, triggering memories of youthful laughter or mature reflection. Allen has been writing about nostalgia at least as far back as *Play It Again, Sam*, always with an awareness of both its seductive charm and potential danger. He shares Proust's conviction that the paradise offered by the memory of an idealised past must be a lost paradise. Like art, nostalgia is, for Allen, a necessary illusion – a respite from the problematic, ugly or disappointing present but an escape that cannot be maintained. In the three films examined below, he surveys the spectrum of nostalgia's appeal to his movie audience, from nearly undiluted reminiscence in *Radio Days* to emotional ambivalence in *The Purple Rose of Cairo* to amused scepticism in *Midnight in Paris*. Apparently, in the postmodernist consumer culture of the twenty-first century with its attendant short-term memory, nostalgia, for Woody Allen, ain't what it used to be.

Radio Days

Made in 1987 at the very apex of Allen's critical acclaim and cultural significance following a string of successes (and immediately preceding the disappointing serious films, *September* and *Another Woman*), *Radio Days* was, for its creator, flushed with a generous budget and control that allowed him numerous re-shoots with a cast of more than 150 speaking parts, 'a purely pleasurable, self-indulgent thing' (Lax 2009: 35). Although he does not rank it among his favourite works, anecdotal evidence suggests that it rates very highly among Woody Allen aficionados. Perhaps seduced by the nostalgic delight it affords, academic scholars and film critics have generally treated *Radio Days* lightly, if at all. Like Fellini's anecdotal memoir *Amarcord* (1973), to which it is sometimes compared (Boitani 2015: 68), the film is lyrical rather than plot-driven, a succession of self-contained stories voiced by an adult narrator (Woody Allen) describing memories of his childhood inspired by radio and popular music of the early 1940s.

Nostalgia colours the reception of *Radio Days* in several ways beyond reflecting the narrator's personal recollection of a bygone era. Many members of the cast, for example, have appeared in Allen's earlier films: Danny Aiello, Jeff Daniels, Gina DeAngeles, Julie Kavner, Renée Lippin, Fred Melamed, Tony Roberts, Wallace Shawn, Michael Tucker and, of course, his former leading ladies, Diane Keaton, Mia Farrow and Dianne Wiest. Recognising each one of them brings to mind earlier movie experiences, almost exclusively positive ones. On the soundtrack over the Windsor font credits the jazz trumpeter Harry James plays an updated version of Rimsky-Korsakov's 'Flight of the Bumblebee', composed for orchestra at the end of the nineteenth century and a familiar piece of music often first heard in childhood. The voice that follows the introductory credits immediately can be recognised (without introduction) as belonging to Woody Allen, whose familiar New York inflections provide a continuous link between the past of the diegesis and the present of the narration. The audience, which might be excused for regretting Allen's absence from the screen for the first time since the ill-fated *Interiors*, likely gathers pleasure from his presence on the soundtrack exercising authorial control and informing their reception of his childhood avatar, whose name, Joe (Seth Green), can barely be discerned in the dialogue. The mischievous red-haired boy is, for all they know or care, 'Woody'. The narrator begins as if reciting a fairy tale, 'Once upon a time many years ago', as the scene opens on a pair of house burglars interrupting their heist by successfully identifying three songs over the phone for a radio quiz called 'Guess that Tune', thereby creating a parable of poetic justice – the very opposite of *Crimes and Misdemeanors* or *Match Point* – when the robbery victims, the Needlemans, awaken the next day in their ransacked apartment to a truckload of new home furnishings. The reconstructed set of the broadcast, complete with enthusiastic audience, full orchestra and the familiar voice of the announcer, Don Pardo, marks the first in a series of radio parodies (the original programme, 'Name that Tune', evolved into a popular television show that would have been remembered by many of Allen's younger fans): 'The Masked Avenger' (= 'The Shadow'), 'Whiz Kids' (= 'Quiz Kids'), 'Bill Kerns' Favorite Sports Legends' (= 'Bill Stern's Sports Newsreel'). More than forty songs create a mnemonic medley of the era as Allen, like a benevolent disc jockey

Fig. 15: The establishing shot of the old neighborhood, recalled 'at its most beautiful'

reaffirming traditional values of family, neighborhood and community, spins out his memories.

The most glorious of these recalled images – the film's 'money shot' – appears after the opening episode as the camera tracks back from the ocean surf lashing a street in Rockaway on a grey afternoon to a high-angle establishing shot of the neighbourhood, lined with telephone poles and dotted with parked cars from the 1940s, the dark sky and bleached colours of the weathered homes creating the nearly monochromatic vision that Isaac had conjured in the prelude to *Manhattan*. The unnamed but unmistakable narrator sets the scene and immediately acknowledges how it has been affected by nostalgia. 'It's my old neighborhood, and forgive me if I tend to romanticise the past. It wasn't always as stormy and rain-swept as this, but I remember it that way because that was it at its most beautiful.' On the soundtrack, a piano plays Kurt Weill's great standard, 'September Song', about an aging man sharing 'these precious days' remaining of his late life in the company of his beloved. Woody Allen has used the plot motif of returning home in numerous films before (*Annie Hall*, *Interiors*, *Hannah and Her Sisters*) and after *Radio Days* (*Another Woman*, *Crimes and Misdemeanors*, *Alice*, *Celebrity*), either for comic effect or to express a character's regret at having grown beyond the comforting past. Here, he returns home for the duration of the movie, as if it were a sustained flashback.

The highlight for young Joe comes at the approximate centre of the film when he visits Radio City Music Hall for the first time, accompanied by Aunt Bea (Dianne Wiest) and her current boyfriend, a scene that was shot on location at the recently refurbished Midtown showcase. As Frank Sinatra sings 'If You Are But a Dream', the narrator describes how entering the lobby, climbing the carpeted stairs and gazing at the Art Deco furnishings 'was like entering heaven. I never saw anything so beautiful in my life.' Allen lingers on the spectacle, which concludes reverently, wordlessly, with the black and white screen image of Katharine Hepburn kissing James Stewart in *The Philadelphia Story* (1940), as an usher closes the door to the theatre. The boy's rapture reprises Cecilia's reverent gaze (despite much diminished circumstances in a far less appealing setting) in *The Purple Rose of Cairo*. Even the bad guys in *Radio Days* are vulnerable to nostalgia. In the very next scene, the mobster hitman Rocco (Danny Aiello) seems about to kill Sally White (Mia Farrow), the hatcheck girl who just witnessed his latest execution ('I don't meet anybody from the old neighborhood in years', Rocco laments when he first confronts her, 'and when I do, I gotta kill her'), but decides instead to take her home to meet his mother and help her career when he discovers they both grew up within a block of each other in Canarsie. In a plot development reprised in *Celebrity*, Sally survives and eventually flourishes after receiving elocution lessons to alleviate her Judy Holiday Brooklyn accent and transforming herself into a sophisticated gossip-show host.

Despite its sentimental patina, *Radio Days* incorporates several reflections of the dark side of the narrator's memory – the racism that freezes a bigoted neighbour when she spies a mixed couple kissing, the anti-Semitism that means 'no Jews in the Stork Club', the threat of Nazi submarines off the Rockaway shore, the 'sudden unexpected human tragedy' of a little girl falling down a well – although Maurice Yacowar seems to overstate the effect when he claims that 'for all its roseate nostalgia, true to form, Woody Allen looks back in dread' (2006: 254). This assessment fails to account for both the *balance* of the episodes depicted and the narrator's pervasive *tone*, exuberant at the outset, wistful at the end. Sander Lee also may miss the point when, more pedantically than Yacowar, he suggests that the boy's discovery late in the film that his father is a cab driver exemplifies 'Allen's ambivalence about the ultimate effects of allowing an overpowering media presence into our homes' (1997: 222). In fact, Lee sounds like the Communist neighbours next door when he adds, 'In a culture dominated by the tales of success and glamour that radio feeds them on a daily basis, people have become dissatisfied with mundane jobs; they are ashamed if they don't reach the same levels of success urged upon them over the airwaves' (ibid.). As the family gathers together in the living room to toast the new year of 1944, the radio prominent in the background broadcasting the celebration in Manhattan, Joe's mother expresses a brief moment of apprehension about the future that her husband quickly dismisses before they both join the party (along with their newborn daughter) in the adjoining room. With hugs all around, they hardly appear to be malcontents.

The film concludes on a doubly nostalgic note, returning to the Broadway rooftop that had been the site of Sally's earlier amorous adventures and allowing the radio celebrities who have gathered there to reflect on the passing of another year. 'I wonder if future generations will ever hear about us', the Masked Avenger (Wallace Shawn) says to Sally, his companion for the evening. 'It's not likely. After enough time, everything passes. I don't care how big we are or how important in their lives.' Allen cuts to the scene in Rockaway and then ends on the now abandoned rooftop, the show people having gone back inside when snow begins to fall, the door having magically closed behind them after the Avenger, restored to his usual effervescence, becomes the last to leave. For the third time, 'September Song' is heard, now played by a melancholy violin. Woody Allen recites the film's benediction: 'I never forgot that New Year's Eve, when Aunt Bea awakened me to watch 1944 come in. And I've never forgotten any of those people or any of the voices we used to hear on the radio. Although the truth is, with the passing of each New Year's Eve, those voices do seem to get dimmer and dimmer.' With this ending, *Radio Days* achieves the kind of ending Sandy Bates could only imagine in *Stardust Memories*, a 'good kind of sentimental'.

The Purple Rose of Cairo

Nostalgia describes a kind of fantasy of the past, enhancing the fiction that is memory. As the narrator of *Radio Days* nostalgically recalls being awakened by Aunt Bea to welcome the new year of 1944, he also acknowledges how the innocent belief in the goodness ('The Masked Avenger') and glamour ('Breakfast with Irene and Roger') of those simpler times, exemplified by his aunt's admiration for a radio ventriloquist, requires a faith that his adult perspective cannot easily sustain. In the penultimate scene of his wistful vision of returning home (*nostos*), Allen resurrects the image of his first muse, Diane Keaton, dressed all in white, on the bandstand singing 'You'd Be So Nice to Come Home To'. It is only a cameo role, but Keaton's ghostly presence after a four-year absence from his films and her displacement from Allen's personal life perfectly suits the elegiac mood of the film's closing minutes. Missing from the gathering of celebrities on the rooftop, she lingers in memory; only her aura remains.

What Diane Keaton might represent for the audience then (in 1987) and now, a romantic ideal becoming 'dimmer and dimmer', Fred Astaire and Ginger Rogers certainly personify for devoted moviegoers from Allen's own generation, a paradigm of physical grace long gone from life but preserved on celluloid. Astaire's disembodied voice singing 'Heaven', with its antique crooning tenor, conjures up the Golden Age of Movies at the beginning of *The Purple Rose of Cairo*, which serves as a kind of companion piece to *Radio Days* in its sentimental evocation of a bygone era. 'There are certain films I make that are best described as cartoons,' Allen told Stig Björkman, 'because people don't bleed and nobody dies really' (2004: 45). This account applies precisely to Tom Baxter, the movie character who escapes the screen and emerges unscathed from Monk's unfair pummeling ('I don't get hurt or bleed', he reassures Cecilia. 'Hair doesn't muss') as well as to Allen's conception of the past in *The Purple Rose of Cairo*. (*Zelig*, although it undoubtedly features a cartooned protagonist, uses archival footage and celebrated 'talking heads' in the present to create a documentary verisimilitude, a cinematic brand of magic realism, in its treatment of the historical period.) As the significance of the war years in *Radio Days* is reduced to the radio announcement of the attack on Pearl Harbor, a brief UFO performance, and the (perhaps) fantastical sighting of a German submarine off the coast of Rockaway, the 'Hard Times' (as they have come to be nostalgically recalled) of the 1930s are largely represented in *The Purple Rose of Cairo* by an unemployed lout pitching pennies and an anonymous bread line. Allen is no more interested in re-creating small-town America in the 1930s than he will be thirty years later to depict the French Riviera of the 1920s in *Magic in the Moonlight*. The film-within-the-film, hereafter referred to as 'The Purple Rose of Cairo', is even more cartoonish, necessarily so to distinguish it from Cecilia's 'real' world, its black-and-white B-movie characters immediately identifiable by details of their costumes: pith helmet, clerical collar, tiara or maid's uniform.

'Home' for the film's beleaguered protagonist Cecilia is the Jewell Theater in her backwater town in New Jersey, not the cramped, drab apartment she regrettably shares with her dissolute husband, Monk. The exterior of the Jewel was built only as a façade for the production, but Allen filmed the interiors of the movie theatre at the real Kent Theater in Brooklyn, a favourite site from his childhood (Lax 2009: 210), now (even in 1985) a relic of a nearly vanished era before the suburban multiplex. Like the eponymous humanities professor in 'The Kugelmass Episode', Allen's O. Henry Prize-winning story first published in 1977 in the *New Yorker*, Cecilia 'lives' for a time with a fictional character, Tom Baxter, magically liberated from the screen. Kugelmass similarly enters Flaubert's *Madame Bovary* through 'The Great Persky's' magical device that transports him to a point in the novel when Charles is away, 'a few pages after Leon and just before Rudolphe' (Allen 1980: 48). Emma proves to be as eager to escape Yonville as Cecilia is to leave New Jersey. 'I've always dreamed that some mysterious stranger would appear and rescue me from the monotony of this crass rural existence' (1980: 45–6). The story's plot inverts the film's: Kugelmass escapes his troubles by first entering the fiction, then escorts Emma back to contemporary New York; Cecilia entertains Tom in New Jersey, then spends 'a night on the town' in black-and-white Manhattan. Both fanciful tales seem to make the same point about the treacherous appeal of fantasy. On the brink of indulging his desire for romance, Kugelmass thinks to himself, 'I'm going to regret this' (1980: 43). In the opening scene of *The Purple Rose of Cairo*, Cecilia is nearly hit in the head by a falling letter from the movie marquee as she gazes enthralled at the lobby poster for the coming attraction. After barely escaping the magician's cabinet and the demanding Mrs. Bovary, Kugelmass declares, 'I've learned my lesson' (1980: 54), but he returns three weeks later to beg Persky to transport him to *Portnoy's Complaint*, only to get projected into an old Spanish textbook where he spends his time running away from an irregular verb. Cecilia, a moral innocent compared to the jaded professor, also fails to learn her lesson. Having rejected her 'perfect' fictional lover for Gil Shepherd, the actor who plays Tom, she is abandoned in the final scene with no other recourse than to indulge her romantic dreams by watching the latest feature at the Jewell, Fred and Ginger starring in *Top Hat* (1935). But while the point of the earlier story, like that of most of the *New Yorker* pieces (as their category as 'casuals' implies), is merely to amuse – 'Who cares what the point of the story is?' Bursky reminds his poker pals at the end of 'The Shallowest Man' (1980: 111) – *The Purple Rose of Cairo* evokes a more complex response to Cecilia's fate.

Because the narrating voice of Woody Allen recalling his childhood does not frame the representation of the Depression, the nostalgia created by *The Purple Rose of Cairo* stems from the audience's recollection of going to the movies or, if they are old enough, of the studio's generic product during Hollywood's heyday, represented here by 'The Purple Rose of Cairo'. Allen knows perfectly well that most of these programme films, like the old radio shows, are '*quite* god-awful' when experienced today (Lax 2009: 36). As Cliff tells his niece in *Crimes and Misdemeanors* as they leave a matinée of *Happy Go Lucky*, 'That was not such a great movie, but it was fun', which is perhaps the best that can be said about movies whose 'point' is simply to entertain. In *Hannah and Her Sisters*, however, a different Allen character will be saved by watching a different kind of Hollywood film, *Duck Soup*, that somehow (most likely through the genius of the Marx brothers) manages to transcend its genre. Cecilia, Allen's avatar in *The Purple Rose of Cairo*, will be similarly saved by Fred and Ginger, contrary to Britta Feyerabend's assertion that the film's ending 'criticizes nostalgia for its numbing effect on individuals' (2009: 54). First of all, *Top Hat* is not nostalgic *for Cecilia*; secondly, she appears *revived* rather than numbed by the shimmering immanence from the screen.

Cecilia's obsessive escape from tedium – somewhat like Emma Bovary's in the prior century – is through romantic fiction. The nostalgia that attaches to *The Purple Rose of Cairo* emanates not from the protagonist's fondness for early-twentieth-century silent cinema or dime novels but from the film audience's fond remembrance of Hollywood's black-and-white movies, not only studio classics like *Top Hat* but also lesser movies like 'The Purple Rose of Cairo'. Cecilia's dreamy absorption in the screen's consolatory images may provide temporary relief from Monk's brutality, but the romantic fantasies she finds inside the Jewell also make her vulnerable to Gil's deceptive blandishments. In eventually choosing Gil (a former cabbie whose real name is Herman Bardebedian) over Tom ('He's fictional, but you can't have everything'), 'Cecilia is only apparently choosing between silver screen images and real life; in fact, Tom and Gil confront her with a choice not between fantasy and actuality but between two different modes of illusion' (Bailey 2001: 146). As a consequence, when Cecilia must 'choose the real world' in the climactic scene back in the theatre, her decision results in regret when Gil immediately betrays her. Cecilia's 'night on the town' with Tom – not the movies – will remain her only truly nostalgic consolation.

Does Cecilia, like so many other protagonists in Allen's cinema, 'make a mistake' by choosing Gil over Tom? Absolutely not. Her reasoning – 'I'm a real person. No matter how tempted I am, I have to choose the real world' – makes perfect sense. To choose otherwise, to lose the distinction between fantasy and reality, would mean insanity. Cecilia's mistake occurs before the movie begins: marrying Monk. Although the story is hers, Allen suggests in a single anomalous cutaway shot, that it might be Gil who has made the biggest mistake within the narrative itself. Allen employs a match dissolve to superimpose Gil's face over Cecilia's as she learns he has returned to Hollywood after surviving a 'close call for his career'. The double exposure transitions to a prolonged close-up of Gil in the airplane taking him 'home' to Los Angeles; as the camera tracks back, his expression turns contemplative, perhaps reflecting on what he has left behind rather than feeling relief and anticipation at the prospect of playing Charles Lindbergh. Peter J. Bailey sees this moment differently, more cynically, describing Gil as 'appearing a little melancholy but never looking out the window, never once looking back' (2001: 151). The melancholy in his expression, however, might reflect the sadness of nostalgia for a simpler conception of 'home' than Hollywood, a possible life now lost in the past. This is precisely the 'look back' that his co-star Ina Beasley warned him not to take when he left for war in the scene from *Dancing Doughboys* that Gil and Cecilia re-enacted in Lawson's Music Store. With Cecilia accompanying him on a ukulele he buys for her, Gil has performed a rousing imitation of Al Jolson singing 'Alabamy Bound' followed by a similarly perfect rendition of 'My Baby Loves Me' with the shopkeeper playing piano. After the line about not looking back, he holds Cecilia in his arms and delivers a romantic kiss as non-diegetic romantic music enhances the effect. Despite having just disclaimed any passion while kissing Ina Beasley on screen, Gil now professes to be overcome by his feelings for Cecilia, a claim on her heart that ultimately wins him her favour over Tom.

But Gil has made a different choice than David Shayne at the end of *Bullets Over Broadway*, opting for celebrity rather than romantic love. Allen makes his 'look back' on the airplane deliberately ambiguous, the length of the shot allowing the audience time to wonder whether Gil might have been carried away by his own performance in the music store when he kissed Cecilia, whether Herman Bardebedian might have left behind his chance for happiness in New Jersey. Does he now regret forsaking Cecilia or simply his act of deception, or (as Bailey suggests) really nothing at all? A sound bridge, Astaire singing 'Heaven' that calls to mind the beginning of *The Purple Rose of Cairo*, takes the audience back to Cecilia, her battered suitcase and the treasured ukulele in hand, as she enters the Jewell during a screening of *Top Hat*. According to Allen, an executive from Orion called him to enquire politely if he might consider a different, presumably happier ending, but for the director, 'The whole reason for *Purple Rose* was for the ending' (Lax 2009: 19). Yes, but *what* ending for Cecilia does he mean, the abandoned waif who enters the movie theatre or the enraptured spectator who smiles through her tears in the closing shot? Allen interprets *The Purple Rose of Cairo* as a 'dark film' with a 'tragic end' (Schickel 2003: 77, 80). Although she certainly does appear bereft at first, a contrary argument might suggest how Cecilia can still cling to her nostalgic memories of her date with Tom, now reflected on the screen in Fred and Ginger's magnificent dance, and embodied by the musical souvenir from Gil she holds in her lap. The extended close-up – rare in Allen's comedies – allows time (more than twenty seconds) to contemplate Cecilia's emotional recovery. 'Neither "crushed" nor psychotic nor tragic,' William Hutch-

Figs. 16-17: Cross-cutting: Gil looks back, while Cecilia gazes at the screen

ings writes, 'she ultimately displays a (fundamentally comic) *resilience* that opposes all of those' (2013: 366). Allen has exhibited elsewhere – with *Casablanca* in *Play It Again, Sam* and *Duck Soup* in *Hannah and Her Sisters* – the power of certain special movies to inspire people, paradoxically, both to indulge and to resist their fantasies in order to live in the real world.

Midnight in Paris

Midnight in Paris is the most recent Allen film to express this ambivalent attitude towards a romanticised image of the past. Combining the nuttiness of 'The Kugelmass

Episode' and *The Purple Rose of Cairo* with the deeply ingrained nostalgia of *Manhattan* and *Radio Days*, Allen's most successful outing to-date of the twenty-first century (measured by box office receipts and contemporary reviews) remains his most expansive exploration of the joys and perils of nostalgia. Although this speculation cannot be confirmed, its conception very likely ensued from the author's habitual practice of reviewing old story ideas in search of his next project. Perhaps Allen came across a copy of 'A Twenties Memory', a short piece he originally published in *The Chicago Daily News* that appeared in his first collection of stories, *Getting Even* (1971). Many of the icons of the 1920s featured in the movie – Scott and Zelda Fitzgerald, Gertrude Stein, Picasso and Dalí – appear in the five-page sketch, the most prominent being Ernest Hemingway, who three times manages to box with the narrator and break his nose. With more opportunities within the film, Allen squeezes in at least nineteen celebrity impersonators, with references to several others, creating (as he did in *Annie Hall*) a kind of cultural literacy test for his audience.

The film begins with a gorgeous three-minute-fifteen-second montage of Paris, consisting of sixty shots during which Sidney Bechet's early 1950s recording of 'Si tu vois ma mère' plays on the soundtrack. The scenes of familiar landmarks – the Seine, Montmartre, the Moulin Rouge, the Louvre, Notre Dame, the Champs-Elysées, Tuileries Gardens – are nostalgic in at least three ways. Most obviously, they create a scrapbook of the city that has been enshrined in countless movies, beginning with the Lumière brothers' *actualités* and including Allen's own *Everyone Says I Love You* (1996) and, a few years before *Midnight in Paris*, the anthology film *Paris, je t'aime* (2006). Secondly, the music of Sidney Bechet, an American expatriate who played at Bricktop's nightclub (with Josephine Baker) in Montmartre during the 1920s and spent the last decade of his life in Paris, transports the movie audience back to the mythic paradise of the Lost Generation. Finally, the formal design of the montage immediately recalls Allen's celebrated prologue to *Manhattan*. As if to confirm the connection, the very last shot of the opening sequence in *Midnight in Paris* views a distant lighted train at night as it appears to pass beneath the Eiffel Tower, beautifully invoking a memory of the subway moving past Yankee Stadium in *Manhattan* as 'Rhapsody in Blue' reaches its crescendo. The editing suggests the passing of a summer's day, Darius Khondji's golden-hued cinematography modulating to record a glistening shower about halfway through the sequence, then gradually shading into twilight and approaching midnight. Ultimately, what remains most nostalgic about the opening to *Midnight in Paris* is simply Allen's old-fashioned commitment to *beauty*, the Romantic ideal abandoned by the postmodernist aesthetic.

For all the familiarity induced by the images of Paris and the remembrance, for many in the audience, of the opening montage in *Manhattan*, Allen introduces a few subtle variations. There is no voice-over commentary, for example, to impose a personal narrator controlling the images. Although the scenes themselves (along with the music) are highly selective and certainly might suggest Woody Allen's artistic choices – no sightings of immigrants or outliers from the *banlieues* – they are presented from the perspective of a contemporary *flâneur*, a tourist's view of a city romanticised in the collective memory rather than that of an individual who has lived there long enough to claim Paris as 'my town, and it always would be'. The title credits follow, another slight variant (despite being the familiar white Windsor font on a black background) in that they come *after* the opening three and a half minutes and incorporate the first bit of dialogue in voice-over. The protagonist, instantly recognisable by his voice (like Woody Allen in *Manhattan*) as Owen Wilson, proclaims how 'drop dead gorgeous this city is in the rain', a colloquialism that most cinephiles will link to Isaac calling New York a 'knockout' and that the montage to *Midnight in Paris* has just illustrated. The female voice replies in far less enthralled language ('What's so wonderful about getting wet?'), thereby setting in motion the essential conflict within this mismatched couple. Wilson's performance adds another dimension of the film's evocative nostalgia: he is the most satisfying incarnation of the Woody Allen persona since ... Mia Farrow.

Gil, a successful Hollywood screenwriter, is visiting Paris with his fiancée Inez (Rachel McAdams) and her wealthy parents. As Owen Wilson stirs memories of Woody Allen's earlier roles, his character here, like Farrow's Cecilia, is a dreamer. Gil yearns to trade his lucrative screenplays and home in Beverly Hills for the life of a true artist in bohemian Paris, his version of 'Heaven' being composed not of white telephones and champagne but simply a clean, well-lighted place. He regards himself as 'a Hollywood hack who never gave literature a real shot' who hopes one day to publish his 400-page manuscript about a guy who works in a nostalgia shop. As the film's narrative begins, he finds himself visiting Versailles with Inez and her 'brilliant' friend from college, Paul (Michael Sheen), who is currently guest lecturing at the Sorbonne. When Inez unflatteringly describes her boyfriend's penchant for Paris in the 1920s in the rain, Paul refers to Gil as 'Miniver Cheevy' – the poet Edward Arlington Robinson's 'child of scorn' who 'wept that he was ever born' – and quickly diagnoses his pathology as a condition similar to the original seventeenth-century understanding of nostalgia: 'The name of this fallacy is called golden age thinking – the erroneous notion that a different time period is better than the one

one's living in. It's a flaw in the romantic imagination of those people who find it difficult to cope with the present.' Gil takes this insulting portrait literally in stride – smiling and silently putting his arms on Inez's shoulders as he follows Paul's walking tour of the grounds.

Although he is every bit the pompous ass, Paul proves right about Gil, whose nostalgia might be more precisely defined as *mythophilia*, 'a longing not for what is remembered, but what is known only through its retelling through story and myth' (Malpas 2012: 169). Gil's knowledge of Paris in the 1920s derives not from personal memory but from what he has learned through schooling and books, from Gertrude Stein's description of the Lost Generation and Hemingway's of 'a moveable feast'; Gil himself has no back story in Paris, other than regretting that he did not stay there on an earlier visit. E. A. Robinson had indeed portrayed his particular kind of yearning (*algia*) a century earlier:

Miniver mourned the ripe renown
That made so many a name so fragrant;
He mourned Romance, now on the town,
And Art, a vagrant.

Miniver loved the Medici,
Albeit he had never seen one;
He would have sinned incessantly
Could he have been one.

The magical plot of *Midnight in Paris* will teleport Gil back to his fantasised cultural paradise, where he personally experiences what had previously been merely a vicarious fantasy of the Left Bank in the 1920s, thereby allowing him to exchange Boym's restorative nostalgia (admiring a lost truth and tradition) for reflective nostalgia, which calls that truth into question (2001: 41–55). The process takes Gil through three ascending stages of nostalgic thinking, as defined by the sociologist Fred Davis: i) from *simple* nostalgia celebrating the beautiful past compared to the unattractive present, through ii) *reflexive* nostalgia that questions and corrects the perfection attributed to the past, to iii) *interpreted* nostalgia that analyses both the truth about the lost home (*nostos*) and the reasons for yearning after it (*algia*) (1979: 16–26). For Gil, this passage backwards in time will lead him to discover the illusory enchantment of the past and the truth that the present is simply 'unsatisfying, because life is unsatisfying'. Ironically, Paul, described by the guide at the Rodin Museum as the 'pedantic gentleman', is himself a nostalgic stock figure in Woody Allen's oeuvre – a descendant of the Columbia professor in the movie line in *Annie Hall*, Leopold (José Ferrer), the pompous philosopher in *A Midsummer Night's Sex Comedy*, Lloyd (Jack Warden), the physicist who regards the universe as a 'temporary convulsion' in *September*, and anyone in the crowd at the Museum of Modern Art opening in *Manhattan* – representing 'the dominant discourse of rationality' versus Gil's romanticism (Szlezák 2015: 177). Gil rightly calls Paul a 'pseudo-intellectual' early on, and proves it so in a delightful put-down over a Picasso portrait after he has met the artist's original model; nevertheless, he will come around to acknowledge something close to what Paul defines as his mistaken glorification of the past and to confront his 'denial of the painful present'.

As Gil embarks on several post-midnight soirées with the luminaries of Parisian culture, his encounters replicate not only his own simple conception of the past (he tells Inez that Zelda Fitzgerald is 'exactly as we've come to know her through everything you've read in books') but also the audience's vague recollection of earlier Woody Allen films. The first famous people he recognises at the party for Jean Cocteau are Cole Porter (glimpsed at the piano in *Bullets Over Broadway*) and Scott Fitzgerald (the first witness to Zelig's transformation). When Scott and Zelda take him to Bricktop's to watch Josephine Baker, Allen recycles Bricktop's 'talking head' testimony and the archival images of the dancer from *Zelig*. And when Gil accompanies Adriana (Marion Cotillard) for a late-night stroll along the Seine, fans may recall Joe's (Woody Allen) magical dance with Steffi (Goldie Hawn) in the same location in *Everyone Says I Love You*. Katherine Fusco suggests in her brilliant account of *Midnight in Paris* how the film's 'depthless citation' – the caricatures of modernist artists and the ethos of modernism – creates a 'recuperative nostalgia' that redeems these figures from certain political and historical unpleasantness and subtly places Woody Allen among their esteemed company (2013: 295–96). As a result, *Midnight in Paris* manages to transform the audience's love for bygone Paris into nostalgic admiration for the director.

The film's plot turns on an inventive complication similar to Cecilia's night on the town in *The Purple Rose of Cairo* when Gil follows Adriana back in time to *La belle époch*, which is her personal site of nostalgia. After dancing at Maxim's and enjoying the show at the Moulin Rouge, he gains 'an insight' after realising that Lautrec, Gauguin and Dégas dream of painting during the Renaissance (an era that was itself fascinated by antiquity), that every generation dreams of an earlier *l'age d'or*.

Confronted by Adriana's decision to remain in the 1890s and armed with Gertrude Stein's advice that 'the artist's job is not to succumb to despair but to find an antidote for the emptiness of existence', Gil halts what he now perceives as 'an infinite regress of unfulfilled longing' (Eubanks 2014) and returns to the present, determined (as Marion was, under the influence of Rilke's recovered poem, in *Another Woman*) to change his life. Magic has temporarily allowed him to live out his fantasy; now luck – the other element in Woody Allen's cosmology empowered with the potential to offset the despair that haunts mortality – provides him the possibility of happiness in the form of Gabrielle (Léa Seydoux), a pretty Parisian purveyor of nostalgia. Thus, *Midnight in Paris* concludes on the same paradoxical note as *The Purple Rose of Cairo*, affirming 'both the futility of looking back and the impossibility of *not* looking back' (King 2013: 202). Nostalgia, which began in the seventeenth century as a disease, has evolved into a cure – or, at least, a palliative – for postmodernity.

Chapter Seven
To Remedy Regret

'It's important to have some laughs, no question about it, but you gotta suffer a little, too. Because otherwise, you miss the whole point of life.'

Broadway Danny Rose

Midnight in Paris became such a successful film largely because it reversed a general perception of the misanthropy, nihilism and despair that had marked Allen's work since *Husbands and Wives*. Gone were the brooding existentialist philosophers (*Anything Else, Whatever Works*) and psychologically disturbed women (*Celebrity, Melinda and Melinda, Vicky Christina Barcelona*) as well as the trivial comic bits (*Small Time Crooks, Hollywood Ending*) and grimly disturbing endings (*Match Point, Cassandra's Dream*) that had suggested creative exhaustion. Gil Pender's 'minor insight' while visiting the past that all was not perfect, his realisation that 'these people don't have any antibiotics', inspires him not to repeat his earlier mistake of leaving contemporary Paris, which in turn makes possible the moral luck of meeting Gabrielle on the Pont Alexandre III in the film's final scene. The bridge, which had been constructed at the end of the nineteenth century, serves as an apt metaphor linking past to present and promising, as the new couple cross in the rain, a hopeful future. Gil's southern-California-bred mellowness precludes the bitterness of regret at having pursued the wrong career with the wrong person in the wrong place, and so *Midnight in Paris* closes on a note of unalloyed sweetness (as Bechet reprises 'Si tu vois ma mère' on the soundtrack), one that produces, as Katherine Fusco has argued, its own kind of nostalgia for Allen's classic period.

In particular, the final image of a newly-formed couple walking away from the camera might recall the director's modest masterpiece of the 1980s, *Broadway Danny Rose*. As distinguished from the complex narrative of *Annie Hall*, the romantic virtuosity of *Manhattan*, the technical skill of *Zelig*, the ensemble performances of *Hannah and Her Sisters* and the philosophical ambition of *Crimes and Misdemeanors*, the artfulness of Allen's perfect little parable for adults has largely eluded extended critical analysis. Its protagonist, a former lounge comic turned 'personal manager' played by Allen, has usually been dismissed as one of the 'lovable losers' of his earliest work. The comic business – Danny's hapless clients (a blind xylophonist, a one-legged tap dancer, etc), his cowardly Bob Hope shtick, the squeaking imprecations of a gun-toting gangster high on helium – while comprising some of the funniest bits in his entire oeuvre, tends to obscure the philosophical dimensions of the story. Like *Radio Days*, which begins with the auteur's voice recalling his memories of a bygone era, *Broadway Danny Rose* originates in the reflections of a group of veteran comics sharing lunch at Manhattan's Carnegie Deli, but this time the myth they bring to life 'is neither a nostalgic overture toward the past nor an attempt to preserve it as a cultural artifact' (Rubin-Dorsky 2003: 264). Except for a couple of early vignettes depicting Danny's career as a performer, the film does not dwell in the 1950s, the heyday of the Catskills resorts, nor does it explore the nostalgia craze of the 1970s that spawned Danny's hottest protégé, the Italian crooner Lou Canova (Nick Apollo Forte). Although they don't fully realise it, his former colleagues fondly remember Danny Rose not out of longing for the good old days but rather for the traditional values of self-sacrifice and loyalty that he embodied ('Where you gonna find that kind of devotion today?' one of them asks), ideals now missing from their world. His story produces 'a lot of laughs, lot of laughs, lot of laughs' in the re-telling but also, as the comics leave the Carnegie and the audience the movie theatre, perhaps a sigh of relief at the film's ultimate affirmation of a common humanity.

Both the setting and the tale trace back to Allen's earliest professional experiences entertaining in the mountains and telling jokes in the city. 'Each night we used to go over to one of those delicatessens around Broadway and 7th Avenue and sit for hours and relax after the show and have some food and talk and tell stories' (Björkman 2004: 143). One of the 'Borscht Belt Scheherazades' (Shone 2015: 124) in *Broadway Danny Rose*, in fact, is Woody Allen's own revered producer, Jack Rollins (although he barely gets in a line during the rapid-fire dialogue). There is also an early reference to Weinstein's Majestic Bungalow Colony, which is where Allen began his career performing magic tricks as a teenager. The film begins at a

Fig. 18: 'Borscht Belt Scheherazades' share Danny Rose stories at the Carnegie Deli

back table with three brief scenes linked by dissolves that depict an expanding group of comics (first two, then five, and finally seven – with Rollins barely visible on the right edge) regaling each other with anecdotes and good-natured complaints about their marginal employment. Despite the failure of their old jokes and the increasing driving distances between their gigs, the guys maintain a boisterous camaraderie as they try to top each other with tales about the legendary agent of low-end acts until one of them, Sandy (Sandy Baron, playing himself), embarks on 'the greatest Danny Rose story', and the movie's framing device gives way to the plot.

Growing out of the shared recollections of the gathered community of comics, Danny Rose's greatest adventure takes on the qualities of a folktale, but rather than remaining a shaggy-dog story like 'The Shallowest Man' with no other point than to amuse, *Broadway Danny Rose* can be understood as a profoundly ethical illustration of faith, fortitude and transcendence. What seems to be yet another tale of a lovable *schlemiel*, in other words, becomes, upon reflection, an homage to a secular saint unlike anything else in Woody Allen's oeuvre. Viewed this way, as a parable instead of a farce, the film more closely resembles Isaac Bashevis Singer's short story 'Gimpel the Fool' than either *Zelig* or *Alice*. In Singer's most famous text, what starts out as a comic tale about the village baker, a hopelessly gullible *shtetl* sap, told in the vernacular style of Sholem Aleichem's Tevye stories, gradually evolves as the hero's credulity becomes a metaphor for unwavering belief in life's possibilities. Similarly, *Broadway Danny Rose* turns out to be a lesson in perseverance and even redemption. Danny's steadfastness in the face of mockery, hostility and deception, much like Gimpel's willingness to endure the tricks of the villagers and his adulterous wife, ultimately reconfigures the joke of his suffering into a testament of faith. Near the end of Singer's story, after a lifetime of being fooled, Gimpel plots his revenge against the town by pissing in the bread he bakes for them, only to be admonished by the ghost of his deceased wife Elka to remain true to his essential goodness. Elka confesses her regret to her cuckolded husband in a dream – 'I deceived Gimpel. That was the meaning of my brief life' (Singer 1983: 12) – prompting Gimpel to renounce his evil plan and choose instead to wander over the land, spinning yarns about 'improbable things that could never happen' (1983: 14) to the delight of children. In a way that reflects Singer's celebrated story, Allen's film tests the integrity of his protagonist's devotion to principles that make him appear foolish in the eyes of the world. Danny's career has been continually thwarted by the disloyalty of his clients once they become successful, yet he remains true to the morality (his Uncle Sidney's 'Acceptance, Forgiveness and Love') of his Jewish roots. Tempted at last by the betrayals of Lou and his hard-bitten mistress Tina (Mia Farrow), Danny overcomes his despondency, achieving a kind of immortality, like Gimpel's, in the memory of his community.

Much of the praise that has attached itself to *Broadway Danny Rose* has centered on Mia Farrow's transformation into a tough Italian broad, plumped up with a diet of daily milk shakes and a bit of padding, but Allen deserves some acting credit as well. Danny Rose is unlike any other character he has played, 'the least narcissistic and most caring avatar of the Woody persona' (Hösle 2007: 48). With his hideous wardrobe and *chai* necklace, he seems a caricature of the New York Jew that he personified in Alvy, Isaac, Mickey and Cliff during the decade that surrounds *Broadway Danny Rose*, but without their urban sophistication or economic success. He also resembles at first glance the cartoon protagonists he played in the early comedies, but without either their acquisitiveness or lasciviousness. Lacking education (as revealed by his comical misuse of words like 'facetious' and 'didactic') or an autodidact's intellectual ambition, Danny might appear to be most like Ray Winkler, the hustler and thief Allen portrays in *Small Time Crooks*, a character whose larcenous impulses are balanced by his devotion to his wife as well as his vocational incompetence. However, Danny's honesty and concern for all his clients set him apart from the comic simplicity of this later incarnation. He occupies an unprecedented status among Allen's roles and, surprisingly enough, remains nearly unique among all of the characters in Allen's cinema of regret (Cheech in *Bullets*

Over Broadway – who is not that film's 'Woody persona' – might be the exception): Danny is a man of principles, the antithesis of a shallow man.

Let's put this rather bizarre claim (given the apparent two-dimensionality of his characterisation) about Danny's integrity to the test. Some critics have compared him with his immediate predecessor, Leonard Zelig, another figure from faux history whose reality has also been testified to by several real-life witnesses. *Zelig*, like *Broadway Danny Rose*, recounts a strange story that purports to be a nearly forgotten fragment of urban myth. But Leonard has no volition of his own. The 'principle' that rules his behaviour is a pathology that must be cured, not a virtuous choice that 'the greatest Danny Rose story' seems unconsciously motivated to preserve. In contrast to Leonard's compulsion to conform, Alvy Singer initially defines himself according to an idea of self-exclusion in *Annie Hall* – 'I would never want to belong to any club that would have someone like me for a member' – that his autobiographical narrative about 'missing' Annie subsequently resists. Danny, however, never wavers from his traditional humanistic principles (though he is sorely tempted at the end). In a variation on Alvy's speculation about his motives for turning off Allison Portchnik, Isaac abandons Tracy because they do not belong to the same age-appropriate club, only to reverse his position in the end. He has integrity, to be sure (as when he resists Mary in the Hayden Planetarium), but his allegiance to principle often proves misplaced. In *Hannah and Her Sisters*, as another example, Mickey tries out a succession of religions in search of 'the whole point' that only leads him to suicidal despair before luck intervenes in the form of a Marx brothers matinée, a chance meeting in a record store and a fertility miracle. Cliff tries to assert some artistic integrity by working on his documentary in *Crimes and Misdemeanors*, but he shows himself ready to violate both his marital vow and his professional agreement with Lester, only to be left alone musing drunkenly about a movie he will never make. By contrast, Danny *hosts* a party (as he does every year) in the film's final scene, rather than being excluded from it, making a self-abnegating decision to uphold his 'philosophy of life' – and redeeming the remorseful Tina in the process.

Danny expounds his philosophy to Tina in a New Jersey diner after they first meet. She asks him about his other acts besides Lou, and he describes a couple of his 'interesting artists' as well as his ethos of personal management: 'I find them. I discover them. I breathe life into them, and then they go. No guilt. I mean, they don't feel guilty or anything. They just … split.' Tina responds with appreciation for his clients' opportunism ('they see something better and they grab it') and contempt for his loyal services ('you must be doing something wrong'). Danny then launches into his defence of guilt that served as an epigraph for Chapter Four: 'It's very important to feel guilty. I'm guilty all the time, and I never did anything.' The absurdity of his confession coincides with a very funny line a minute earlier when Danny had mentioned one of his current acts, a parrot that sings 'I Gotta Be Me'. Like Camus' version of Sisyphus, the bird transcends his fate by choosing a singular tune; in the world of parrots, his is the voice of integrity. By analogy, Danny's sense of responsibility amid a world of deceit, his choice to engage with others and 'waive his commissions' while still feeling guilty, becomes an act of good faith in a fallen, self-absorbed world. Like a good existentialist, he does not believe in God, as he tells Tina in the diner; like a good Jew, he quickly adds, 'I'm guilty over it.' Tina's counter philosophy foretells precisely Flender's in *Bullets Over Broadway*: 'You gotta do what you gotta do', she advises. The greatest Danny Rose story hinges on the conflict between these two worldviews.

Danny's faith transcends the managerial imperative to sell his clients and appears instead as an instinctual belief in the best about everyone else who comes under his wing. Thus, he calls his water glass virtuoso 'the Jascha Heifetz of the instrument' and advises another client that 'you're gonna become one of the great balloon-folding acts of all time'. Despite her judgement while briefly stopping at his apartment that he is 'livin' like a loser', Danny encourages Tina's interest in interior decorating ('nobody ever liked my African jungle idea before', she responds in pleased surprise when he approves her tacky ideas for improving his place) and offers to manage her implausible career ('I don't see you, honey, just decorating little joints…'). His sense of guilt primarily consists of *not doing enough* for his clients, even a married philanderer like Lou, whose 'integrity' he defends when Tina becomes jealous over the 'cheap blonde' she suspects he sees on the side ('He cheats with one person at a time, only', he reassures her). Nevertheless, Danny is not entirely free from regret. The film depicts two comic moments early on when he violates his own principles. The first occurs when he devotes himself entirely to Lou's preparations for appearing before Milton Berle in hopes of landing an extended contract, and Danny inadvertently neglects one of his more vulnerable acts, Herbie's Birds, whose star singer has been eaten by a cat. 'I admit, it's my fault. I've been remiss, lately', Danny tells the distraught Herbie. The second is when he reluctantly agrees to play 'the beard' so that Lou's mistress, Tina, can attend his performance for Uncle Miltie at the Waldorf Astoria. He has tried to persuade Lou to give up the affair – memorably quoting his Aunt Rose: 'You can't ride two horses with one behind' – but the mistaken identity that ensues when he agrees to front for Lou provides the plot's broad comedy in which Tina and Danny escape her former boyfriend's Mafia family's vendetta.

After the comic hijinks involving Danny and Tina barely managing to flee their captors in the helium balloon warehouse, the film takes a moral turn and the jokes all but disappear. Danny sits wearily in the rear of a taxi at night. Lou's familiar hit song from the 1950s, 'Agita', is heard on the soundtrack, playing slowly and in a minor key. Danny turns his head and, in a favourite shot of Woody Allen's – recalling various concert scenes or the celebrated horizontal pan across the front seat of Dwayne's car to a terrified Alvy in *Annie Hall* – the camera pans to Tina sitting lost in thought. In the flickering darkness, she returns Danny's offscreen gaze with a subdued smile. Although the two characters can be seen only in separate close-ups, the panning shot links them more subtly than the kidnappers' ropes that bound them on top of one another during their enforced captivity. Tina will attempt to sever their relationship in the subsequent scene at the Waldorf Astoria, after Danny revives her inebriated lover with his special hangover cure and Lou delivers a successful performance, but this intimate moment in the taxi returning to the city proves to be indissoluble.

The aftermath of Lou's triumphant audition stirs Tina's heretofore dormant conscience and brings the motif of regret to the forefront for the remainder of the film. In an interview with Stig Björkman, the director remarked how 'Jack Rollins has often said that it's a tragedy of a manager's job that the more successful the manager becomes doing what he's doing, the less the client needs him' (2004: 33). Illustrating this sad irony, Lou's popular lounge act in front of Berle (and Howard Cosell, in another cameo role) dooms his business relationship with Danny. Allen carefully composes the crucial break-up scene, which begins with a long shot of Danny, Tina and Lou walking towards the camera down a long shopping corridor inside the Waldorf. As Danny chatters about that afternoon's adventure he wants to share with Lou, the singer talks about 'some changes' he and Tina have decided to make. 'Like what?' Danny asks, as the couple swings off camera to the left, leaving Danny in an unusually tight close-up. Lou replies, 'like management'. The close-up lingers (a chandelier creates a subtle halo effect on Danny) as Lou explains that he has decided to switch agents to Sid Bacharach (Gerald Schoenfeld), a much more suave and successful manager. When the shot finally changes after more than fifteen seconds to a two-shot of the couple in the adjoining darkness, Tina lowers her head as Lou rationalises his deception ('we've got this special rapport') and she walks out of the frame, denying any responsibility ('leave me out of this'). Now in the centre of the hotel's mezzanine, Lou complains that Danny turns everything into 'a

Fig. 19: Lighting creates a halo effect as Danny discovers another client has abandoned him

personal situation', a rebuke that, for once, leaves Danny outraged. 'Of course I make it personal', he replies. 'That's the point!' Tina repeats her pragmatic philosophy – 'You gotta do what you gotta do, and Danny's gotta understand it' – at which point the exasperated and furious manager abruptly descends the staircase, leaving Lou to call out his name.

For all he might regret his wasted efforts on behalf of Lou, Danny's most serious concern – his only cause for *remorse* – immediately follows. Brooding on his latest case of being abandoned by a client, Danny sits alone in the Carnegie Deli when he learns that Barney Dunn, a stuttering ventriloquist too incompetent for even him to handle, has been sent to the hospital after being attacked by a couple of thugs. Earlier in the day, Danny had fingered Barney as Tina's 'lover' while being roughed up by the kidnappers, believing that the hapless entertainer was out of the country working a cruise and never intending to 'betray' him, as Nancy Pogel mistakenly claims (1987: 196). Still, Danny can't help but feel guilty: earlier, as he had ratted out the presumably safe-at-sea Barney during the warehouse scene, he instinctively turned heavenward to pray for God's forgiveness. These two consecutive scenes in the Waldorf and the Carnegie illustrate the distinctions between regret and remorse. Danny undoubtedly regrets his fate, the unpleasant outcome of Lou deserting him on the brink of success, but he is clearly not the agent of this result and his apparent anger in the moment demonstrates that he does not feel responsible. 'Although regret does focus on the feeling that we wish the state of affairs had turned out differently,' Stephen De Wijze argues, 'it need not imply that we wish we had acted differently' (2005: 460). When he hears about Barney, however, whose three-week cruise was unexpectedly cancelled, Danny feels immediately guilty, even though he was under considerable physical threat from the hitmen and had no way of knowing Barney was still in town. Perhaps this is why Pogel, internalising his sense of moral responsibility, considers Danny's innocent act of 'naming names' a betrayal. Although he did not *intentionally* betray Barney, Danny realises that his *action* resulted in the assault. Unlike Lou, who regrets hurting Danny's feelings but has no compunctions about taking necessary steps to advance his career, Danny is overwhelmed with remorse, which requires that he take some compensatory action (Taylor 1985: 99). Thus, he immediately visits Barney in the hospital and, in a brief scene that totally inverts the superficial motives of Lenny Mendel's hospital visits in Allen's story 'The Shallowest Man', offers to pay all his bills. Allen concludes the episode with a long shot of Danny standing outside in the darkness and the rain, the black-and-white image of abject despair possibly recalling one of Allen's favourite films, Vittorio De Sica's *The Bicycle Thief* (1948). One of the comics in the deli interrupts Sandy's narration to protest his tale's unexpected shift of tone: 'I thought this was a funny story. It's terrible!'

The dénouement that follows focuses on Tina, who suffers psychosomatic symptoms of what Janet Landman defines as *neurotic* regret, which 'occurs when the source of the regret goes unacknowledged, or when it involves unacknowledged ambivalence or marked self-hatred, or both' (1993: 218). Tina moves in with Lou, whose career flourishes under new management, but she begins drinking heavily and experiencing headaches and insomnia. Her fortune-teller Angelina (Olga Barbato) diagnoses her problem as 'bad conscience' and envisions her standing before a mirror, precisely the dream Tina says she had the previous week. The film cuts from Angelina's parlour to a close-up of Tina staring at herself in the bathroom mirror as Lou complains from the shower about how she is 'always so edgy'; the camera tracks in on her distressed reflection, the sight/site of a shame/remorse she can no longer bear. 'I want to rest easy again', she had told Angelina, but she has not yet fully acknowledged her moral transgression against Danny after what she describes as their shared 'adventure', confessing only to 'some little wrong' she did to a man she hardly knew. Over time, Tina has come to regret her influential role in Lou's desertion, but her self-consciousness has not yet fully curdled into remorse. The film demonstrates how her imperfectly repressed guilt can only be resolved through what the psychiatrist Melanie Klein calls *reparation*, a process of transcending the ego and reconciling with the other. Landman explains: 'The concept of reparation brings to the Freudian concept of working-through a greater emphasis on the interpersonal nature of the final resolution of internal conflict. Reparation takes resolution outside the confines of the head and heart of the individual (as in the coping literature) and outside the confines of the therapy room (as in Freudian transference) into the wider world of others' (1993: 219). In a similar vein, Emmanuel Levinas employs Tina's particular word to describe this journey in *Time and the Other* as the 'ethical adventure of the relationship to the other person', a necessary shift from 'ontological identity to ethical subjectivity' (qtd. in Girgus 2010: 5). For Tina, reparation requires a face-to-face encounter with Danny Rose.

Sandy continues the narration in voice-over after Tina and Lou have split, as she sullenly watches the Macy's Thanksgiving parade with her latest boyfriend, a small-time actor in commercials she had met during her escapade with Danny. The spectacle of the gigantic balloons (Uncle Miltie presides over a float) triggers her memory of their daring escape from the warehouse. Reduced to tears, she breaks away from her date and seeks out Angelina, who is gone for the holiday. 'Before one can possibly cope with, work through, resolve, or transcend regret,' Landman writes, 'one must first experience fully the painful fact of regret itself' (1993: 251, 252). Tina feels both the guilt of having betrayed Danny and the emptiness his absence brings. 'I missed an opportunity, I've regretted it ever since', Andrew, Allen's character in *A Midsummer Night's Sex Comedy*, had said to Farrow's character, Ariel, two years before *Broadway Danny Rose*. 'That's the saddest thing in life, a missed opportunity.' Now the actors' roles are reversed. The scene switches from the parade on Central Park West to the small apartment near the Carnegie Deli where Danny is hosting his annual Thanksgiving dinner party for his clients. Just as he begins serving the frozen turkey TV dinners to his merry guests, Tina appears at his door, seeking reconciliation. 'I came to apologise', she whispers in the darkness of the hallway and recites his Uncle's Sidney's catechism: 'Acceptance, Forgiveness and Love.' In a separate close-up, Danny resists her entreaties, deciding that Tina's offer of friendship would not be 'such a great idea' – the same phrase Isaac had used in the Hayden Planetarium to spurn Mary's offer to spend more time together, but with a different motivation this time. Isaac was resisting the temptation to become more involved with his best friend's mistress (just as Danny had earlier resisted Tina's flirting out of consideration for Lou). Now Danny turns away Tina out of resentment and spite. The camera remains on him as he returns to the party, only to contemplate his uncharacteristic rejection of a fellow human being. With the intuition that 'a good life is a life without cause for regret' (Rosati 2007: 234), Danny chases after Tina and finds her in front of the deli, where, in a long shot that prohibits hearing their conversation, he persuades her to return to the Thanksgiving gathering. 'The greatest Danny Rose story' thus ends very similarly to *Manhattan*, with the Allen character running into the street to express his regret, but *Broadway Danny Rose* extends the narrative one extra beat, allowing the audience to witness Tina's acceptance of his offer of reconciliation.

The framing device returns to provide the film's conclusion, in which the secular communion in Danny's apartment receives confirmation in the communion among the comedians. Their voices resume over the final exterior shot and the closing credits, as they celebrate Broadway's 'living legend' and the great honour bestowed upon him by the Carnegie Deli, the 'Danny Rose Special', 'probably a cream cheese on a bagel with marinara sauce', one of the comics says. Note that 'probably': the menu is right in front of them, but the honorary sandwich remains fabled in their imaginations. (Incidentally, you can now purchase a 'Woody Allen Special', pastrami and corned beef piled on rye, at the Carnegie Deli for the truly fabulous price of $29.99. Better hurry, though. The Carnegie Deli recently announced it will soon be closing.) The 'Danny Rose' recipe suggests an enduring 'mixed marriage', although nothing more is heard about Danny's relationship to Tina, as befits his current mythic status. The last laugh, however, conjures his generous spirit when Corbett (Corbett Monica), Danny's unconscious disciple, picks up the cheque ('a national holiday!' his companion proclaims). Danny has redeemed not only Tina but the beleaguered comedians and, as Jeffrey Rubin-Dorsky appealingly argues, the lost Jewish culture of the Catskills, 'by finding within it the spiritual component that all the nostalgia in the world could not recover' (2003: 275). The last words of dialogue that can be heard are Corbett's claim that 'for these kinds of laughs, I figure it's worth the price', with another comic adding, 'Well, we'll do it again tomorrow.' 'Agita' plays happily, harmoniously over the credits.

With *Broadway Danny Rose*, Allen most gracefully achieves his artistic ambition of synthesising comedy with drama while redeeming life's inevitable regret – *shallow* regret ('You gotta do what you gotta do') – through remorse and responsibility. Danny's story induces 'a lot of laughs', to be sure, but his suffering demonstrates as well 'the whole point of life' embodied in Uncle Sidney's homiletic formula, 'Acceptance, Forgiveness, Love'. In this 'subtly eloquent' (Yacowar 1991: 242) fairy tale for adults, a film that runs barely more than eighty minutes, Allen, like Nathaniel Hawthorne, has created a masterpiece on a totally human scale, trusting that 'the Beautiful idea has no relation to size', and thereby realising (although hardly recognising it) his own dream of becoming 'the Artist of the Beautiful' (1987: 361). *Broadway Danny Rose* stands apart from his other great works about nostalgia by preserving the humanistic ideal of authentic community and compensating for the regret that follows the passage of time. 'Hey, Danny, thanks a lot', Barney Dunn's dummy says in the closing line heard at the party. 'Boy, Thanksgiving sure rolls around fast.' Sure does, about as fast as the next Woody Allen movie.

Postscript
Speculations

'My conflict is between what I really am and what I would really like myself to be. I'm forever struggling to deepen myself and to take a more profound path, but what comes easiest to me is light entertainment. I'm more comfortable with shallower stuff [*laughter*]. I'm basically a shallow person.'

– Woody Allen (Lax 1991: 285)

'There are many people I know at my age who say, "I have no regrets". [*Big laugh.*] I have nothing but a million regrets. [*Smiles.*]'

– Woody Allen (Lax 2009: 329)

I began writing this book shortly after the release of *Irrational Man*; as I compose this post-script, *Café Society* has just opened in America months after its premiere at Cannes. Like the unmistakably aging but still familiar voice of the director narrating the story, the new film shadows its own cinematic progenitors, recycling (and sometimes plagiarising) numerous moments from earlier Woody Allen movies: the voice-over that accompanies the nostalgic invocation of a bygone era immediately recalls Allen's narration of his boyhood in *Radio Days*; Vonnie's (Kristen Stewart) anniversary gift to Phil (Steve Carrell), a framed love letter signed by Rudolph Valentino, recalls the allure of nostalgia, particularly as envisioned in

Adriana and embodied by Gabrielle (Léa Seydoux) in *Midnight in Paris*; Phil's confession to his nephew Bobby (Jesse Eisenberg) about being 'consumed by guilt' over his extramarital affair echoes precisely the situation and dialogue in *Bullets Over Broadway* when David confides in Flender about sleeping with Helen Sinclair; the Dorfman family's Passover discussion about love and the afterlife parallels the philosophical argument about guilt at the Seder table in *Crimes and Misdemeanors*; Bobby's regret over not being able to play a musical instrument reprises the pool hall conversation when David recalls his classmate's skill on the accordion in *Bullets Over Broadway*; Vonnie's conversations with Bobby about their aborted Hollywood romance take up the sadness of a 'missed opportunity' explored in *A Midsummer Night's Sex Comedy* and *Another Woman*; Bobby's taking Vonnie for a final night on the town conjures memories of *The Purple Rose of Cairo*, while the culminating romantic carriage ride through Central Park (accompanied by the Rogers and Hart song 'Manhattan') clearly alludes to *Manhattan*; the bittersweet ending on New Year's Eve similarly evokes directly the ending to *Radio Days*.

Undoubtedly, further screenings of *Café Society* would reveal more examples of such self-citation, but the regrettable truth in every case, which even the harshest reviewers have generally avoided (presumably out of respect for his age and output) is that Allen repeats himself shallowly, without either fresh wit or new insight. The voice-over, for example, contributes nothing to the resonance of the film but instead seems simply a lazy form of exposition. Unlike the monologist in *Annie Hall*, the anonymous narrator of *Café Society* has no 'key jokes' to illuminate his themes; unlike the retrospective storytellers in *Another Woman* or *Radio Days*, he is not reflecting back on his own insensitive or innocent past. Only the film's sustained close-ups of first Vonnie and then Bobby preceding the conclusive fade to black express something like the poignancy and profundity – the wistfulness – of the long take down a windswept Rockaway street seen in high-angle tracking shot at the beginning of *Radio Days* or the close-up of Chris's rueful contemplation at the end of *Match Point*. In *Café Society*'s closing moments, the protagonists finally seem to emerge from their mannequin roles in a screenplay 'written by a sadistic comedy writer', as Bobby describes it, to consider their disorienting transformation into fully realised adults, wondering about their own lost selves.

Questioned by his nephew about the identity of his young mistress, Phil testily responds, 'She's not a movie star. I'm not shallow. I'm not seduced by cheap glamour', and insofar as he subsequently marries Vonnie, apparently maintains a loving relationship, and provides her with an appealing, fashionable life, his actions (no less than Woody's towards Soon-Yi) suggest real depth in his emotional attraction. At the same time, however, his compulsive name-dropping without the appearance of a single client, combined with how his character essentially drops out of the story, attests to a certain professional superficiality as well as his cartoon status within the film. The protagonists, Bobby and Vonnie, have promised each other a more authentic life together as a bohemian couple in Greenwich Village, yet they each compromise their dreams and consequently live with their regrets, uncertain in the end, as Vonnie puts it, whether feelings that never die are a good thing or a bad thing.

Meanwhile, Woody Allen presses on, his six-part comedy for Amazon Prime completed – presumably 'very lucrative', as his avatar in *Crisis in Six Scenes* Sidney J. Munsinger describes his venture into writing for television after a long, mediocre career as a novelist – and his next feature in post-production. As a comprehensive study of his oeuvre, *Woody Allen's Cinema of Regret*, I regret to say, therefore must remain incomplete. Throughout my writing project, I have attempted to preserve a personal distance appropriate for an academic book, largely avoiding both a reviewer's tone of appreciation or criticism and a moralist's appraisal of Allen's character or public life. In this conclusion, however, I will speak in my own voice about some of the issues that continue to influence any appraisal of Woody Allen's character and cinematic achievement. Rather than cite specific quotations in order to refute certain arguments, I will refer here to generally held opinions (Allen's best work is behind him) and widely known facts (Mia and Ronan Farrow are determined to ruin his reputation) in order to speculate about three topics that occupy the current popular discourse about Woody Allen: What kind of a person is he? Will he ever make a(nother) great movie? Where is his place in the history of cinema?

The Woody Allen I Don't Know

During my professional life, I have tried to contact Woody Allen three times through letters on my college's stationery inviting him to participate in a seminar I was teaching or to receive an honorary degree. I can recall crafting each of these one-page queries with meticulous care and personal charm, even offering him a game of tennis during his visit. Despite my best efforts, I received no responses, although this result might very well be attributable to my not using the correct contact address. It hardly matters, except to suggest that Allen remains a very private person who seems content – 'obliged' would be the better term – only to reply to questions at press conferences or to professional collaborators and to correspond with higher-ranking journalists or scholars than myself. My training in literature during the 1960s, the heyday of New Criticism, has conditioned me to focus on the text as the object of study and to avoid autobiographical or historical interpretation. Art and literary criticism has, of course, evolved since then, and I have learned to contextualise the works that interest me according to their cultural moment and to integrate other disciplines in seeking out the complexities of a particular film, but I remain fundamentally committed to a formalist analysis that subordinates an author's intentions or interpretations regarding his or her own creation. Perhaps this training partly explains why I have written books about three notoriously reclusive film artists who were alive at the time – Ingmar Bergman, Terrence Malick and now Woody Allen – none of whom granted me access while I was writing or acknowledged my work after it was published. (I did spend a long and pleasant afternoon interviewing Elia Kazan (Michaels 2000: 218–31), the subject of my first book and also something of a recluse in later life, but he agreed to see me only after my manuscript was completed and I had sent him an earlier article I had published about his final film, *The Last Tycoon* (1976)).

Woody Allen has been a public figure for sixty years. Audiences first thought they got to know him through his self-presentation as a cabaret comedian and through his comic persona in the early movies. Some of the attributes of this caricature – claustrophobia, a preference for urban living rather than the country, an aversion to driving – are apparently true for Allen, but certain other more significant qualities – timorousness, ineptitude around women, neurotic insecurity (particularly prominent in his stand-up routines) – are manifestly untrue. His appearances *as himself* – in numerous published interviews and press conferences related to the release of his latest movie, in two full-length documentaries (Barbara Koppel's *Wild Man Blues* (1997) and *Woody Allen: A Documentary* (2012), and, most notoriously, in the child custody court case involving Mia Farrow and the 2014 *New York Times* opinion piece responding to the renewed charges against him of having sexually abused his daughter – have been as carefully constructed as his movie roles to portray a rational if somewhat morose, affable if somewhat reserved, thoughtful if somewhat glib, and utterly self-contained artist figure.

Koppel's film, which proves surprisingly stagnant given her Academy Award credentials, depicts Allen on tour in Europe with his jazz band and accompanied by Soon-Yi, to whom he was not yet married. The only time Woody seems entirely at ease is when he is on stage playing his clarinet. Otherwise, he seems like a neurotic, *kvetching* American tourist – nauseated on the motorboat entering Venice, complaining about the hotel beds, warning a press conference about his claustrophobia, searching for sweets in a fine restaurant – when he is not chattering rather charmlessly with fans. A gondola ride with Soon-Yi, which recalls the romantic carriage ride through Central Park to celebrate Tracy's birthday in *Manhattan*, proves dreary and mirthless, despite the couple's hand-holding. Wiede's documentary, which aired in two parts on PBS, presents essentially the same person fifteen years older. Allen seems a bit more relaxed (almost certainly because he is on his home turf) and reflective, quietly covering his entire life and career without ever truly letting down his guard, so the film has the effect of visually recapitulating a half century of interviews. Both films might be most interesting during the brief glimpses of Allen awkwardly interacting with his parents. In *Wild Man Blues*, his mother offers a perfectly apt summation of her son's use of autobiography in his films: 'He adds or subtracts from his life. He doesn't want to make a movie of his life.' Wiede's film includes a home movie clip of Nettie Konigsberg, shot by Allen in 1986, in which she describes her doubts about not sufficiently nurturing her son: 'I was very strict with you, which I regret because if I hadn't been that strict, you might have been not so impatient, what should I say, not *better* – you're a good person – but maybe softer, maybe warmer.'

Critics who complain about the repetitiveness of Allen's films should be forced to read his interviews over the past four decades, which have remained monotonously consistent and personally unrevealing. Virtually everyone who reads this book knows the key points in Allen's account of himself: in real life, he is nothing like the characters he portrays; he uses art to distract himself from the tragic fact of human mortality; he attributes his success more to luck than to talent; he regrets not having made a masterpiece; he believes the inclinations of the heart always conquer the restraints of reason. This last point, of course, formed the basis of his public self-defence for falling in love with Mia Farrow's adopted daughter and reappears as a central theme in several of his most celebrated films ('The heart is a very, very resilient little muscle', Mickey says at the end of *Hannah and Her Sisters*). As a facile excuse for impropriety, it can be found again in *Café Society* ('In matters of the heart, people do foolish things'). Any discussion of Allen's moral and legal culpability for the scandal that broke in 1992 should separate his 'infidelity' (if that is the right term, and I do not think it is) from the charges of sexually abusing his daughter Dylan. Whatever moral objections one might raise against a 55-year-old man having an affair with a 20-year-old woman living in the same home with her mother, who happens to be his longtime lover and professional collaborator (and I certainly share with others a distaste for the unseemliness of these circumstances), it is also true that Allen was unrelated to Soon-Yi by either blood or law, that he never married or actually lived with Mia Farrow, and that (by implication in her autobiography and subsequent accounts from both parties) their sexual relationship had been dormant for some time (Farrow 1997: 260, 269). And while it does not excuse his behaviour, the fact that he has remained married to Soon-Yi for twenty years – apparently 'happily', to invoke Emmet's question to Hattie in *Sweet and Lowdown* – does speak to the endurance of his feelings for her. Like Boris at the end of *Whatever Works*, Allen appears to have 'lucked out' in his mid-life marriage.

The second, more repugnant, charge raised in 1992 by Mia Farrow and renewed to this day by Ronan Farrow, hinges on the discrepancy between the verdict of the investigation conducted by the Yale-New Haven Hospital that, 'It is our expert opinion that Dylan was not sexually abused by Mr. Allen', and the opinion of the presiding judge in the custody case, Justice Elliott Wilk, who wrote about the molestation charge, 'We will probably never know what occurred' (Allen 2014: SR9). The testimony at the custody trial leaves little doubt that Allen was a neglectful, not to say reprehensible, father figure for his adopted children, including Dylan. Nevertheless (and as would be expected from such an accomplished writer), his 2014 statement in *The New York Times* in response to Nicholas Kristof's column in the same newspaper re-hashing Dylan's account does make it seem very unlikely that he abused his daughter on the afternoon in Connecticut that she had described. If that is true, then he has nothing to apologise for, except for the fact that he never acknowledges *any* wrongdoing in his relations with his adopted children. His only regret ('I was heartbroken', he says in the *Times* piece) is that he lost the custody case and was separated – permanently in the case of Ronan and Dylan – from his children. I don't believe Allen attributes this consequence to *agent* regret but rather *bad luck* in the appointment of Judge Wilk to the case. Among his 'million' regrets, in other words, he apparently does not include his private behaviour in 1991–92.

Although he continues to insist that he has not read his son Ronan's screed in *The Hollywood Reporter* (Farrow 2016), timed to coincide with the Cannes premiere of *Café Society*, Allen does acknowledge that he gets 'harassed all the time' about the allegations of child abuse and that his resistance has become 'weaker' with age. 'But it doesn't affect me', he paradoxically asserts. 'I just have no interest in it' (Shoard 2016). My own assessment of Ronan Farrow's persistent accusations on behalf of his sister against his father, his film collaborators, and the movie industry press coincides with the letter of rebuttal self-published two weeks later by his film biographer, Robert B. Wiede (2016):

> Woody Allen wasn't tried and found 'not guilty' nor was he exonerated by way of some obscure legal loophole. Rather, two separate, thorough investigations, conducted by highly-regarded teams of professionals, whose job it is to determine whether there is credible evidence to charge someone of a crime, *concluded that the incident never happened*. Your father was never tried for any crime, because no charges were ever brought against him. Yet you're essentially asking the media to treat him as a pariah who never faced up to the charge, or was convicted of a crime and managed to negotiate his way out of a proper sentencing. For someone with your background in law, that's a very interesting position to take.

To summarise my view of his fall from grace in 1992, Allen's personal conduct during this volatile period may justifiably be subjected to many ethical questions, but his legal responsibility has been definitively resolved.

In his otherwise largely unrevealing biography, David Evanier quotes one of Allen's boyhood friends, Jerry Epstein, about Woody's characteristic attitude regarding his own behavior: 'There's no feeling of guilt in him, nor of conscience. It's always your fault' (2015: 153). Despite how this observation might appear to contradict the premise of my book regarding the protagonists of his films, it has the ring of truth. Allen himself has frequently commented on his sometimes audacious self-confidence, especially early in his career in setting his own professional ambitions, and then expressed his surprise at having achieved them. At the end of Wiede's documentary, for example, he acknowledges how, 'I've lived out all these childhood dreams. I wanted to be a movie actor, and I became one. I wanted to be a movie director and a comedian, and I became one. I wanted to play jazz in New Orleans, and I played in street parades and joints in New Orleans, and I played in opera houses and concerts all over the world. There was nothing in my life that I aspired toward that hasn't come through for me.' That self-confidence made possible Allen's autonomy as an artist and his indifference to the critical success or failure of his films, but it also could have devolved into the self-regard and consequent ruthlessness that has marked his personal and professional life. Perhaps this quality was what his mother had in mind when she wished that he might have been 'warmer' and when Woody himself confessed to being 'a shallow person'. Along with his philosophical doubts, whatever personal regrets he may harbour, as I have suggested in my discussions of his films, have apparently been sublimated into his work.

The Auteur at Eighty

As Woody Allen has known since he was a child, the ultimate regret is death, a topic that has been a touchstone of his humour since his stand-up days. His quip from 'Death (A Play)', the source for *Shadows and Fog*, remains one of his most famous one-liners: 'It's not that I'm afraid to die,' his hero explains, 'I just don't want to be there when it happens' (1976: 106). As Boris explains at the end of *Love and Death*, to be dead is 'worse than the chicken at Tresky's restaurant', indeed a regrettable fate. After repeating another of his well-known jokes about preferring not to live on in the hearts of his countrymen but rather to live on in his apartment, Allen turned serious about the subject of 'aging and perishing' while talking with Stig Björkman: 'It's such a horrible, horrible thing for humans to contemplate, that they don't contemplate it. They start religions, they do all kinds of things not to contemplate it. They try to block it out in every way. But sometimes you can't block it out' (2004: 105). Nor has the passage of time alleviated his dread: 'You don't beat that anxiety,' he reported recently. 'You don't mellow when you get older and gain a Buddhist perspective' (Fragoso 2015). Above all, human beings want to live, and if our lives did not end, the mistakes and losses that cause regret might be corrected or restored over time.

With a father who lived to be 100 and a mother who made it to 97, Allen has reason to believe that he has inherited the longevity gene, and so he can hope that by continuing to be productive he may yet get 'lucky' enough (as he thinks he was with *Match Point*) to direct another meritorious film – he seems to have given up on directing an authentic masterpiece. The prospect of another 'great' Woody Allen movie – measured either by box office receipts or Academy Award nominations – seems remote, however, if for no other reason than the negative publicity that continues to shadow him in America. More to the point, the history of the cinema (or any of the arts, in truth) does not provide many examples of artists who created masterpieces beyond the age of eighty. Ingmar Bergman wrote and directed his last film, *Fanny and Alexander* (1982), when he was 64; Akira Kurosawa, another of Allen's favourite filmmakers, directed *Ran* (1985) when he was 75. Manoel de Oliveira, the Portuguese director whose career spanned from the silent era to the digital age and who made films after turning 100, might serve him as a private model, although I have not come across any reference Allen has made to de Oliveira's work. Furthermore, given the narrowness of his material and his stylistic conservatism – the physical conflict at the climax of *Irrational Man* proved a shocking departure; the Sony Alta F65 digital cinematography of *Café Society* marks a similarly unprecedented choice – Allen is unlikely to capture a younger audience or a new generation of critics.

Ty Burr, writing in *The Boston Globe* on the eve of the American premiere of *Café Society*, expressed the current assessment of Allen's place in popular culture by declining to comment on Ronan Farrow's renewed public attacks against his father's character but offering the professional opinion that he is 'the most overrated film director working' (2016: N1) – this despite subsequently identifying four 'legitimate masterpieces' (*Zelig, Hannah and Her Sisters, Crimes and Misdemeanors, Husbands and Wives*), one other 'major' work (*Deconstructing Harry*), and excluding *Annie Hall* only because of its muddled 'provenance' (2016: N9). Without bothering to challenge his list (readers will surmise that I would exclude *Zelig* and include *Manhattan, Broadway Danny Rose, Sweet and Lowdown* and *Match Point* among the masterpieces), I might ask how many other active filmmakers – or, for that matter, novelists, playwrights or composers – have produced at least five certified master works? Given the current ambivalence about Allen's moral authority and cultural relevance, he almost certainly will not regain the astounding renown he enjoyed during the 1970s and 1980s, but there seems no need to diminish his achievements on screen over more than four decades. We measure artists by the highlights in their body of work, not by the mediocrities or failures.

Despite the daunting odds, I speculated at the end of the first chapter that Woody Allen might still produce a fifth act for his career. What form could that final achievement take? I consider here two possibilities that might thrust him into the limelight again. Having already created so many films that imagine a romanticised or otherwise distorted perception of a world quite different from what it really is, the one remaining option for Allen's cinema of regret is a movie explicitly about death, something on the order of Michael Haneke's *Amour* (2012) that could quite possibly star himself. It may seem surprising that, for all his films concerned with the *fear* of death, Allen has never directly addressed the subject of *dying*. In retrospect, this fact appears as a rather startling omission. Perhaps his movie career might finally turn toward this topic, tracing a pattern also found in the late fiction of Philip Roth (*The Dying Animal, Everyman, Exit Ghost*), a novelist Allen has read and admired (Björkman 2004: 324). Given his persistent belief that, 'If you focus on mortality the house always wins' (Galloway 2016), however, the more likely masterwork that still lies ahead might take a literary form. Woody Allen has always been a writer – of jokes, comedy sketches, plays, *New Yorker* casuals, screenplays and, less frequently, book reviews, obituaries and op-editorials – but the obvious missing entry in his bibliography is an *autobiography*. Ingmar Bergman once more has set a high standard for Allen to follow if he chooses. Allen wrote a lengthy review of *The Magic Lantern* for *The New York Times* when Bergman's autobiography was published in 1988 ('The voice of genius!' it begins). The other great model he might follow is Elia Kazan, whose magisterial 800+-page autobiography appeared in the same year as Bergman's and is widely regarded today as one of the best books of its kind written by an American director of stage or screen.

The general impression one gets from his own account of himself at the end of Robert Weide's *American Masters* documentary and David Evanier's recent biography is that Woody Allen has become accustomed to getting what he wants from life. Writing an autobiography would afford him the chance to set the record straight about the controversies that have occupied the public's impression of him as well as to detail some of those million regrets he claims to harbour. *That* project (and, I suspect, that project alone) would return him to the very centre of American culture that he occupied during the 1970s and 1980s. Such a book may never happen, but I would still bet that Woody Allen is considering it.

The Pantheon

In a culture that has grown suspicious of aesthetic standards and the very idea of artistic 'greatness', a society that has largely adopted his own formula by measuring 80 per cent of success as simply 'showing up', Woody Allen deserves extraordinary credit. He has shown up for more than sixty years. It makes no sense to compile a list of his greatest films because that ranking would change with each re-viewing, and art works are not like batting averages, precise measurements of a certain skill. The movies I have discussed at length in this book, to make an obvious point, all seem worthy of attention, in addition to several others – *A Midsummer Night's Sex Comedy, Mighty Aphrodite, Vicky Cristina Barcelona, Blue Jasmine* – that did not receive extended analysis but nonetheless contribute to the magnitude of Allen's cinematic legacy. His own assessment of that achievement has not likely changed from the ultimate self-appraisal he offered to Eric Lax:

> My objective feeling is that I haven't achieved anything significant artistically… I feel I've made no real contribution to cinema. Compared to contemporaries like Scorsese or Coppola or Spielberg, I've really influenced no one, not in any significant way… I never had a big audience, was never a big moneymaker, never did controversial themes or paid any attention to current fashion. My films have not stimulated the talk of the country on social, political, or intellectual issues. They're modest pictures done for modest budgets making extremely modest returns and making no real ripple in the show business world… I never had enough technique or sufficient depth to my ideas to start anybody thinking. I'm a Brooklyn-Broadway wisecracker who's been very lucky. (Lax 2009: 365)

These remarks are made without regret, he adds, because 'I'm smart enough to know I've maximized my limited gifts' (ibid.). Through a combination of luck and a highly developed work ethic, he has transformed his supposedly shallow ideas into film art. *And yet* (to invoke Professor Levy from *Crimes and Misdemeanors* once again), there is nothing quite as remarkable about Woody Allen's cinema as the totality of its effect. Certainly I can think of no filmmaker, American or international, who has written and directed so many films over a span of forty years (from *Love and Death* to *Café Society*) that can be watched today with such pleasure.

If Allen has failed his own test – borrowing from John Keats – of beauty ('technique') and truth ('ideas'), it could be because he is an unduly harsh grader. Throughout this study, I have tried to highlight the visual brilliance of moments like the long shots of Rockaway in the rain (*Radio Days*) and the Eiffel Tower in the darkness (*Midnight in Paris*), the emotional pull in close-ups such as Tracy in the malt shop (*Manhattan*) and Cecilia in the Jewel Theater (*The Purple Rose of Cairo*), and the expressive composition of scenes like Judah at the lectern (*Crimes and Misdemeanors*) and Emmet under the telephone pole (*Sweet and Lowdown*). Few American films in the past thirty years have had their ideas discussed as thoroughly as *Crimes and Misdemeanors*; the complex narrative structure of *Annie Hall* has been similarly analysed in several film textbooks. But I take Woody Allen at his word when he says that his place in the pantheon of American cinema does not really matter to him, that he would prefer to achieve immortality by not dying. But when that day inevitably arrives, I like to speculate that his dying words will be spoken without regret but merely matter-of-factly, echoing his character's questions at the end of *Husbands and Wives*: 'Can I go? Is this over?'

Bibliography

Allen, Woody (1971) Getting Even. New York: Random House.
_____ (1976) *Without Feathers*. New York: Warner.
_____ (1980) *Side Effects*. New York: Random House.
_____ (1988) 'Through a Life Darkly', *The New York Times*, 18 September; http://www.nytimes.com/1988/09/18/books/through-a-life-darkly.html. (accessed 19 May 2016)
_____ (2007) 'The Man Who Asked Hard Questions', *The New York Times*, 12 August; http://www.nytimes.com/2007/08/12/movies/12alle.html (accessed 23 February 2016)
_____ (2014) 'Woody Allen Speaks Out', *The New York Times*, 7 February, SR9.
Ames, Christopher (2013) 'Jazz Heaven: Woody Allen and the Hollywood Ending', in Peter J. Bailey and Sam B. Girgus (eds) *A Companion to Woody Allen*. Malden, MA: Wiley-Blackwell, 207–26.
Asensio Aróstegui, María del Mar (2006) 'Hlenka Regained: Irony and Ambiguity in the Narrator of Woody Allen's *Another Woman*', in Charles L. R. Silet (ed.) *The Films of Woody Allen: Critical Essays*. Lanham, MD: Scarecrow Press, 256–67.
Bailey, Jason (2014) *The Ultimate Woody Allen Film Companion*. Minneapolis, MN: Quarto.
Bailey, Peter J. (2001) *The Reluctant Film Art of Woody Allen*. Lexington, KY: University Press of Kentucky.
Bailey, Peter J. and Sam B. Girgus (eds) (2013) *A Companion to Woody Allen*. Malden, MA: Wiley-Blackwell.
Baron, Marcia (1988) 'Remorse and Agent-Regret', *Midwest Studies in Philosophy*, 13, 259–81.
Bergson, Henri (2008) *Laughter: An Essay on the Meaning of the Comic*. Rockville, MD: Wildside.
Bittner, Rudiger (1992) 'Is it Reasonable to Regret Things One Did?', *The Journal of Philosophy*, 89, 5, 262–73.
Björkman, Stig (2004) *Woody Allen on Woody Allen*, revised edition. New York: Grove Press.

Bloom, Harold (1997) *The Anxiety of Influence: A Theory of Poetry*, second edition. Oxford: Oxford University Press.

Boitani, Giacomo (2015) 'Two and a Half: Nostalgia, Modern Parody, and Fellini in *Stardust Memories*, *Radio Days*, and *To Rome with Love*', in Klara Stephanie Szlezák and D. E. Wynter (eds) *Referentiality and the Films of Woody Allen*. New York: Palgrave Macmillan, 68–84.

Boym, Svetlana (2001) *The Future of Nostalgia*. New York: Basic Books.

Brode, Douglas (1985) *Woody Allen: His Films and Career*. Secaucus, NJ: Citadel.

Buber, Martin (1996 [1923]) *I and Thou*, trans. Walter Kaufmann. New York: Touchstone.

Burr, Ty (2016) 'Here's why Woody Allen is overrated', *The Boston Globe*, 17 July, N1-N8-9.

Davis, Fred (1979) *Yearning for Yesterday: A Sociology of Nostalgia*. New York: The Free Press.

de las Carreras-Kuntz, María Elena (2015) 'Magical Tricks and Ingmar Bergman: Referentiality in *Magic in the Moonlight*', in Klara Stephanie Szlezák and D. E. Wynter (eds) *Referentiality and the Films of Woody Allen*. New York: Palgrave Macmillan, 210–26.

De Wijze, Stephen (2005) 'Tragic Remorse – The Anguish of Dirty Hands', *Ethical Theory and Moral Practice*, 7, 5, 453–71.

Eubanks, Peter (2014) 'Memory and Nostalgia in Woody Allen's "Midnight in Paris"', *Revista de Humanidades*, 23, September-December; http://www.revistadehumanidades.com/articulos/65-memory-and-nostalgia-in-woody-allen-s-midnight-in-paris (accessed 5 November 2016).

Evanier, David (2015) *Woody: The Biography*. New York: St. Martin's.

Farrow, Mia (1997) *What Falls Away: A Memoir*. New York: Doubleday.

Farrow, Ronan (2016) 'My Father, Woody Allen, and the Danger of Questions Unasked'. *The Hollywood Reporter*, 11 May; http://www.hollywoodreporter.com/news/my-father-woody-allen-danger-892572 (accessed 5 November 2016).

Faulkner, William (1990 [1932]) *Light in August*. New York: Vintage.

Feyerabend, Britta (2009) Seems Like Old Times: Postmodern Nostalgia in Woody Allen's Work. Heidelberg: Universitätsverslag Winter.

Fingarette, Herbert (1977) *Self-Deception*. New York: Routledge and Kegan Paul.

Fragoso, Sam (2015) 'At 79, Woody Allen Says There's Still Time to Do His Best Work', NPR; http://www.npr.org/2015/07/29/426827865/at-79-woody-allen-says-theres-still-time-to-do-his-best-work (accessed 17 May 2016).

Fusco, Katherine (2013) 'Love and Citation in *Midnight in Paris*', in Peter J. Bailey and Sam B. Girgus (eds) *A Companion to Woody Allen*. Malden, MA: Wiley-Blackwell, 359–80.

Galloway, Stephen (2016) 'The Woody Allen Interview (Which He Won't Read)', *The Hollywood Reporter*, 4 May; http://www.hollywoodreporter.com/print/889678 (accessed 19 December 2016).

Girgus, Sam B. (1993) *The Films of Woody Allen*. Cambridge: Cambridge University Press.

_____ (2010) *Levinas and the Cinema of Redemption: Time, Ethics, and the Feminine*. New York: Columbia University Press.

Gordon, Jill (2004) 'Self-Knowledge in *Another Woman*', in Mark T. Conrad and Aeon J. Skoble (eds) *Woody Allen and Philosophy*. Chicago and La Salle, IL: Open Court, 218–42.

Guenther, Lisa (2011) 'Shame and the temporality of social life', *Continental Philosophy Review*, 44, 23–39.

Guthrie, Lee (1978) *Woody Allen: A Biography*. New York: Drake Publishers.

Harland, Pamela and Jenny Peters (1999) 'The *Sweet and Lowdown* from Woody Allen on His New Film…' *If*, 10, 3, 23 December.

Hawthorne, Nathaniel (1987) *Selected Tales and Sketches*. New York: Penguin.

Hösle, Vittorio (2007) *Woody Allen: An Essay on the Nature of the Comical*. Notre Dame, IN: University of Notre Dame Press.

Howard, Scott Alexander (2012) 'Nostalgia', *Analysis*, 72, 4, 641–50.

Hutcheon, Linda (2000) 'Lyrical Emotions and Sentimentality', *Philosophical Quarterly*, 62, 546–68.

Hutchings, William (2013) 'Woody Allen and the Literary Canon', in Peter J. Bailey and Sam B. Girgus (eds) *A Companion to Woody Allen*. Malden, MA: Wiley-Blackwell, 359–80.

Ingle, Zachary T. (2015) '"A full meal with a vitamin pill and extra wheatgerm": Woody Allen, Dostoevsky, and Existential Morality', in Klara Stephanie Szlezák and D. E. Wynter (eds) *Referentiality and the Films of Woody Allen*. New York: Palgrave Macmillan, 119–36.

Jones, Kent (2011) 'Woody Allen: The Film Comment Interview (Expanded Version)', *Film Comment*, May/June; http://www.filmcomment.com/article/woody-allen-the-film-comment-interview/ (accessed 29 October 2015).

King, Claire Sisco (2013) 'Play It Again, Woody: Self-Reflexive Critique in Contemporary Woody Allen Films', in Peter J. Bailey and Sam B. Girgus (eds) *A Companion to Woody Allen*. Malden, MA: Wiley-Blackwell, 73–94.

Knight, Christopher J. (2013) '"Raging in the Dark": Late Style in Woody Allen's Films', in Peter J. Bailey and Sam B. Girgus (eds) *A Companion to Woody Allen*. Malden, MA: Wiley-Blackwell, 73–94.

Lahr, John (2006) 'The Imperfectionist', in Robert E. Kapsis and Kathie Coblentz (eds) *Woody Allen: Interviews*. Jackson, MS: University Press of Mississippi, 143–68.

Landman, Janet (1993) *Regret: The Persistence of the Possible*. New York: Oxford University Press.

Lawrence, D. H. (1923) *Studies in Classic American Literature*. New York: Thomas Seltzer.

Lax, Eric (1991) *Woody Allen: A Biography*. New York: Alfred A. Knopf.

_____ (2009) *Conversations with Woody Allen*. New York: Alfred A. Knopf.

LeBlanc, Ronald (2000) 'Deconstructing Dostoevsky: God, Guilt, and Morality in Woody Allen's *Crimes and Misdemeanors*', *Film & Philosophy*, July, 84–101.

Lee, Sander (1997) *Woody Allen's Angst: Philosophical Commentaries on his Serious Films*. Jefferson, NC: McFarland.

―――― (2001) 'Existential Themes in Woody Allen's *Crimes and Misdemeanors* with Reference to *Annie Hall* and *Hannah and Her Sisters*', in Kimball King (ed.) *Woody Allen: A Casebook*. New York, Routledge, 55–80.

Levinas, Emmanuel (2003) *On Escape*, trans. Bettina Bergo. Stanford, CA: Stanford University Press.

Macready, John Douglas (2013) 'A Difficult Redemption: Facing the Other in Woody Allen's Exilic Period', in Peter J. Bailey and Sam B. Girgus (eds) *A Companion to Woody Allen*. Malden, MA: Wiley-Blackwell, 95–115.

Malpas, Jeff (2012) *Heidegger and the Thinking of Place*. Cambridge, MA: MIT Press.

McClelland, Tom (2011) 'The Philosophy of Film and Film as Philosophy', *Cinema*, 2, 11–35.

McGrath, Douglas (2006) 'If You Knew Woody Like I Knew Woody', in Robert E. Kapsis and Kathie Coblentz (eds) *Woody Allen: Interviews*. Jackson, MS: University Press of Mississippi, 116–29.

Meade, Marion (2000) *The Unruly Life of Woody Allen*. New York: Scribner.

Melville, Herman (1992 [1851]) *Moby-Dick*. New York: Penguin.

Michaels, Lloyd (2000) 'Interview with Elia Kazan', in William Baer (ed.) *Elia Kazan Interviews*. Jackson, MS: University of Mississippi Press, 218–31.

Parmerleau, William C. (2000) 'Rethinking Raskolnikov: Exploring Contemporary Ethical Horizons in Woody Allen's *Crimes and Misdemeanors*', *Film & Philosophy*, July, 102–14.

Pogel, Nancy (1987) *Woody Allen*. Boston: Twayne.

Polhemus, Robert M. (2013) 'Comic Faith and Its Discontents: Death and the Late Woody', in Peter J. Bailey and Sam B. Girgus (eds) *A Companion to Woody Allen*. Malden, MA: Wiley-Blackwell, 116–44.

Rapf, Joanna E. (2013) '"It's Complicated, Really": Women in the Films of Woody Allen', in Peter J. Bailey and Sam B. Girgus (eds) *A Companion to Woody Allen*. Malden, MA: Wiley-Blackwell, 257–76.

Roche, Mark W. (2006) 'Justice and the Withdrawal of God in Woody Allen's *Crimes and Misdemeanors*', in Charles L. P. Silet (ed.) *The Films of Woody Allen: Critical Essays*. Lanham, MD: Scarecrow Press, 268–83.

Rorty, Amelie Oksenberg (ed.) (1980) *Explaining Emotions*. Berkeley, CA: University of California Press.

Rosati, Connie S. (2007) 'Mortality, Agency, and Regret', *Studies in the Philosophy of the Sciences and the Humanities*, 94: 231–59.

Royal, Derek Parker (2012) 'Falsifying the Fragments: Narratological Uses of the Mockumentary in Woody Allen's *Husbands and Wives* and *Sweet and Lowdown*', *Post Script*, 31, 54–66.

Rubin-Dorsky, Jeffrey (2003) 'The Catskills Reinvented (and Redeemed): Woody Allen's *Broadway Danny Rose*', *Kenyon Review*, 25, 3/4, 264–81.

Sartre, Jean-Paul (2003 [1943]) *Being and Nothingness*, trans. Hazel E. Barnes. New York: Routledge.

Schickel, Richard (2003) *Woody Allen: A Life in Film*. Chicago: Ivan R. Dee.

Shoard, Catherine (2016) 'Woody Allen: "There are Traumas in Life that Weaken Us. That's What Has Happened to Me"', *The Guardian*, 25 August; https://ronanfarrowletter.wordpress.com/2016/05/30/hard-questions-for-ronan-farrow-an-open-letter/ (accessed 5 November 2016).

Shone, Tom (2015) *Woody Allen: A Retrospective*. New York: Abrams.

Singer, Isaac Bashevis (1983) *The Complete Stories*. New York: Farrar Straus Giroux.

Szlezák, Klara Stephanie (2015) '"Hi Mr. Hemingway": Time and Space, Travel, and Literary Heritage in *Midnight in Paris*', in Klara Stephanie Szlezák and D. E. Wynter (eds) *Referentiality and the Films of Woody Allen*. New York: Palgrave Macmillan, 173–89.

Taylor, Gabrielle (1985) *Pride, Shame, and Guilt: Emotions of Self-Assessment*. Oxford: Clar-endon.

Trigg, Roger (1971) 'Moral Conflict', *Mind*, 80, 317, 41–55.

Vigliotti, Robert (2000) 'Woody Allen's Ring of Gyges and the Virtue of Despair', *Film & Philosophy*, July, 154–62.

Walker, Alexander (2006) 'Woody Allen', in Robert E, Kapsis and Kethie Coblentz (eds) *Woody Allen Interviews*. Jackson, MS: University Press of Mississippi, 92–105.

Wallace, James M. (2004) 'The Mousetrap: Reading Woody Allen', in Mark T. Conrad and Aeon J. Skoble (eds) *Woody Allen and Philosophy*. Chicago: Open Court, 69–88.

Weide, Robert E. (2011) *Woody Allen: A Documentary*. Los Angeles: docuramafilms. DVD.

_____ (2016) 'Hard Questions for Ronan Farrow – An Open Letter', 30 May; https://ronanfarrowletter.wordpress.com/2016/05/30/hard-questions-for-ronan-farrow-an-open-letter/ (accessed 19 December 2016).

West, Nathanael (1957) 'The Dream Life of Balso Snell', in *The Complete Works of Nathanael West*. New York: Farrar, Straus & Giroux, 1–62.

Williams, Bernard (1982) *Moral Luck*. Cambridge: Cambridge University Press.

Wilson, Janelle L. (2005) *Nostalgia: Sanctuary of Meaning*. Lewisburg, PA: Bucknell University Press.

Yacowar, Maurice (1991) *Loser Take All: The Comic Art of Woody Allen*. New York: Continuum.

_____ (2006) 'The Religion of *Radio Days*', in Charles L. P. Silet (ed.) *The Films of Woody Allen: Critical Essays*. Lanham, MD: Scarecrow Press, 250–5.

Zahavi, Dan (2012) 'Self, Consciousness, and Shame', in Dan Zahavi (ed.) *The Oxford Handbook of Contemporary Phenomenology*. Oxford: Oxford University Press, 304–23.

Zoch, L. N. (1986) 'Remorse and Regret: A Reply to Philips and Price', *Analysis*, 46, 1, 54–7.

Index

Academy Award xv, 2, 14, 43, 53, 89, 92, 140, 144
aesthetic: aesthetic goal 84, 100; aesthetic standards 146; foregrounds aesthetics 7; postmodernist aesthetic 120
agency 11, 22, 56, 67–8; acknowledgment of agency 56; denying agency 7; guilty agency 5; personal agency 43
Alice xv, 13, 40, 50–2, 81, 112, 127
Alvy 6–7, 11, 17, 32, 40–50, 52, 89, 104, 106–7, 109–10, 128–9, 131
Amarcord 111
American Film Institute 43
American Masters 2, 146
Amour 145
Anna Karenina 35
Annie Hall xi, xiv, xv, 1, 6–7, 11, 13–4, 17, 22–3, 27, 29, 35, 40–4, 46–7, 49, 52, 64–5, 71–2, 85, 89, 106–8, 112, 120, 123, 126, 129, 131, 138, 145, 147; *see also* montage and voice-over
Another Woman xiii, xv, 39, 44–50, 54, 57, 82, 86, 106–7, 110, 112, 124, 138
anti-Semitism 113
Anything Else xv, 42, 83, 96, 125
Aristotle xii, 83, 90
artist: artistic mediocrity 81; artist immortality xvi; audience memory 109; autonomy as an artist 143; caricature of an artist 22; interesting artists 129; limitations as an artist xiv, 13; modernist artists 123; narcissistic artist xii, 94, 96; older artist 54; representation of artists xv; would-be artists 81; young artist 35
audience: audience memory 109; audience recognition 29; Broadway audience 96; enthusiastic audience 111; frustrated audiences 70; ideal audience 16; portrait of audiences 88; stimulate an audience 86; voyeurism of the audience 85, 89; younger audience 145
auteur xi, 19, 29, 52, 144–7 ; auteur signature xii, 108; auteur voice 126; fictional auteur 87; international auteur 1; self-discipline as an auteur 82; status as an auteur 28
autobiography: autobiographical film 20; autobiographical or historical interpretation 140; autobiographical interpretation 14, 88; autobiographical narrative 129; autobiographical scenario 59; autobiographical speculation 54; autobiographical story 40

Bad Faith 12
Baker, Josephine 120, 123
Bakhtin, Mikhail 63
Bananas 28–9
Barrett, William 78
Battleship Potemkin 28, 34
Beauvoir, Simone de 79
Being and Nothingness 7, 10
Benchley, Robert xiv, 28
Bergman, Ingmar xii, xiv, 6, 8, 19–21, 28, 34–5, 37, 68, 82–3, 86, 90, 92, 108, 140, 144, 146
Bergson, Henri xii
Bewitched, Bothered, and Bewildered 109
Bicycle Thief, The 133
Björkman, Stig 22, 32, 40, 88, 106, 115, 131, 144
Blue Jasmine xii, 2, 20, 47, 50, 59, 146
Bogart, Humphrey 6, 32, 51
Bonnie and Clyde 26, 28
Boston Globe, The 145
break-up xiii, 1, 7, 9, 11, 40, 49, 51, 58, 92, 105, 107, 131
Brickman, Marshall 31
Broadway Danny Rose xi, xvi, 1, 12, 14, 40, 61, 67, 97, 106, 125–9, 134–6, 145
Brooklyn Bridge 106
Brothers Karamazov, The 33, 36, 63
Buber, Martin 46–7, 49, 52, 55, 59, 66
Bullets Over Broadway xiii, 7, 11, 15–16, 62, 81, 96–101, 109, 118, 123, 130, 138

Café Society xv, 20, 52, 59, 137–8, 141–2, 145, 147
Cannes 137, 142
Carnegie Deli 14, 126–7, 132, 134–5
cartoon: cartoonish cinematic presentation 62; cartoon protagonists 115, 128; cartoon version of life 27; two-dimensionality of a cartoon 22
Casablanca 6, 119

Casino Royale 25, 28, 97
Cassandra's Dream xi, xii, xiii, xv, 4, 11, 61, 63, 73, 75–7, 125
Catholicism 52, 85
celebrity xi, 3, 10, 25, 29, 85, 88, 101, 118, 120; *see also* audience
Celebrity 48, 82, 88, 112–13, 125
Chicago Daily News, The 120
childhood 23, 27, 40, 81, 109, 111, 115–16, 143
cinematic subjectivity 89–90
Citizen Kane 26, 98
clarinet 19, 99, 140
classic period 1, 6, 40, 44, 50, 125
claustrophobia 140–1
Cloquet, Ghislan 32
comedy 4, 13, 25, 27, 32, 33, 40, 43, 50, 52, 62, 70, 81–4, 88, 131, 135, 139, 146; American romantic comedy 40; art of comedy 70; Catskill-style comedy 106; Hollywood film comedy 37; paranoid comedy 96; physical comedy 29, 31; plotless comedy 29; romantic comedy 44, 49, 54, 107; sadistic comedy 138
comic persona 3, 140
Cool Hand Luke 26
cosmic screwing 31, 33
crabs at Sam Wo's, the 107
Cries and Whispers 21, 90
Crimes and Misdemeanors xi, xii, xiii, xv, 1, 5–6, 19, 29, 36, 56, 61–2, 63–77, 79, 84, 104, 109, 111–12, 116, 126, 129, 138, 145, 147
Crime and Punishment 33, 63, 68, 74
Crisis in Six Scenes 82, 110, 139
Curse of the Jade Scorpion 82

Day of the Locust, The 88–9
Death 28, 32–4, 70
death 12–13, 31, 33, 59, 68, 78, 85, 92, 101, 105, 144–5

Death (A Play) 144
Death Knocks 28, 82
Deconstructing Harry xiii, 3, 13–14, 16, 20, 63, 74, 82, 88–9, 91–6, 98, 145
depression xii, 93, 116
de Oliveira, Manoel 144–5
De Sica, Vittorio 133
Dickinson, Emily 70, 73
diegesis: diegetic behaviour 48; diegetic dialogue 58; diegetic film festival 85; diegetic music 22; diegetic scenes 92; extradiegetic intrusion 42; extradiegetic repetition 42; non-diegetic romantic music 118; past of the diegesis 111
Di Palma, Carlo 55
Dostoyevsky, Fyodor 19, 32–3, 35–7, 63, 68, 74
dramatic storytelling 83
Dr. Strangelove 29
Duck Soup 29, 104, 109, 117, 119

Eisenstein, Sergei 28, 33–4, 37
Eliot, T. S. 12–13, 36, 40, 56, 60
Epstein, Jerry 143
Evanier, David 143, 146
Evergreen Review 28
Everyone Says I Love You 120, 123
Everything You Always Wanted to Know about Sex* (*But Were Afraid to Ask) 30, 35
existentialism 46

Fanny and Alexander 144
Farrow, Mia xiii, 2, 10, 15, 47, 49–50, 53–4, 58–9, 64, 66, 78, 91, 96, 111, 113, 121, 128, 134, 140–1; lawsuits 13, 88, 139, 142, 145; *see also* break-up
Farrow, Ronan 139, 142–3, 145
Faulkner, William 85
Feldman, Charles 23–5
Fellini, Federico xiv, 19, 86, 89, 92, 111

Film & Philosophy 63
Fitzgerald, Ella 58
Fitzgerald, Scott and Zelda 120, 123
flâneur 121
Flight of the Bumblebee 111
Freud, Sigmund 5, 23, 46, 134
furtiva lagrima, Una 109

Gershwin, George 7, 107
Getting Even 28, 120
Gimpel the Fool 127
Godfather, The 30, 109
Greenwich Village 2, 22, 97, 139
guilt xii, xiii, xv, 3–8, 10–12, 14, 18, 21, 36, 51, 56, 61, 63, 64, 67, 69, 72–3, 75, 77–8, 101, 138; acceptance of guilt 56; admission of guilt 15; collective guilt 5; defence of guilt 130; guilty agency 5; guilty of nihilism 68; mock guilt 6; repressed guilt 133; sense of guilt 64

hamartia xii, 6
Hannah and Her Sisters xi, 1, 47, 52–59, 64, 89, 108–9, 112, 116, 119, 126, 129, 141, 145
Happy Go Lucky 68, 116
Hawthorne, Nathaniel 135
Heidegger, Martin xi, xii
Hemingway, Mariel 4, 7, 92
Hitchcock, Alfred xii, 62
Hollow Men, The 12, 13, 60
Hollywood Ending 11, 41, 125
Hollywood Reporter, The 142
Hope, Bob 23, 32, 35, 126
humour: appropriate humour 27; burlesque club humour 30; dark humour 88; humourless 39; over-the-top humour 13; political humour 23; slapstick humour 43 superficial beyond the humour 26; *see also* parody

Husbands and Wives xi, xv, 1, 11, 26, 39, 58–63, 83, 105, 109, 125, 145, 147

I Am a Fugitive from a Chain Gang 26
I and Thou 46–7, 52
If You Are But a Dream 113
I Gotta Be Me 130
I'll Be Seeing You 71, 109
infidelity 56–7, 101, 141
insomniac list 84
Interiors 28–9, 39, 45, 50, 81–2, 85, 88, 104, 108, 111, 112
IQ 87; creative IQ 82
Irrational Man xi, xiii, xv, 13, 35, 37, 61, 63, 74, 76, 77–80, 86, 137, 145

James, Henry xiv
jazz 14–15, 20, 31, 108, 111, 140, 143
Jazz Baby, The 22
Jazz Heaven 87
Jewel Theater 115–18, 147
Jews: good Jew 130; Hasidic Jew 43; Jewish ambiance 24; Jewish assimilation 24; Jewish background 63; Jewish culture 135; Jewish roots 128; New York Jewish writer 88, 128; self-hating Jew 93; urban Jewish experiences 2
Joffe, Charles H. 22, 25
jokes 19, 22, 23, 27, 33, 40, 83, 87, 99, 126–7, 131, 138, 144, 146; in-jokes 28; philosophical jokes 106
Joyce, James 6, 8, 70

Kael, Pauline 53, 86
Kant, Immanuel 37, 79, 86
Kazan, Elia 2–3, 140, 146
Keaton, Diane 6–7, 29–31, 33, 91, 111, 114–15
Kenyon Review 12
Khondji, Darius 120
Kierkegaard, Søren 86

Konigsberg, Nettie 141
Kugelmass Episode, The xv, 115–16, 119–20
künstlerroman 97
Kurland, Jeffrey 59
Kurosawa, Akira 144
kvetching 33, 44, 81, 141

Lady from Shanghai, The 62
Landman, Janet x, xiii, xvi, 4, 27, 37, 43, 48–9, 53, 56, 73, 103, 133–4
Laughter xii
Levinas, Emmanuel xiii, 8, 47, 55, 67, 71, 77, 134
Levi, Primo 71
Light in August 85
longevity 144
Lost Generation 120, 122
Love and Death xiv, 1, 14, 32–7, 40, 61–2, 82, 84, 87, 108, 144, 147
Love fades xiv, 41, 44
Lumière brothers 120

Madame Bovary 116
Magician, The 82–3, 91
Magic in the Moonlight 82–3, 115
Magic Lantern, The 146
magic realism 115
Manhattan 3, 9, 11, 20, 22, 24, 30, 46, 51, 65, 108, 116, 120, 126, 138; Manhattan lifestyle 50, 81
Manhattan xi, xii, 1, 4, 6–8, 10, 13, 18, 21, 31–2, 44, 47, 53–4, 62, 64, 66, 75, 82, 85–6, 92–3, 97, 106–9, 112–13, 120–1, 123, 126, 135, 138, 141, 145, 147
Manhattan Murder Mystery xiii, 2, 62, 68, 109
Marx brothers 29, 88, 104, 107, 117, 129
Match Point xi, xii, xiii, xv, 2, 13, 20, 61–2, 67, 72–6, 84, 109, 111, 125, 138, 144–5
Max Pincus's Dark Secret 93
McGrath, Douglas 96

Melinda and Melinda 2, 84, 97, 125
melodrama xii, 4, 50, 96; humourless melodrama 39
Melville, Herman xv, 11, 8
memory xv, xvi, 17, 42, 43, 50, 65, 67, 73, 90, 92, 103–4, 107, 110, 114, 120, 122, 128, 134; collective memory 107, 112; idealised memory 91; mixing/Memory 40; narrator's memory 113; nostalgic memory 105; short-term memory 110; testimony of memory 104
Mendelssohn, Felix 108
meta-commentary 26
Midnight in Paris xv, xvi, 2, 15, 20, 108, 110, 119–25, 138, 147
Midsummer Night's Sex Comedy, A xiv, 54, 83, 123, 134, 138, 146
Mighty Aphrodite 35, 75, 91, 146
misanthropy xii, xvi, 54, 57, 125
mise-en-scène 8–9
Miss Lonelyhearts 88–9
mockumentary 10, 14; *see also Zelig*
modernism 123
Modern Times 28, 34
monochromatic vision 112
Monsieur Beaucaire 35
montage 7, 42–3, 51, 71, 107, 108, 121; clichéd montage 68; montage of memories 106; retrospective montage 71; sentimental montage 11; three-minute-fifteen-second montage 120; three-shot montage 34
Murder He Says 68
Murder Quartet 62, 64, 76
My Apology 36
My Baby Loves Me 118
mythophilia 122; *see also* nostalgia

narcissism xii, 15, 42, 66, 82, 92, 128; artist as narcissist 94, 96;; Freudian narcissism 46

narration: closing narrations 86; consequential narration 23; first-person narration 49, 79; narrating voice 45, 116; nostalgic narration 42; present of the narration 111; retrospective narration 44; voice-over narration 10, 42, 45, 46, 134
narrative: autobiographical narrative 129; metafictional narrative 87; relationship narratives 50
narrator: adult narrator 111; anonymous narrator 138; modernist narrator 40; narrator's memory 113; personal narrator 121; *see also* nostalgia
neurotic insecurity 140
Never Say Die 35
New Jersey 115–16, 118, 129
New Yorker 3, 23, 26–7, 115–16, 146
New York Post 22
New York Times, The 3, 19, 23, 83, 140, 142, 146
nihilism xii, xvi, 68, 125
nostalgia: cinephiliac nostalgia xvi; fantasy of the past 114; interpreted nostalgia 122; nostalgically Greek 103; nostalgic consolation 117; reflective nostalgia 107, 122; reflexive nostalgia 122; restorative nostalgia 107, 122; sadness of nostalgia 118; simple nostalgia 122; vulnerable to nostalgia 113

On Escape 77
Other 7–8, 10, 18, 71, 77, 134

Paris 3, 120–5
Paris, je t'aime 120
Parlez-Moi d'Amour 15
parody 6, 14, 26–37; grotesque parody 26; ingenious parody 6; resisting parody 43; self-parody 28
Passion of Anna, The 83

Passover Seder 63, 67, 138
Perelman, S. J. 28
Persona 35
Philadelphia Story, The 113
philosophy: existentialist philosophy 31, 63, 69; philosophical doubts 144; philosophy of existence 3; philosophy of hope 72; philosophy of life 129; philosophy of regret 12; philosophical satire 31; pragmatic philosophy 132
Platonic vision 104
Play It Again, Sam xiv, 5, 6, 30, 51, 109–110, 119
Poetics 83, 90
Porter, Cole 123
pragmatism 84, 132; pragmatism over aesthetics 97
Previn, Soon-Yi 2, 20, 59, 139–42
Prokofiev, Sergei 33–4, 108
Proust, Marcel 108, 110
punishment 3, 18, 68–9, 77
Purple Rose of Cairo, The xi, xii, xv, 1, 2, 15, 40, 50–1, 82, 97, 109–10, 113–20, 123–4, 138, 147

Radio Days xvi, 1, 110–15, 120, 126, 137–8, 147
Ran 144
Rhapsody in Blue 7, 108, 120
Rimsky-Korsakov, Nikolai 111
regret: agent regret xv, 4–5, 44, 48, 55, 61, 75, 82, 104, 142; character regret 4–5, 12, 48, 56, 82, 104; cinema of regret 41, 48, 57, 61, 104, 128, 139, 145; emotion of remorse 56; human regret 13; neurotic regret 133; philosophy of regret 12; shallowness of regret 61
remorse xii, xiii, xiv, xv, 3–14, 18–21, 25, 36, 42, 44, 48, 56, 61, 63, 67–8, 73, 75, 77, 101, 103, 129, 132–3, 135; buyer's remorse 5; comic remorse 5; fullness of remorse 48; no true remorse 17, 63; public remorse 3; remorseless 74, 77, 90–1; shallow remorse 56; tragic remorse 5, 11
Rollins, Jack 22, 126–7, 131
Rose, Mickey 26, 28
Rosenblum, Ralph 26, 29
Ross, Herbert xiv, 5, 30
Roth, Philip 2, 145

Sahl, Mort 23–4
Sartre, Jean-Paul xiii, 7, 10, 12, 46, 55, 63, 77, 86
schlemiel xii, xiv, 1, 24, 27, 29, 31, 33, 127
Schubert quartet 67
Scoop 2, 11, 84
Seems Like Old Times 42–3, 106
self-: self-abnegation 44; self-aggrandising style 70; self-appraisal 146; self-assessment xv, 4, 36–7, 81, 83; self-assured 65; self-citation 138; self-congratulation 32, 91; self-contained stories 111; self-deprecation 25, 93; self-destructive behaviour 77; self-doubt 41; self-education 47; self-examination 47; self-indulgent filmmaking 89; self-knowledge 48; self-referential 2, 91; self-reproach xii, 55–6, 61, 68; self-vindication 42
September 5, 39, 48, 76, 81–2, 104, 110, 123
September Song 112, 14
Seventh Seal, The 8, 19, 21, 28, 33–4, 82
Seven Year Itch, The 26
sexual abuse 13, 140–2
Shadows and Fog xv, 39, 62, 89, 144
Shallowest Man, The xiv, 11–14, 23, 54, 59, 94, 116, 127, 133
Shallow Indifference of Wealthy Celebrities, The 88

shallowness   xii, xiv, 1–20, 29, 37, 61, 72, 82, 92–3, 108
shame   xii, xiii, xiv, xv, 3–12, 18, 51, 55–6, 61, 63, 66, 73–4, 77, 101, 133
Shame   83
Side Effects   xiv, 12
Singer, Alvy *see* Alvy
Si tu vois ma mère   120, 125
Sleeper   30–2, 35
Small Time Crooks   104, 125, 128
Smiles of a Summer Night   83
Socrates   36–7
Stardust   90
Stardust Memories   xv, xvi, 16, 39, 82, 85–92, 94, 96, 105, 107, 114
Star Wars   43, 94–5
Stein, Gertrude   25, 120, 122, 124
Strangers on a Train   62
suicide   36, 45, 47, 50, 57–8, 65, 71–2, 77, 79, 88, 104
Sunday in the Country, A   87
Sweet and Lowdown   xi, xii, xiv, 2–3, 14–20, 21–2, 26, 82, 87, 92, 141, 145, 147

Take the Money and Run   xii, 25–8; *see also* parody
Tavernier, Bertrand   87
Taxi Driver   107
Tolstoy, Leo   35–7
Top Hat   116–118
To Rome with Love   2, 84
Tracy's face   8, 17, 107
2001: A Space Odyssey   30

United Artists   22, 28, 31

Vicky Christina Barcelona   xvi, 47, 52, 125
Viva Vargas   28

voice: auteur's voice   126; familiar voices 109, 111, 137; female voice   121; narrating voice   116; off-camera voice 71; passive voice   10, 52; Socratic voice   86; voice of genius   146; voice within the dream   48
voice-over   6–7, 19, 26–7, 33, 42, 45–6, 56, 66, 71–2, 77–8, 98, 121, 134, 137–8

Waldorf Astoria   68, 130–1
War and Peace   35
Waste Land, The   40, 49
Weill, Kurt   112
Weinstein's Majestic Bungalow Colony 126
Welles, Orson   26, 62
West, Nathanael   88
West Side Story   26
Whatever Works   57, 83–4, 91, 97, 104, 125, 142
What is This Thing Called Love?   58
What's New Pussycat?   23–5, 30, 97
What's Up, Tiger Lily?   25, 70
Wild Man Blues   140–1
Wild Strawberries   19, 82, 92, 105
Willis, Gordon   86, 107
work ethic   83, 147
Writers Guild of America   43

You'd Be So Nice to Come Home To   114
You Will Meet a Tall Dark Stranger   41, 82

Zelig   xii, 1, 10, 26, 115, 123, 126–7, 129, 145
Zelig, Leonard   xii, 10–11, 16, 21, 104, 123, 129
Zhao Fei   22

GPSR Authorized Representative: Easy Access System Europe, Mustamäe tee 50, 10621 Tallinn, Estonia, gpsr.requests@easproject.com